Financial and Management Accounting

Third Revised and Enlarged Edition

Volume I

C.L. Tyagi
Madhu Tyagi

PUBLISHERS & DISTRIBUTORS (P) LTD

Published by

ATLANTIC

PUBLISHERS & DISTRIBUTORS (P) LTD

7/22, Ansari Road, Darya Ganj, New Delhi-110002
Phones : +91-11-40775252, 40775214, 23273880, 23275880
Fax : +91-11-23285873
Web : www.atlanticbooks.com
E-mail : orders@atlanticbooks.com

First Edition, 2003
Second Revised and Enlarged Edition, 2017
Third Revised and Enlarged Edition, 2022

Disclaimer

- The author and the publisher have taken every effort to the maximum of their skill, expertise and knowledge to provide correct material in the book. Even then if some mistakes persist in the content of the book, the publisher does not take responsibility for the same. The publisher shall have no liability to any person or entity with respect to any loss or damage caused, or alleged to have been caused directly or indirectly, by the information contained in this book.
- The author has fully tried to follow the copyright law. However, if any work is found to be similar, it is unintentional and the same should not be used as defamatory or to file legal suit against the author.
- If the readers find any mistakes, we shall be grateful to them for pointing out those to us so that these can be corrected in the next edition.
- All disputes are subject to the jurisdiction of Delhi courts only.

Printed & bound in India by Atlantic Print Services

Preface to the Third Edition

Seeing the overwhelming response of the previous edition, the third revised edition of the book is being presented to the students. It could not be brought out on anticipated time due to COVID-19 pandemic. Now, it is ready for the students with new updates. Additional matters are added in the topics like Break-even Analysis, Operation Research, and Accounting Changing for Price Level. New topics such as Human Resource Accounting, Inflation Accounting, and Management Accounting in Non-Profit Organisations are included. The reason is that there is no agreement among writers as to which topics should be included in a book on Management Accounting because of its wide scope. Various definitions of this discipline have ended in emphasizing some of its facets only to the exclusion of others.

The book has been designed with a specific objective of fulfilling the needs of graduate and post-graduate students of Indian universities. Students appearing for C.A., I.C.W.A., and I.C.S.I. examinations may also find it useful.

We hope that the book will come to the expectations of the students. Errors and deficiencies pointed out by the readers are welcome. We thank Atlantic Publishers and Distributors Pvt. Ltd., New Delhi, without whose efforts the book would not have seen the light of the day.

C.L. Tyagi

Madhu Tyagi

Contents

1
Accounting Theory

In accounting, just like any other subject, one should first know the basics. They include the following:

1. Definition of Accounting
2. Divisions of Accounting
3. Accounting Terminology
4. Functions and Utility
5. Systems of Accounting
6. Accounting Principles
7. Basic Financial Reports

1. Definition of Accounting

Accounting is the language of business. It has been defined as "the art of recording, classifying and summarising in a significant manner and in terms of money, transactions and events which are, in part at least, of a financial character and interpreting the results thereof" (American Institute of Certified Public Accounting). Once the system has been designed and installed, recording and classifying data may become somewhat routine and repetitive. The accountants direct most of their attention to summarising data i.e. reporting and interpreting meaningful implications of data.

Accounting as an Information System

Accounting is a process of identifying, measuring and communicating economic information to permit informed judgements and decisions by users of information. Accounting is an information system necessitated by the great complexity of modern business. Many persons and agencies outside the organisation require financial data e.g. investors, creditors, labour unions, analysts and legal authorities. As an information system, the accounting process serves both inside and outside an organisation.

The reporting process, comprising four main channels of information flow, is presented in Exhibit 1.1.

Origin

Existence of accounting is found in the Western countries of Italy, France and Germany as early as 1340 A.D. But the general agreement

TYPICAL FLOWS OF ACCOUNTING INFORMATION

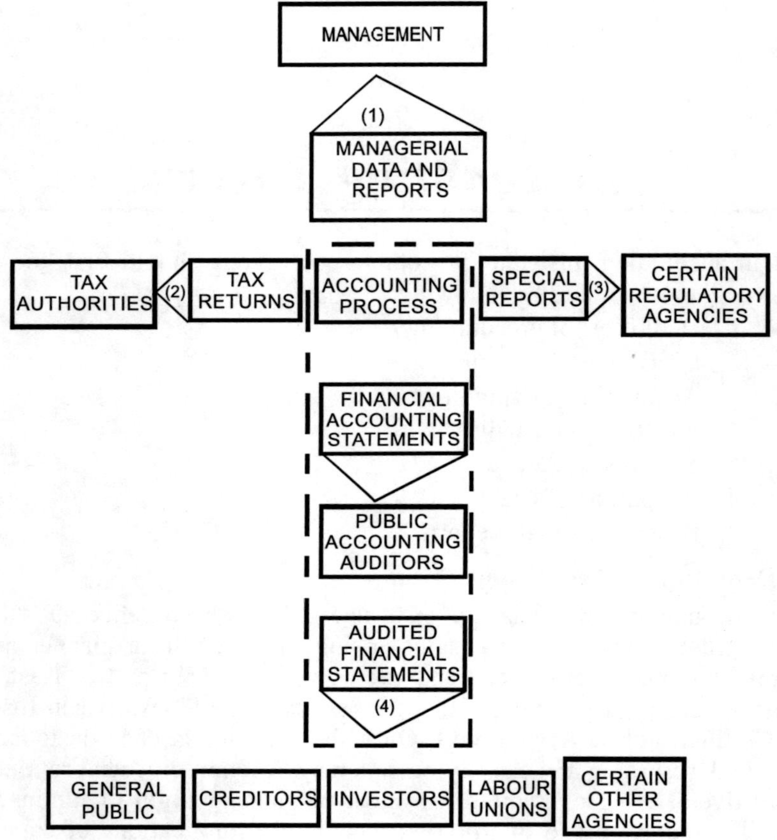

Exhibit 1.1

Notes: 1. Dotted lines show reporting area governed by generally accepted accounting principles.

2. The above four channels provide information for managerial data and reports, tax returns, special reports and financial accounting statements.

---

is that it was Luca Paciolo, a mathematics teacher in Venice, who first made known in 1494 the double entry accounting system to the Western world. Leonardo da Vinci wrote illustrations and Paciolo did the text. The German poet, Goethe, also mentions about this system. In India, Kautilya, mentions about the keeping of accounts from the period of 321 to 296 B.C. The old Indian system of accounting of maintaining books is on double entry bookkeeping system.

2. Divisions of Accounting

Accountants who render accounting services on a fee basis, and staff employed by them are engaged in Public Accounting. Accountants working with any organisation are engaged in Private Accounting. The phrase 'Public Accounting' is also used for accounting of government departments, public sector undertaking and NGOs. Commercial Accounting refers to accounting of business organisations. The following are specialised accounting fields:

(a) Financial Accounting. It is concerned with recording of transactions for a business enterprise or other economic unit and periodic preparations of various reports from such records. Such accounting is governed by "Generally Accepted Accounting Principles".

(b) Auditing. It is a field of activity involving an independent review of the accounting records.

(c) Cost Accounting. It refers to determination and control of costs, particularly of manufacturing concerns.

(d) Management Accounting. It employs both historical and estimated data in assisting management in daily operations and in planning future operations. It deals with specific problems that confront enterprise managers at various organisation levels.

(e) Tax Accounting. It encompasses the preparation of tax returns and tax planning.

(f) Accounting Systems. It is a special field concerned with the design and implementation of procedures for the accumulation and reporting of financial data.

(g) Budgetary Accounting. It presents the plan of financial operations for a period and through records and summaries, provides comparisons of actual operations with predetermined plan.

(h) Others. There is not-for-profit (non-profit) accounting that maintains the accounting records of various NGOs and social institutions. Social Accounting and Human Resource Accounting are the new fields of accounting. It is difficult to describe them succinctly. Former is concerned with costs and benefits that a society pays and gets, the latter is about measuring in money terms the costs and efficiency benefits of workers. *International Accounting* is a modern term used for accounting employed for MNCs.

Bookkeeping and Accounting are related. Bookkeeping is the recording of business data in prescribed manner and is clerical in nature. Accounting is concerned with the design of the system of records, the preparation of reports based on data and interpretation thereof.

3. Accounting Terminology

There are some special terms used in special sense and meaning in accounting. Some of them are given below:

(a) Business Transaction. Any exchange of money and/or goods and services (money's worth) between two persons. It may be sale or purchase of goods, receipt and payment of cash (cheque) or rendering of service by one person to another. If payment for such transaction is made immediately, it is called *cash transaction.* If payment is promised to be made later, it is called *credit transaction.*

(b) Goods (merchandise). It means all those things or articles in which a businessman deals. For a paper merchant paper is goods, furniture is goods for a furniture dealer. But paper for a furniture dealer is not goods or furniture is not goods for a paper merchant. They will treat them as an asset.

(c) Debtor and Creditor. Debtor is a person who has to pay money, called debt, to another person. This another person who has to receive the money is called a creditor. *A* buys goods on credit from *B*. *A* is debtor of *B* and *B* is creditor of *A*. If *A* does not pay, the irrecoverable debt is called Bad Debt. In U.S.A. debtor is called accounts receivable and creditor is called accounts payable.

(d) Turnover. It means total sales, both credit and cash.

(e) Expense and Expenditure. Expenses are costs incurred by a firm in the process of earning revenue. Generally, they are measured by the costs of assets consumed or services used during an accounting period. Depreciation on machinery, rent, salaries, power and light are examples.

Since expenses are deducted from revenue in determining net income, the accounting process relates expense in a period to the revenue of that same period e.g. January rent, no matter when it is paid, should be related to January revenue in determining net income for that month. If an annual rent of ₹ 6,000 is prepaid on January 1, only 1/12 of ₹ 6,000 or ₹ 500 is considered expense for January. At the end of January, the remaining prepayment of ₹ 5,500 constitutes an asset (called Prepaid Rent) to be apportioned over the remaining 11 months.

Expenditure means spending of money for acquiring any asset or payment of a liability, *Drawings or Withdrawals* (money or goods taken by owner from the business) are not expenses. So, remember expenses are directly related to the earning of revenue. They are measured by the amount of assets or services consumed (or expired) during an accounting period. Expenditure results in acquiring any asset or payment of liability. Expenses are also called Revenue expenditure and expenditure is also called Capital expenditure.

(f) Revenue. Any money received in business either from sale of goods in which firm is dealing or from rendering any service. Revenue is not earned when business borrows money or when owner contributes assets. Revenue is also reflected when goods are sold on credit or services are rendered on credit. Subsequent receipt of money from the customer on account of credit given to him, does not represent revenue. There is a shift of one asset to another.

(g) Owner's Equity or Capital. The amount of investment made by the owners (shareholders) in business. The creditors' equity or liabilities represent debts of the business.

(h) Voucher. Any written document in support of a business transaction e.g. receipt, counterfoil, copy of deed and bill of exchange etc.

(i) Purchases and Sales. Purchases refers to buying of those goods in which firm is dealing. Sale means transfer of ownership of goods in which firm is dealing.

(j) Assets and Liabilities. Assets are the economic resources of the business that can be expressed in money terms. They may take many forms e.g. (1) *Fixed assets* (i.e. physically identifiable) example land, machinery etc., (2) *Current assets* they represent claims for payment or services example Debtors (also called accounts receivables) or prepayment for future services, example prepaid rent, (3) *Liquid assets* example cash in hand or at bank.

Assets are recorded in Balance Sheet in established order as given in Schedule III of Companies Act 2013. They are recorded at purchase or cost price. They are depreciated for many reasons. Any increase in their market value is ignored according to GAAP. Liabilities are the obligations or debts to be paid either in money or services. They are listed in prescribed order and may be short term example Bills payable (Notes payable) or long term example debentures (bonds).

(k) Bill of Exchange. It is an unconditional order in writing in which creditor calls upon debtor to pay a particular sum after a time. It is a credit negotiable instrument. The debtor has to write the word "accept" on it and return it to creditor. From the creditor's point of view, it is bills receivable and from debtor's point of view, it is bills payable. In U.S.A., they are called notes receivable and notes payable.

4. Functions and Utility

All those who are interested in an organisation are also interested in its working and results. They can know all about an organisation through accounting records and financial reports. Besides owners, other parties who are interested in accounting data of an organisation are creditors, employees, investors, government, managers, research scholars and the public.

The following are main functions objectives of accounting:

(a) To keep systematic records.
(b) To protect business properties.
(c) To ascertain the operational profit or loss.
(d) To ascertain the financial position of the business.
(e) To facilitate decision-making and to exercise control.

5. Systems of Accounting

(A) Double Entry Bookkeeping System. Under this system each business transaction has two aspects and therefore, is recorded twice. The two aspects are that if something comes in business, something goes out also i.e. if there is a receiver, then there is a giver also. If there is an income, there is some loss or sacrifice. The recording of this *Dual Aspect* is done by *Debit* and *Credit* rule. Each account has two sides (a) Debit (abbreviation Dr.), (b) Credit (Cr.). The following accounting equation is based on this system:

Assets = Liabilities + Owner's Equity

The double entry bookkeeping system can be applied in two basis:

(a) Cash basis

(b) Accrual or Mercantile basis.

(a) Cash basis. In case of cash system entry in account books is made only when cash is received or paid. If a payment or receipt is due, no entry is made. Government accounts or accounts of non-trading concerns are kept on cash basis. Receipt and payment account is an example.

(b) Accrual basis. In case of accrual or mercantile basis, all outstanding and prepaid incomes or expenses are taken into account. This system takes into account the payment or receipt the moment they become due, even if the receipt or payment will be at a later date. This system is followed by most business concerns.

(B) Single Entry System. This is as such not a system. It is incomplete double entry system in which only personal accounts of Debtors and Creditors and Cash (Bank) accounts kept. It is not a reliable system unless it is converted into double entry system.

6. Accounting Principles

The standards adopted by accountants all the world over while recording accounting transactions are called 'generally accepted accounting principles'. The word 'generally' shows that they are not binding. These standards or principles are divided into two categories:

(a) Accounting Conventions

(b) Accounting Concepts or Postulates.

(a) Accounting Conventions

The conventions i.e. traditions or customs followed by accountants are four:

(i) Conservatism, (ii) Full disclosure, (iii) Consistency, (iv) Materiality.

(i) Conservatism. This convention means 'play safe' i.e. anticipate no profits and provide for all possible losses. Under this convention e.g. Inventory is valued at cost price or market price whichever is lower or provision is made for bad and doubtful debts.

(ii) Full disclosure. It means transparency in accounting. All information should be fully, honestly and fairly disclosed. On the basis of this convention Companies Act 1956 requires that financial statements shall give a 'true and fair' view of the state of affairs of the company.

(iii) Consistency. It means that once an accounting policy or practice is adopted should not be changed without valid reasons. For example, there are many methods of depreciation. Once a particular method is adopted should not be changed next time without valid reasons.

(iv) Materiality. It means important details must be disclosed and ignore minute details. Any item or fact is material whereby its disclosure is likely to influence the judgement of any person interested in accounts and firm.

(b) Accounting Concepts or Postulates

Concepts mean basic conditions which must be followed. The following are some concepts:

(i) Separate entity concept. Business is regarded as a separate entity from the owners. If *A* starts a business with ₹ one lakh, then *A* is a creditor of business. Business is regarded as an artificial person—be it a company or partnership or role proprietorship.

(ii) Going concern concept. It is presumed that the business will continue for a long time. It is regarded not permanent. A business one day or the other will close, but in accounting it is assumed that it will have a long period existence.

(iii) Money measurement concept. Only those transactions that can be expressed in money are recorded. Fictitious assets like goodwill or trademarks or patents are recorded after calculating their value in money terms. Section 134(5)(d) of Companies Act 2013 makes it compulsory.

(iv) Accounting period concept. Actual or net loss or profit from a business can be known only after the business is closed. But at that time it will involve lot of work. So for convenience the accounting period is fixed either one year or six months or any other period at the end of which profit or loss is calculated.

(v) Cost concept. It means that the asset is to be recorded at cost price. Any appreciation in value is not taken into account, unless the management feels to revalue them due to some reason. According to conservative approach the depreciation is charged on asset at the end of a period.

(vi) Dual aspect concept. It has already been explained in connection with double entry bookkeeping system.

(vii) Realisation concept. Except in case of hire purchase or contracts undertaken, revenue is recorded when sale is made though cash may be received later.

(viii) Matching concept. Due to double entry system and dual aspect of each transaction, costs and revenues are matched to find loss or profit. Costs and revenues of an accounting period are compared. When actual expense is incurred or revenue is received is irrelevant. The moment they become due are considered e.g. salary of December 2000 becomes due in December, though it is paid in January 2001. Salary of December will be recognised in year 2000.

(c) Accounting Standards

In 1973, International Accounting Standards Committee was formed. It consisted of 95 members representing 32 countries. India's Institute of Chartered Accountants and Institute of Cost and Works Accountant are its members. In India, has standards, recently made mandatory under Section 133 of the Companies Act 2013 and an recommendation of National Financial Reporting Authority.

Accounting's Unlimited Capacity for Service

Accounting is capable of supplying financial information that is essential for the efficient operation and for the evaluation of performance of any economic unit in society. Changes in the environment in which such organisations operate will inevitably be accompanied by alterations in accounting concepts and techniques. Although long range predictions as to environmental changes are risky and of doubtful value, there are two areas that promise to receive increased attention in the immediate future—international accounting and socio-economic accounting.

The rapid growth of MNCs is certain to have a significant impact on accounting because of different environments existing in various countries in which such firms operate. Currently a major problem is the need to develop more uniform accounting standards among countries.

The term socio-economic accounting refers to the measurement and communication of information about the impact of various organisations on society. Three major areas of social measurement can be identified. First, at the societal level the interest is on the total impact of all institutions on the matters that affect the quality of life. The second area is concerned with the programmes undertaken by the government and society oriented non-profit organisations to accomplish specific social objectives. The third area is "corporate social responsibility". Section 135 of Companies Act 2013 focuses on the public interest in corporate social performance in areas such as reduction of water and air pollution, conservation of natural resources, improvement in the quality of product and customer service, and employment practices regarding minority groups and females. The concept of social measurement is relatively simple as a theory, but much additional study and research is needed before measurement can be expressed in terms of monetary costs and benefits.

7. Basic Financial Reports—The Balance Sheet and Profit and Loss Account

One of the major functions of accounting is to provide periodic reports to management, owners and outsiders. The two principal reports resulting from the process of financial accounting are Balance Sheet and, Profit and Loss Account (also called Income Statement). Although the contents of these financial statements may vary among different firms, their basic purpose is the same.

In case of a company their form is prescribed under **Indian Companies Act, 2013 in Schedule III**. According to the Standards, no ASI issued by Institute of Chartered Accountant prescribes disclosure of Accounting policies. The Balance Sheet is designed to portray the financial position of the organisation at a particular date i.e. (point in time). The P and L Account is designed to portray the operating results for a period of time. These financial statements may be prepared monthly or quarterly or half-yearly or yearly.

The Balance Sheet, sometimes called the statement of financial position, is a listing of firm's assets, liabilities and capital (owner's equity) on a given date.

Following is the specimen Balance Sheet of Mr. Anand Printers a sole proprietor, as on December 31, 20XX.

ANAND PRINTERS
Balance Sheet
As on 31st December, 20XX

Liabilities	₹	Assets	₹
Anand's Capital (owner's equity)	4,00,000	Land	40,000
Bills Payable (Notes payable)	10,000	Building	2,00,000
Creditors (Accounts payable)	1,000	Machinery	2,20,000
Bank Loan	1,00,000	Debtors (Accounts Receivables)	9,500
		Bills Receivable (Notes receivable)	1,000
		Closing Stock (Supplies on hand)	20,500
		Cash in hand	20,000
	5,11,000		5,11,000

Notes: (i) In U.S.A., assets are written on left side and liabilities on the right side.
(ii) Names in brackets are used in U.S.A.
(iii) It can be prepared in vertical form also.

The proper heading of a Balance Sheet consists of the name of the organisation, the title of the statement and the date on which it was prepared.

Note that the body of the statement contains three major sections: Assets, Liabilities and Capital (owner's equity). This presentation makes it very convenient for the reader to tell at a glance that the resources of the firm total ₹ 5,11,000 and that these assets are financed by two sources: ₹ 1,11,000 by creditors (liabilities) and ₹ 4,00,000 by the owner's Capital (owner's equity). Sometimes left side of the statement is called Equities, with sub-divisions called creditor's equity and owner's equity. An important aspect of this statement is that the total assets always equal the sum of the creditor's and owner's equities. This balancing is described as accounting equation.

Accounting equation. It is an equation that dictates that all of the listed resources are attributed to claims of creditors and owners. This relationship can be shown as follows:

Technical Terms	:	Assets = Liabilities + Owner's Equity (A = L + O)
Basic Meanings	:	Business Resources = Outsiders claims + Owner's claims
Amount	:	₹ 5,11,000 = ₹ 1,11,000 + ₹ 4,00,000

Note that the owner's equity is equal to net assets of the business i.e. it is residual claim. Net assets mean the difference between total assets and liabilities. The expression "net worth" is no longer used for owner's equity. Net worth is owner's equity plus reserves and surpluses (retained earnings).

There are transactions in business that "do not affect" owner's equity and transactions that "affect owner's equity".

Transactions not affecting owner's equity. Certain transactions may change the character and amounts of assets liabilities or both, but have no effect on owner's equity e.g. if Mr. Anand purchases an equipment for ₹ 5,000 in cash, the machinery and equipment will increase by ₹ 5,000 but cash will decrease by that amount. Similarly collection of Debtors (Accounts Receivables) results in a shift of assets. Debtors will decrease and cash will increase by ₹ 10,500.

Transactions changing the amount of owner's equity are of four types:

	Effect on owner's equity
1. Owner's Contributions	Increase
2. Owner's Drawings (withdrawals)	Decrease
3. Revenues	Increase
4. Expense	Decrease

Profit and Loss Account (Income Statement)

To show the results of operations for a period, an income statement is prepared. It shows income and expenses for the period. The difference between income and expenses tell the net profit (income) or loss. The Balance Sheet and Profit and Loss Account are complement to each other.

QUESTIONS

1. Write full words for the following abbreviations:
   DR; CR; GAAP; P and L; NGOs; O.E.; B/P; A/R; B/R; N/P; A = L + O; C.E.
2. Fill in the blanks:
   (a) Accounting is recording, classifying and ________ transactions.
   (b) The double entry bookkeeping system was first given by _______ in Italy.
   (c) Assets are of many types e.g. ______.
   (d) In Balance Sheet assets can be written in _______ order.
   (e) Balance Sheet is prepared on ________.
3. Which of the following statements is true?
   (a) There is no difference between bookkeeping and accounting.
   (b) Accrual and Mercantile basis are not the same.
   (c) Accounting conventions are not binding.
   (d) Single entry system is good.
   (e) Balance Sheet can be prepared only in horizontal form.
4. What are the various specialized accounting fields?
5. Explain the following accounting terminologies:
   Goods, Expense, Expenditure, Revenue, Sale, Asset, Voucher, Dual Aspect, Postulates, Entity, Drawings.
6. What is the utility of accounting? For whom is it beneficial?
7. Explain the various accounting principles.
8. What transactions do or do not affect owner's equity?

2

Management Accounting—Theory

DEFINITION OF MANAGEMENT ACCOUNTING

Management or Managerial Accounting consists of two words, "Management" and "Accounting" which are both composite and elastic terms. A comprehensive explanation of the concept 'Management' poses many difficulties. Invariably it leads to many descriptive phrases. E.F.L. Brech says that management is "seeing that the job gets done efficiently. It takes all centre on decisions for planning and guiding the operation that are going on in the enterprises."[1] The functions of management are planning, organising, direction and control. Accounting is a collection, classification and interpretation of the financial information relevant to the operation of an organisation.[2] By merging these two definitions, we can define management accounting. A typical merged definition describes management accounting as "the application of professional knowledge and skill in the preparation and presentation of accounting information in such a way as to assist management in the formulation of policies and in planning and control of the operations of the undertaking".[3]

Accounting must accumulate financial data for two widely different objectives:

(i) External reporting for those who have an interest in the company but do not participate in running the enterprise; and

(ii) Internal reporting to meet the needs of those who are actively engaged in managing the undertaking.

External reporting, called Financial Accounting, must be made to conform the generally accepted accounting principles. Internal reporting is called Management Accounting. Internal reporting need not conform to any rigid set of rules. Any workable concept or technique, whether it is drawn from accounting, economics, mathematics, or statistics, may be applied. The data need not be objective, conservative or verifiable. They may be facts, estimates, approximations or projections. So the management

---

1. *Principles and Practices of Management*, p. 9.
2. *Accounting—An Introduction*, K.W. Perry, p. 3.
3. *Terminology of Management and Financial Accounting* (I.C.M.A.), p. 9.

accounting "has looser constraints than financial accounting".[1] As a result, there is no common agreement among management accountancy writers for the topics to be included in it.

Some more standard definitions are given below:

(a) "Management Accounting is the term used to describe the accounting methods, systems and techniques, which coupled with special knowledge and ability, assist management in the task of maximizing profits or minimizing losses. Management Accountancy is the blending together into a coherent whole financial accounting, cost accounting and all aspects of financial managements."

—Batty, J.

(b) "Managerial Accounting, sometimes referred to as management accounting, is a division of accounting that deals specifically with how accounting data or other financial data can be used in the management of business or non-business entities."

—Moore, C.L. and Jaedicke, R.K.

(c) "The application of accounting and statistical techniques to the specific purpose of producing and interpreting information designed to assist the management in its functions of promoting maximum efficiency and in envisaging, formulating and coordinating future plans and subsequently in measuring their execution."

—Association of Certified and Corporate Accountants of U.K.

OBJECTIVE AND SCOPE OF MANAGEMENTS ACCOUNTING

Management Accounting is a term applied to a fairly recent development in the field of accounting. It is used to describe an expanded role of accounting in the management scheme in which the accountant, as an active member of the management team, focuses attention on the collection and presentation of information that will be useful in the day-to-day operations of the company.

Seldom costs that have been determined for financial statements can be used in planning, decision-making or control. The management accountancy enters into these phases at several points. As the functions of management can be grouped in the above three categories so the management accountants participate in all three phases of (a) planning, (b) control, and (c) decision-making.

In the overall planning phase, management accountant assembles, classifies and presents the economic and financial data concerning employees, money, materials, machines and methods into a coordinated plan or plans for the considerations and decisions of the management. This data can be used in budgeting, deciding about the products to be sold in what markets, at what prices, and evaluating proposals for capital

1. *Cost Accounting*, Charles T. Horngren, p. 4.

expenditures. This data is based on company's past costs or others economic forecast information originating outside the company. To coordinate the internal and external information and to chart for management a course of expected trend levels constitute the most important contribution to planning.

In control phase, the management accounting's function is the result of a need for checks and balances within the business. Actually management accounting does not control, but through the issuance of performance reports, advises all levels of management where and what activities require corrective action. These reports should make possible "management by exception". Emphasising the exceptions to or deviations from a pre-determined plan expedites managerial control. The management accounting sets predetermined standards by which performance can be judged, reports difference between planned and actual performance and aids in fixing the responsibility for departures from a plan.

Decision-making, which is problem-solving, is largely a matter of choosing between alternative course of action. The questions that arise are many and varied. Although the management accountant has no ready and easy answers, profitability will be a factor in each instance and accounting data, properly accumulated and applied, will play a large part in the ultimate answer.

FUNCTIONS AND SIGNIFICANCE OF MANAGEMENT ACCOUNTING

The nature of management accounting functions is clearly presented in its definitions and scope discussed above. Management accounting is a service function. It is sometimes called higher cost accounting. A good management accounting system should perform the following functions:

1. Facilitate the preparation of reports for management to (a) assess company profitability; (b) financial status of the business; (c) anticipated future progress of the business; (d) stability and security of investment in the business; and (e) company liquidity and ability to pay debts.
2. Ensure that, within reason, those financial factors which should influence a business decision are readily available.
3. Make possible the provision of consistent information for the preparation of management reports in a uniform manner.

In order to perform its functions, management accounting draws help from the following disciplines:

1. Finance, financial accounting and economics.
2. Mathematics and quantitative techniques.
3. Behavioural and social sciences.
4. Management information systems and computer science.

QUALITIES OF SOUND MANAGEMENT ACCOUNTING SYSTEM

In the provision of information for management, the essential qualities which underlie a sound management accounting system are as follows:[1]

1. Relevance—the system should assist in the provision of useful information to achieve a desired result.
2. Comprehensiveness—the system should cover the basic features of business activity.
3. Flexibility—the system should be adaptable to the needs of a variety of users.
4. Realism—the system should recognize the practical limitations in the business situation regarding provision of financial data and its potential use.
5. Accuracy—the system should recognize the degree of accuracy required for source data to provide output within the prescribed limits of accuracy to meet the objectives laid down by management.

ORGANISATIONAL STRUCTURE AND THE MANAGEMENT ACCOUNTANT

Management Accountant performs an advisory service and may be one member of chief accountant's staff. The American title for chief accountant is 'Controller'. A breakdown of this advisory service could provide a statement of the responsibilities of a controller. This confusion is only resolved in each company by the clear definition of the responsibilities of each individual, whatever may be the title. The title is not important, what the individual does is important.

The accounting department does not exercise direct authority over line departments. This department's advice help in the areas of budgeting, controlling, pricing and special decisions. The top line management delegates the authority to the controller, the chief management accountant, about uniformity of accounting and reporting. When the controller prescribes the line department's role in supplying accounting information, he is a 'staff person'. "The modern controller does not do any controllership in terms of line authority except over his own department. Yet the modern concept of controllership maintains that controller does control in a special sense. By reporting and interpreting relevant data, the controller exerts a force or influence that impels management towards logical decisions consistent with objectives."[2]

Reporting to management places the management accountant in a difficult position with his colleagues because the information issued must

1. *Management Accounting*, Norman Thornton, p. 11.
2. *Cost Accounting*, Charles T. Horngren, p. 10.

ORGANISATION STRUCTURE

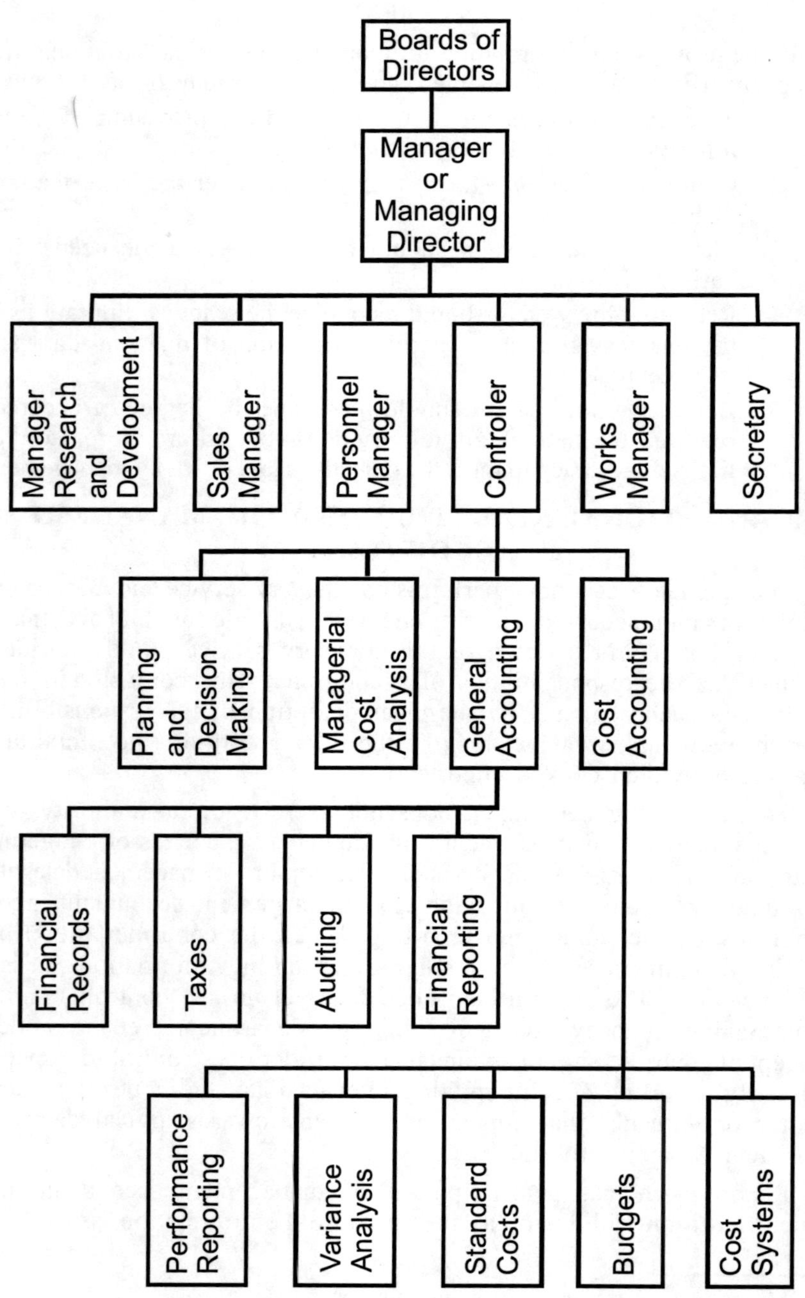

Exhibit 2.1

reflect upon individual performance and most of the information must be reported to the individual's supervisor. Therefore, he should report facts, with standard assessment, objective comments and detailed checking. The functions of controllership sector of a business are shown in Exhibit 2.1.

REPORTING TO MANAGEMENT

The type of financial information reports depend upon the responsibilities of different managers. The reporting procedure must be clearly defined. There should be schedules which explain, in greater detail, sections of an overall report for management. The overall report for management should break down into reports for different levels of management. The report should explain the accounting terms that are capable of misinterpretation. The reporting system should be flexible and should contain facts. A regular review of reports should be made. The time within which the reports are produced depends on the extent effective action can be taken as a result of interpreting the information contained in the statements.

THE FRAMEWORK OF MANAGEMENT ACCOUNTING

The basic classification of data relating to financial information for business management can be considered from two points of view:

1. An analysis of data on the basis of manager(s) actions in the business.
2. An analysis of data on the basis of economic cycle of activities of the business.

The analysis of data on the basis of manager(s) actions, sometimes called management cycle of planning and control, is shown in Exhibit 2.2.[1]

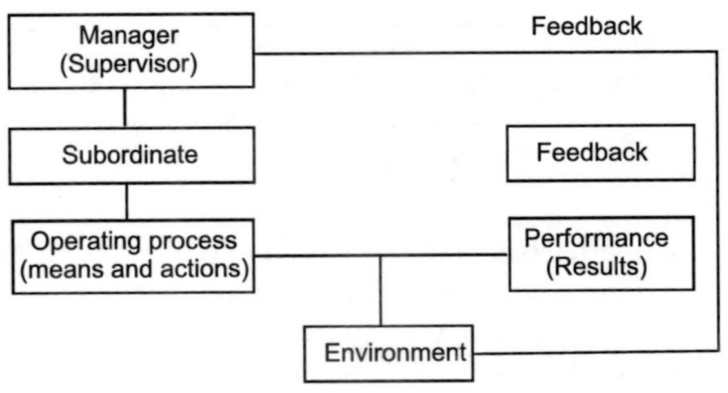

Exhibit 2.2

The operating process includes planning plus the action. The performance and feedback represent control. Two major accounting tools for helping managers are budgets and performance reports. These reports may sometimes consist of comparisons of budgets with actual results from

1. *Adaptive Behaviour*, H. Itami, p. 9.

the budget called variances. The variances help and facilitate "management by exception". The environment here means the uncontrollable factors that affect the success of a process. Feedback indicates how managers learn to improve the unending sequence of predictions and decisions that are embedded in the operating process. In control system, feedback often consists of a comparison of the budget with actual results. Feedback is used for a variety of purposes and is very important. Many control systems are weak, not because the feedback is weak, but because of the managers themselves, who are a part of the system.

The analysis of data on the basis of economic cycle of activities of the business is shown in Exhibit 2.3. It is the actions of managers that produce the economic cycle.

ECONOMIC CYCLE

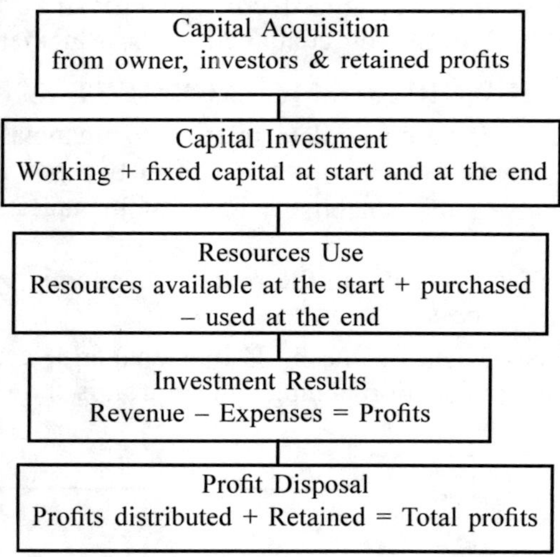

Exhibit 2.3

The above two approaches may be merged into one. The above framework of management accounting is reasonable framework capable of further development. It may be noted that there is no consistent framework of management accounting because it is not an organized discipline of study.

THE DATA INFORMATION TRANSFORMATION[1]

The data gathering, processing and transmission from several different points of view—those of information systems, information theory, measurement theory, decision theory and organisation theory.

1. Adapted from *Management Accounting*, L.R. Amey and D.A. Egginton.

Accounting is an information system. A system is a set of parts coordinated to accomplish a set of goals. It is necessary to spell out in detail what the whole system is, the environment in which it lives, what its objective is and how this is supported by the activities of the parts. The systems analyst is to identify, observe, analyse and specify the requirements for information in the decision-making activities throughout the organisation (i.e. define the information system) to determine source of data, and to match information requirements with appropriate data sources. An integrated information system would consist of sub-systems spanning all activities of the firm and all-time frames of interest to management in planning, decision and control. The information used by decision-makers is never complete or accurate within the firm. The data collection, data processing and communication are not costless. Faulty expectations may come about because too little information is collected or too little of the available information is used because they are based on irrelevant data of data is biased. These reasons are not exhaustive but indicative.

Information theory defines information in a special way and is concerned with providing a quantitative measure of information conveyed in a message (which may be a set of business data). Information is defined as a function of the probability that a certain "event" will occur, before a defined and reliable message, saying whether or not it has occurred, is received. Information content of the message has to do with uncertainty of the event occurring, as indicated by its prior probability. In order to measure information in this sense we need to be able to specify all possible events and their associated probabilities. The greater the probability that an event will occur, the smaller will be the amount of information in a message saying it has occurred and *vice versa*. The value of information has no relation to the amount of information. To measure the value of information, we have to see the decision theory. It is only worth buying information if value to the user exceeds the cost.

"Measure" is the development of a method of generating a class of data/information which will be useful in a wide range of problems. Measurements seek to express quantitative difference in attributes by bringing them into a certain relationship with a set of numbers. The set of numbers in accounting is expressed in terms of money. In measurement theory to qualify as measures the numbers must show certain formal properties. In accounting there is no measurement confirming to the requirements of measurement theory e.g. there must be a consistent relationship between attributes and numbers. Every measurement is subject to some error. It may be fundamental measurement, which is based on direct observation of attribute measured and derived measurement, which involves a transformation of a fundamental measure. Most accounting numbers are of second type. Though accounting measures do not constitute a measurement system in the strict sense, yet some of the desirable features of accounting measures are kept in mind e.g. accuracy, reasonable cost etc.

FINANCIAL ACCOUNTING AND MANAGEMENT ACCOUNTING

Accounting figures provide four types of information: (a) Historical i.e. actual costs are recorded; (b) Planning i.e. to enable management plan, and finance resources to achieve a profit accounting information is required; (c) Other decision information e.g. buy a new equipment; (d) Control i.e. the accounting information is useful in controlling the future.

The main difference between financial and management accounting lies in their purpose. The former is concerned with recording historic events and the latter with financial reports based on those records. Management accounting is concerned with the present and future, whereas the financial accounting deals with the past. Cost accounting is the essential foundation for the development of management accounting system. Management accounting information is only for internal use of the firm, where financial accounting information may for the use of outsiders like creditors.

COST CLASSIFICATION

Accounting system should serve multiple decision purposes. There are different measures of cost for different purposes. The most economically feasible approach to designing a management accounting system is to assume some common wants for a variety of decisions and choose cost objectives for routine data accumulation in light of these wants. Because costs must be tailored to the decision at hand, many terms have arisen to describe different types of cost. Among other categories classifications of cost can be made by:

1. Time when computed
   - (a) Historical Costs (Actual Costs)
   - (b) Budgeted or Predetermined Costs or Forecasted Costs
2. Behaviour in relation to fluctuations in activity
   - (a) Variable Costs
   - (b) Fixed Costs
   - (c) Other Costs
3. Degree of averaging
   - (a) Total Costs
   - (b) Average Costs
4. Management function
   - (a) Manufacturing Costs
   - (b) Selling Costs
   - (c) Administrative Costs

5. Ease of traceability to cost objective
   (a) Direct Costs
   (b) Indirect Costs
6. Timing of charges against revenue
   (a) Product Cost or Functional Cost
   (b) Period Costs

If a given cost changes in total in direct proportion to changes in activity (also called volume); it is variable.

A cost that is uniform per unit of volume so that it fluctuates in total in direct proportion to the changes in total volume e.g. sales commission and most of the materials.

If total cost remains unchanged for a given period despite wide fluctuations in activity, it is fixed. It does not fluctuate in total over a wide range of volume during a given time span, but that becomes progressively smaller on a per unit basis as production increases e.g. rent, insurance, depreciation.

A fixed cost is fixed only in relationship to a given period of time and a given, though wide, range of activity, called 'relevant range'. Fixed costs may be reduced substantially if activity levels fall drastically. In practice, the task to classification is very difficult and always necessitates nearly some simplifying assumptions e.g. that cost behaviour is linear.

An average cost is computed by dividing some costs by some denominator e.g. by units of production hours, number of invoices, unless total cost is averaged the cost is difficult to interpret. Average cost of making a finished goods is computed by totalling manufacturing costs and then dividing by number of units produced. Unit costs are averages and they must be interpreted with caution. Note that for decision purposes the fixed cost per unit must be distinguished from variable cost per unit. All average costs are not variable costs. Changes in activity will affect total variable costs but not all fixed costs. These relationships are shown below:

	Total Cost	Average Cost per unit
Variable Cost	Change	No change
Fixed Cost	No change	Change

There are three elements in the cost of manufactured product: (a) Direct material i.e. materials that are being identified with the finished goods, (b) Direct labour i.e. labour directly identified with the finished product, (c) Indirect manufacturing costs or factory overhead or factory burden or manufacturing overhead or manufacturing expenses. Prime cost is equal to direct material and direct labour costs. Conversion cost consists of direct labour plus factory overhead.

Product costs are those identified with goods purchased or produced for resale (also called inventoriable costs). They are initially identified as part of inventory in hand. They form the cost of goods sold only when the inventory is sold. Period costs are deducted as expenses (shown on debit side of Profit and Loss Account) during the current period. Selling and administrative expenses are example of period costs. They are deducted from revenue as expenses. The direct material, direct labour and factory overhead are examples of product costs.

Besides the above, costs may be classified:

(a) In relation to manufacturing departments
- (i) Producing Department Costs
- (ii) Service Department Costs

(b) According to their nature as
- (i) Common Costs
- (ii) Joint Costs

(c) Costs for planning and control
- (i) Standard Costs
- (ii) Actual Costs

(d) Costs for analytical processes
- (i) Differential and out of Pocket Costs
- (ii) Imputed Costs < Opportunity Costs / Outlay Costs

(e) According to shifting capacity
- (i) Postponable Costs
- (ii) Avoidable/Sunk Costs

A producing department is one in which manual and machine operations are performed directly upon any part of the product manufactured. A service department is one that renders a particular type of service for the benefit of other departments. Factory overhead is indirect cost with regard to a product or job. Actual factory overhead expenses are incurred and charged to either a producing or a service department, if readily identifiable with any of these departments. Service department expenses are prorated to producing and/or service departments. These prorated costs are called indirect departmental charges. When all service department expenses have been prorated to producing departments, each producing department's overhead will consist of its own direct and indirect departmental expense and the prorated or apportioned charges from service departments.

Common costs are costs of facilities or services employed in two or more accounting periods, operations, commodities or services e.g. depreciation of building. Joint costs occur when production of one product may be possible only if one or more other products are manufactured at the same time e.g. soap and glycerine, kerosene and gasoline.

Standard costs are predetermined costs for direct materials, direct labour and factory overhead. They are established by using information based on past experience and data. A standard states the costs under given conditions which are held constant in order to observe and measure fluctuations.

Differential and out of pocket costs, a short run concept, are those costs that entail current or future outlays for the decision at hand. Such costs are estimated costs which may be incurred if any one of several alternative courses of action is adopted. An imputed cost is the result of a process that recognizes a cost as it pertains to a particular situation, although the cost may not be routinely recognized by ordinary accounting procedures. Assigned or imputed cost may either be opportunity cost or outlay cost. Opportunity cost is the maximum amount that might have been earned if productive goods, service or capacity had been applied to an alternative use. Outlay cost means cash disbursement, as distinguished from opportunity cost.

Postponable costs are those that may be shifted to the future with little or no effect on the efficiency of current operations e.g. repairs. Avoidable costs are those that may be saved by not adopting a given alternative. Sunk cost, a term for past cost, is unavoidable because it cannot be changed, no matter whatever decision is taken. The term sunk cost is misleading one. Example: If old asset has a book value of ₹ 600,000 and scrap value of ₹ 70,000, then ₹ 530,000 is sunk cost. Sunk costs are historical costs that are irrevocable in a given situation.

Costs on which management has a control are called ‘controllable’.

The first step in preparing accounting data for decision-making is a separation of data into relevant and irrelevant costs. Relevant costs are those costs that would be changed by decision and irrelevant costs are not affected by the decision. Sunk costs are irrelevant costs. Relevant costs are incremental or differential costs. The incremental cost is the difference in total costs between two volumes. Committed costs remain constant at all levels unless facilities are expanded or contracted.

Programmed costs must be budgeted in steps to fit different ranges of activity. In some decisions, costs not acceptable for financial reporting are substituted for recorded costs e.g. replacement costs. They are the costs measured in terms of current prices i.e. what would have to be paid where the assets acquired at present price levels.

FINANCIAL DATA DIVISION

The financial information for the management is provided by accounting function. The accounting function gathers this information on the basis of economic cycle of business and/or the basis of functions of management, as shown in Exhibits 2.2 and 2.3.

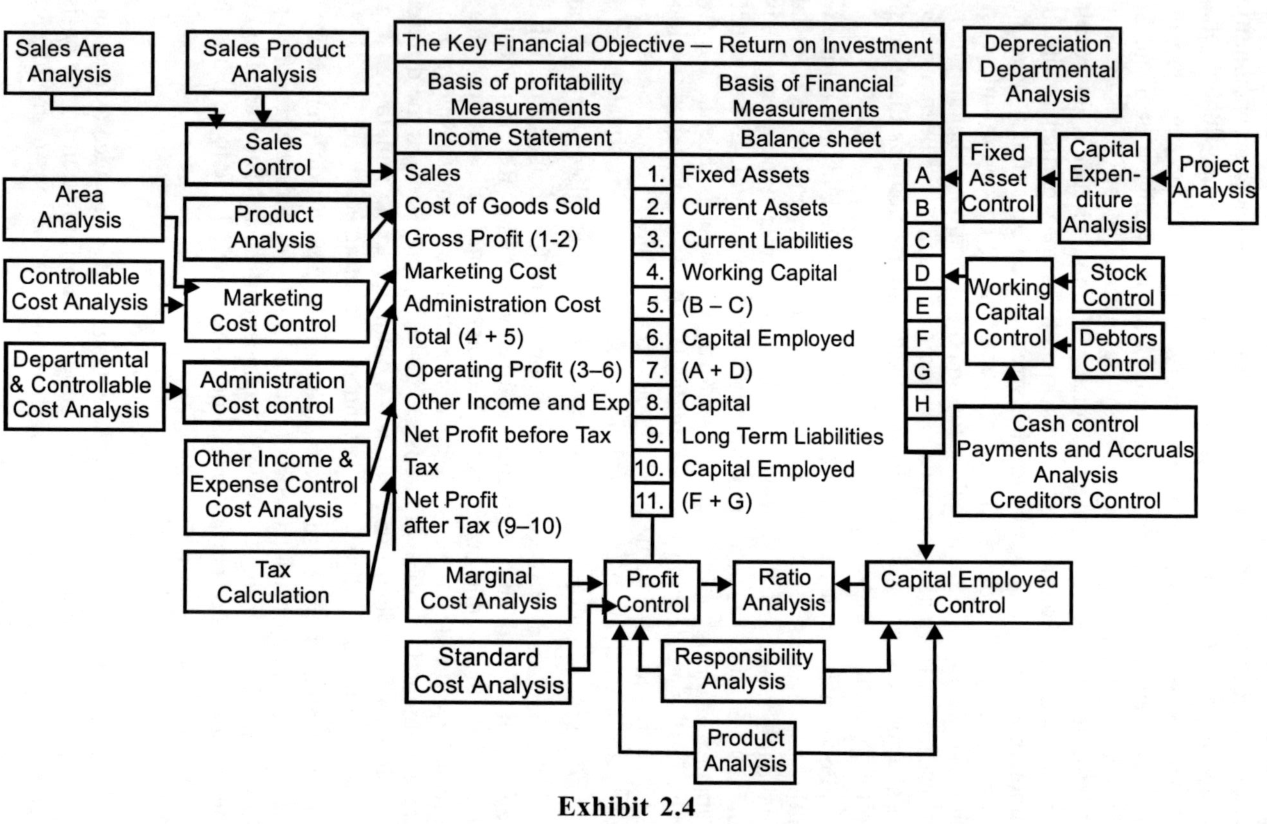
ACCOUNTING INFORMATION FOR CONTROL
Sales Area Analysis
Sales Product Analysis
Sales Control
Area Analysis
Product Analysis
Controllable Cost Analysis
Marketing Cost Control
Departmental & Controllable Cost Analysis
Administration Cost control
Other Income & Expense Control Cost Analysis
Tax Calculation
The Key Financial Objective — Return on Investment
Basis of profitability Measurements
Basis of Financial Measurements
Income Statement
Balance sheet
Sales
Cost of Goods Sold
Gross Profit (1-2)
Marketing Cost
Administration Cost
Total (4 + 5)
Operating Profit (3–6)
Other Income and Exp
Net Profit before Tax
Tax
Net Profit after Tax (9–10)
1. Fixed Assets
2. Current Assets
3. Current Liabilities
4. Working Capital
5. (B – C)
6. Capital Employed
7. (A + D)
8. Capital
9. Long Term Liabilities
10. Capital Employed
11. (F + G)
A
B
C
D
E
F
G
H
Depreciation Departmental Analysis
Fixed Asset Control
Capital Expen-diture Analysis
Project Analysis
Working Capital Control
Stock Control
Debtors Control
Cash control Payments and Accruals Analysis Creditors Control
Marginal Cost Analysis
Profit Control
Ratio Analysis
Capital Employed Control
Standard Cost Analysis
Responsibility Analysis
Product Analysis

Exhibit 2.4

PRODUCTION COST INFORMATION FOR CONTROL

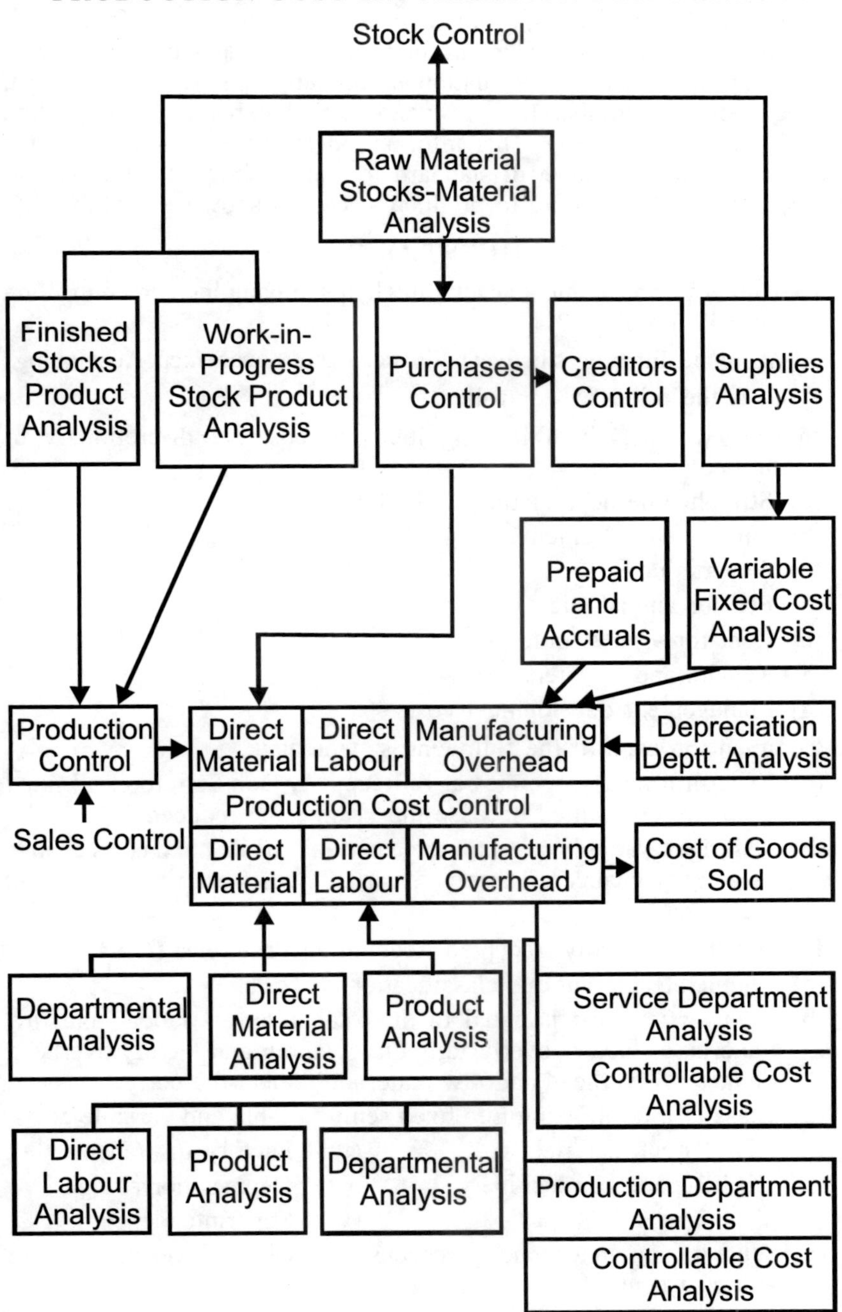

Exhibit 2.5

The information on the basis of economic cycle consists of information relating to capital acquisition, capital investment, resources use, investment results and profit disposal. The information on the basis of functions of management may relate to information about market cost, production cost, working capital, administration cost and capital expenditure (including research and development). This information may be related to income statement and balance sheet of standard format as shown in Exhibit 2.4. The increased detail relating to production cost is shown in Exhibit 2.5.

QUESTIONS

1. Explain how management accounting helps in planning and controlling and in trial problems?
2. What are the differences between Financial and Management Accounting?
3. What is the role of a controller?
4. Indicate whether the following items of cost are discretionary or committed:
   (a) Straight line depreciation on buildings
   (b) Salaries of salesmen
   (c) Advertising
   (d) Fee for annual audit
   (e) Rent for a new cooler
   (f) Repairs and maintenance
   (g) Management development costs.
5. Comment on each of the following statements:
   (a) "The firm nearly operates at full capacity, and therefore, all fixed costs are committed because they cannot be reduced."
   (b) "All right, variable costs are same per unit, while fixed costs change as activity changes. Therefore, variable costs are fixed and fixed are variable."
6. Explain the Generally Accepted Accounting Principles (GAAP):
   (a) Enumerate the various classification of costs.
   (b) "Conversion cost is equal to the total of direct labour and raw material or factory overhead; indirect labour and factory overhead or factory overhead and raw material." Select the correct answer.
   (c) Classify the following into fixed semi-variable and variable costs:
      (i) Direct material
      (ii) Repairs of machinery
      (iii) Rent
      (iv) Factory insurance
      (v) Depreciation straight line
      (vi) Superintendence.
   (d) What do you understand by responsibility centre, investment centre and cost centre?

7. The following accounts of manufacturing company appeared in Balance Sheet of 30-12-2019 and 30-12-2020:

	30-12-2019	30-12-2020
	₹	₹
Raw material inventory	1,30,000	1,46,000
Goods-in-process inventory	1,17,500	1,19,000
Finished goods inventory	1,23,000	1,18,200
Accrued factory salary	13,100	12,400
Accrued interest on Bills Receivable	1,120	1,180

The following amounts appeared in the income statements for 1999:

	₹
Raw material used	13,00,000
Cost of goods sold	19,20,000
Factory labour	12,75,000
Interest income	10,400

Calculate:

Raw material purchased, cost of goods manufactured, factory labour paid and interest received on bills receivable in 2019.

8. (i) Is there any difference between total manufacturing cost and cost of goods manufactured?

   The latter refers to cost of goods brought to completion (finished during the year.)

   (ii) What do you understand by feedback?

   (iii) If the work-in-process inventory has increased during the period, (a) Cost of goods sold will be greater than cost of goods manufactured. (b) or *vice versa* or (c) manufacturing costs will be more (or less than) than cost of goods manufactured. Which statement is correct?

3
Accounting Process—The Practical

Accounting Cycle. The double entry bookkeeping system provides a basic framework for the analysis of business transactions. The accounting procedures of most businesses involve certain basic steps that are accomplished in a given order. This sequence of procedures is known as accounting cycle. The accounting cycle can be divided into following steps:

Flow of Accounting Data

(1) Analyse transactions from source documents (vouchers)
(2) Record in Journal
(3) Post to Ledger accounts
(4) Prepare Trial Balance
(5) Prepare financial statements
(6) Close temporary accounts

The various steps in accounting cycle do not occur with equal frequency. Steps 1 to 3 take place during each operating period, whereas steps 4 and 5 are either taken at the end of month or quarter or six months or annually. Step 6 is taken at the close of the accounting year.

Business firms may end their accounting year either in calendar year basis or financial (fiscal year basis) (April to March) or festival Diwali basis.

Source Document (Voucher). They are usually printed or hand written forms that are generated when the firm enters into business transactions. It should contain the amount, date, possibly the party dealing with the firm and the name of the article. Examples are sales invoice, cheque, counterfoil, receipt, pay in slip etc. The bookkeeper is able to analyze the transaction by examining the voucher. Sometimes certain transactions can be analyzed by making further inquiry or old documents or records or contract or registers.

JOURNAL

"Journal", a French word, means 'a day'. It is a daily record and hence is a book of "original entry". Journalising means recording a transaction in the Journal. The form and manner in which it is recorded is called

"Journal entry". Before we see the Rules of Journal, we should know the type of accounts involved in any transaction.

Types of Accounts

Under British system, also followed in India, accounts are of following types:

1. Personal Account, 2. Impersonal Accounts. They are of two types: (a) Real Accounts, and (b) Nominal Accounts.

1. Personal Accounts. They are accounts of: (i) natural persons e.g. Ram's accounts, Peter's account, Hanif's account, and (ii) artificial persons e.g. Tata Tea Company's account, Punjab National Bank account.

2. Real Accounts. These accounts relate to tangible or intangible assets e.g. land, building, machinery, goodwill, patent.

3. Nominal Accounts. These accounts deal with expenses, gains, losses and incomes e.g. rent, salary, tax, discount, commission etc.

Note: If any prefix or suffix written with the name of any nominal account, it becomes representative personal account e.g. outstanding salary, prepaid wages, rent due, rent paid in advance etc.

RULES OF JOURNAL

Type of Account		Rules
(1) Personal account	(i)	Debit the Receiver
	(ii)	Credit the Giver
(2) Real account	(i)	Debit what comes in
	(ii)	Credit what goes out
(3) Nominal account	(i)	Debit all expenses (Losses)
	(ii)	Credit all gains (Incomes)

Each transaction in business, any of the above two accounts are involved always, not a single account. It may be as follows:

		Rule
(A) Personal and Real	(i)	Dr. the receiver, Credit what goes out
	(ii)	Dr. what comes in, Cr. the giver
(B) Personal and Nominal	(i)	Dr. the receiver, Cr. all gains
	(ii)	Dr. all expenses, Cr. the giver
(C) Nominal and Real	(i)	Dr. what comes in, Cr. all gains
	(ii)	Dr. all expenses, Cr. what goes out.

Examples

(1) Purchased goods from Meenu ₹ 1,00,000

Debit—Goods and Credit Meenu

Goods is a real account. Meenu is a personal account. Rule No. A(ii) applies here.

(2) Paid Rent ₹ 5000

Debit Rent and Credit Cash. Paid means paid Cash. Cash is a real account; and Rent is a nominal account. Rule C(ii) applies here.

The steps in making a Journal entry are three:

(*a*) Find the two accounts involved in the transaction.

(*b*) Find to which class of account they belong.

(*c*) Apply the rule.

If both the accounts involved in a transaction are of same class, any of the Rule No. 1, 2 or 3 will apply. If both accounts are the different classes, any of the rule A, B or C will apply.

TYPES OF ACCOUNTS AND RULES OF JOURNAL UNDER AMERICAN SYSTEM

Types of Accounts. Under American system the accounts are of five types: (1) Assets, (2) Liabilities, (3) Owner's equity, (4) Revenues, and (5) Expenses. They have been explained in Chapter 1.

Rules of Journal

(*a*) Debit if there is increase in Assets, and Expenses

(*b*) Credit if there is increase in Liabilities, owner's equity and revenues

(*c*) Debit if there is decrease in Liabilities, owner's equity and revenues

(*d*) Credit if there is decrease in Assets and Expenses.

Type of Account	Increase	Decrease	Normal Balance
1. Asset	Debit	Credit	Debit
2. Liability	Credit	Debit	Credit
3. Owner's Equity (Capital + Reserves)	Credit	Debit	Credit
4. Revenues	Credit	Debit	Credit
5. Expenses	Debit	Credit	Debit

Note: Balance means the difference between debit and credit. Debit balance means that Debit is more than credit and *vice versa*.

First find whether item affected in which account. Second, find the item affected increases or decreases. Lastly, see whether the transaction should be recorded as debit or credit.

Examples. (1) Purchased goods from Meenu ₹ 1,00,000 on 1-1-2021.

Increase in asset (goods) and increase in liability, so debit goods and credit Meenu. Rule (a) and (b) apply here.

(2) Paid Rent ₹ 5000 on 3-1-2021. For December 2020.

Decrease in asset (cash) and increase in expenses (rent) Dr. Rent and Credit cash. Rule (a) and (d) apply here. The rules are based on accounting equation

Assets = Liabilities + Owner's equity.

☞ **Warning.** Students to follow either British or American system in the beginning, otherwise they will be confused.

Form of Journal. After knowing what is to be debited and credited, the recording is made in the Journal (two column) in a prescribed manner. The format or ruling of Journal is given below, along with the method to record the Journal entry. The form of Journal is same under British and American systems.

JOURNAL

Date	Particulars		L.F.	Debit Amount	Credit Amount
2021 January 1	Goods A/c To Meenu (Goods bought on credit from Meenu)	Dr.		1,00,000	 1,00,000
January 3	Rent A/c To Cash A/c (Being rent paid for December 2021)	Dr.		500	 5000

The above procedure is as follows:

1. Recording the date. Year at top only, the below month and then date.

2. Recording the debit. Title of the account to be debited is inserted at extreme left of the particulars column and amount in the debit column.

3. Recording the credit. Title of the account is below the account debited (leaving some space on left) and writing the word "To". Some accountants do not write the word 'To'. Amount is entered in the credit column, exactly in line. The word 'To' is not written after the name of a person.

4. Writing narration. The explanation is called narration. This may be written in brackets or without brackets. The word 'Being' is written before the explanation.

☞ **5.** Modern trend is not to write the word 'Being' and not to put brackets. Putting brackets and writing the word 'Being' is old practice. Even the word "to" is out of use now in Journal entry only.

Example 1

Typical entries. Journalise the following transactions:

Year 2020

January 1 Jose Mompilli started business with Cash ₹ 50,000, Building1,00,000 and Goods ₹ 10,000

2 Withdrew cash 2,000 for personal use

4 Bought goods from Ali for ₹ 30,000 on a discount of 2%

5 Sold goods to Ram for Cash ₹ 35,000, allowed him discount of 2.5%

6 Bought table ₹ 500, paid Cartage on it ₹ 10

8 Gave Loan of ₹ 100 to X

9 Mr. X is unable to pay due to insolvency

10 Goods given as free sample ₹ 200

Notes: (1) Word account (A/c) is not written after the name of a person. The letter "A" should be capital in "A/c".

(2) Two Journal entries can be combined. It is called 'Compound Journal entry'. See below entry of January 5.

(3) Trade discount is not recorded in any account as it is already deducted in the invoice itself from the gross value of goods. See the entry of January 4. Only cash discount is debited, if given, or credited if allowed. See entry of January 5.

(4) All expenses incurred on the purchase of an asset (Except goods) is included in the cost of the asset. *See* entry January 6.

Solution

JOURNAL ENTRIES

Date	Particulars		L.F.	Debit (Amount) ₹	Credit (Amount) ₹
2020					
Jan. 1	Cash A/c	Dr.		50,000	
	Building A/c	Dr.		1,00,000	
	Goods A/c	Dr.		10,000	
	To J. Mompilli Capital A/c				1,60,000
	(J. Mompilli started business)				
Jan. 2	Drawings A/c	Dr.		2,000	
	To Cash A/c				2,000
	(Cash withdrawn for self use)				

Date	Particulars		L.F.	Debit (Amount) ₹	Credit (Amount) ₹
Jan. 4	Goods A/c	Dr.		30,000	
	To Ali				30,000
	(Goods bought on credit from Ali)				
Jan. 5	Cash A/c	Dr.		34,125	
	Discount A/c	Dr.		875	
	To Goods A/c				35,000
	(Goods sold for cash)				
Jan. 6	Furniture A/c	Dr.		510	
	To Cash A/c				510
	(Bought table for cash)				
Jan. 8	X	Dr.		100	
	To Cash A/c				100
	(Gave ₹ 100 to X)				
Jan. 9	Bad Debt A/c	Dr.		100	
	To X				100
	(Loan not paid by X)				
Jan. 10	Advertisement A/c	Dr.		200	
	To Goods A/c				200
	(Goods given free samples)				

Example 2

Journalise the following transactions in the books of Messrs. Haldi Ram and Sons:

2021			₹
March	1	Started business with cash	1,00,000
	3	Cash purchases	30,000
	5	Sales to Shyam	30,000
	6	Cash sales	10,000
	9	Shyam pays	20,000
	13	Purchases from Ram	20,000
	20	Paid to Ram	10,000
	25	Office rent paid	2,000
	31	Paid Salaries to Staff	10,000
	31	Returns in by Shyam	5,000

Solution

IN THE BOOKS OF HALDI RAM AND SONS

Date	Particulars		L.F.	Debit (Amount) ₹	Credit (Amount) ₹
2021					
March 1	Cash A/c	Dr.		1,00,000	
	To Capital A/c				1,00,000
	(Started business with cash)				
March 3	Goods A/c	Dr.		30,000	
	To Cash A/c				30,000
	(Purchased goods for cash)				
March 5	Shyam	Dr.		30,000	
	To Goods A/c				30,000
	(Sold goods on credit to Shyam)				
March 6	Cash A/c	Dr.		10,000	
	To Goods A/c				10,000
	(Goods sold for cash)				
March 9	Cash A/c	Dr.		20,000	
	To Shyam				20,000
	(Cash received from Shyam)				
March 13	Goods A/c	Dr.		20,000	
	To Ram				20,000
	(Goods bought on credit from Ram)				
March 20	Ram	Dr.		10,000	
	To Cash A/c				10,000
	(Cash paid to Ram)				
March 25	Rent A/c	Dr.		2,000	
	To Cash A/c				2,000
	(Rent paid)				
March 31	Salaries A/c	Dr.		10,000	
	To Cash A/c				10,000
	(Salaries paid)				
March 31	Goods A/c	Dr.		5,000	
	To Shyam				5,000
	(Goods returned by Shyam)				

Note: After the journal entries posting of entries in the ledger. The abbreviation 'L.F.' stands for 'Ledger Folio' which means the page number of the ledger where this Journal entry is posted.

LEDGER

Ledger is the principal book of account. It contains all accounts, their details and amount date-wise. One can know at a glance whether a person is debtor or creditor, and whether it is an expense or income. Ledger can be either in bound form or loose leaf form. Loose Leaf cards are common in banks or where mechanised accounting system is in use.

After Journal entries are made in Journal, each Journal entry is posted in Ledger. The debit entry on the debit side and credit entry on credit side of the relevant account: An index is provided at the beginning in alphabetical order to know on which page (folio) a particular account appears.

Account — T Form

An account has two sides, divided by a vertical line. The left hand side is called the Debit side and the right hand is called Credit side. It is like letter "T" and is called two column account. The debit and credit sides are denoted by writing abbreviation "Dr." and "Cr." on left and right top of the account. Each side is further divided into four columns—date, particulars, folio and amount. The rulings will appear thus:

NAME OF ACCOUNT

Dr. Cr.

Date	Particulars	Folio	Amount	Date	Particulars	Folio	Amount

Alternate Form

An alternate form will appear as follows:

NAME OF ACCOUNT

Date	Particulars	Folio	Dr. Amount	Cr. Amount	Balance	
					Dr. or Cr.	Amount

The advantage of this ruling is that balance of an account is done after every transaction. It is usually followed by banks.

POSTING FROM JOURNAL TO LEDGER

This can better be explained by an example. Suppose on January 2, 2021, Mr. Haldi Ram sold goods for cash ₹ 10,000. Its Journal entry will be:

		₹	₹
Jan. 2	Cash A/c Dr. To Goods A/c (Goods sold for cash)	10,000	 10,000

Now we post it in the ledger. We will open two accounts, one of cash and another of goods. Cash account will be debited and goods account will be credited. When we debit, the letters "To" and when we credit the letters "By" are written. See the following:

GOODS ACCOUNT

Dr. Cr.

Date	Particulars	Folio	Amount	Date	Particulars	Folio	Amount
2021 Jan. 2	To Cash A/c		10,000				

CASH ACCOUNT

Dr. Cr.

Date	Particulars	Folio	Amount	Date	Particulars	Folio	Amount
				2021 Jan. 2	By Goods		10,000

The date is recorded in date column on the side on which posting is done. Folio is page number of Journal where entry has been recorded. Writing "To" or "By" is compulsory.

Posting of Compound Journal Entry

In example 1, compound entry on January 5 in J. Mompilli Journal was:

Cash A/c	Dr.	34,125	
Discount A/c	Dr.	875	
To Goods A/c			35,000

(for goods sold in cash allowing discount 2½%)

The posting of this Journal entry will be as follows:

CASH ACCOUNT

Dr. Cr.

Date	Particulars	Folio	Amount	Date	Particulars	Folio	Amount
	To Goods A/c		34,125				

DISCOUNT ACCOUNT

Dr. Cr.

Date	Particulars	Folio	Amount	Date	Particulars	Folio	Amount
	To Goods A/c		875				

GOODS ACCOUNT

Dr. Cr.

Date	Particulars	Folio	Amount	Date	Particulars	Folio	Amount
					By Cash " Discount		34,125 875

Note: There is no need to write "To" or "By" if in the Ledger there are many postings e.g. in goods account above, just put " ditto sign.

Balancing of Accounts

Balancing of Accounts is made at regular intervals i.e. daily, monthly or annually. The *procedure* of balancing accounts is given below:

1. Total up the two sides of the account on a rough page.
2. Find out the difference or balance between the totals of two sides.
3. Enter the difference or balance in the amount column of the shorter side, "To Balance c/d" (c/d means carried down) on the left hand or debit side of the account if debit side is shorter and "By Balance c/d" on the right hand or credit side of the account, if shorter side is credit side.
4. Then total of the two sides will be the same, which is now written at the bottom of either sides in the same horizontal line. A single line is drawn across the amount column before writing the total and double lines across the amount columns after writing the total.
5. The balance is brought forward at the beginning of the next period. If "To Balance c/d" is written on the debit side before balancing, then it will be brought forward on the credit side and "By Balance b/d" will be written in the particulars column and *vice versa*.

If the total of the debit side of an account is more than the credit side of that account, such an account is said to have a *debit balance*. If, on the other hand, the total of the credit side of an account is more than the debit side of that account, then it will have a *credit balance.* Or if, balance b/d is on debit side it is debit balance and if balance b/d is on credit side, it is credit balance.

Balances of Various Accounts

Personal Accounts. The debit balance of a personal account means the person is our debtor. The credit balance means the person is our creditor. Hence the rule Dr. the receiver, Cr. the giver.

Real Accounts. The debit balance of a real account represents an asset i.e. the value of an asset on hand. Hence the rule Dr. what comes in Cr. what goes out.

Nominal Accounts. The debit balance of a nominal account represents expense or loss and credit balance gain or income. Hence the rule Dr. all expenses, Cr. all gains.

Real and Personal accounts are required to be balanced, if their total is not equal for the purpose of preparing Trial Balance and Balance Sheet. They are not closed, but are carried next year. The nominal account also be balanced and ultimately they are closed by transferring their balances to the Profit and Loss Account.

Example 3

Post entries into ledger from the journal prepared in case of example 2.

Solution

HALDI RAM
CASH ACCOUNT

2021		₹	2021		₹
March 1	To Capital A/c	1,00,000	March 3	By Goods A/c	30,000
" 6	" Goods A/c	10,000	" 20	" Ram	10,000
" 9	" Shyam	20,000	" 25	" Rent A/c	2,000
			" 31	" Salaries A/c	10,000
			" 31	" Balance c/d	78,000
		1,30,000			1,30,000
April 1	To Balance b/d	78,000			

CAPITAL ACCOUNT

2021		₹	2021		₹
March 31	To Balance c/d	1,00,000	March 1	By Cash A/c	1,00,000
			April 1	" Balance b/d	1,00,000

GOODS ACCOUNT

2021		₹	2021		₹
March 1	To Cash A/c	30,000	March 5	By Shyam	30,000
" 13	" Ram	20,000	" 6	" Cash A/c	10,000
" 31	" Shyam	5,000	" 31	" Balance c/d	15,000
		55,000			55,000
April 1	To Balance b/d	15,000			

SHYAM

2021		₹	2021		₹
March 5	To Goods A/c	30,000	March 9	By Cash A/c	20,000
			" 31	" Goods A/c	5,000
			" 31	" Balance c/d	5,000
		30,000			30,000
April 1	To Balance b/d	500			

RAM

2021		₹	2021		₹
March 20	To Cash	10,000	March 31	By Goods A/c	20,000
" 31	" Balance c/d	10,000			
		20,000			20,000
April 1	By Balance b/d	10,000			

RENT A/C

2021		₹	2021		₹
March 25	To Cash A/c	2,000	March 31	By Balance c/d	2,000
April 1	To Balance b/d	2,000			

SALARIES A/C

2021		₹	2021		₹
March 31	To Cash A/c	10,000	March 31	By Balance c/d	10,000
April 1	To Balance b/d	10,000			

Notes: (1) In practice, use of Journal is rarely made. Transactions are directly posted in the ledger only much transactions are Journalised that do not occur frequently in the business e.g. opening entries, closing entries, adjusting entries, transfer entries, rectifying entries and purchase of fixed. Such Journal then is known as General Journal or Journal proper.

(2) Since cash transactions are many, cash account of the ledger is kept separately in a book form. It is called cash book. It may also include bank and discount accounts also. Then it is called "Three column" cash book.

Trial Balance

The fundamental principle of Double Entry Accounting is that for every debit, there must be a corresponding credit. Thus, for every debit or a series of debits to one or several accounts, there must be a corresponding credit or a series of credits for an equal amount. It follows, therefore, that the sums of the debit amounts must be equal to the sums of the credit amounts of the Ledger at any date. But when an account is balanced, equal debits and credits are cancelled against each other, and the difference is called the balance.

Thus, even if all the accounts of the Ledger are balanced, the total of all debit balances must be equal to the total of all credit balances on the same date. The statement in which debit and credit balances are noted down and finally totalled up to ascertain, if they are equal, is called a Trial Balance. Thus, Trial Balance can be defined as *a statement of debit and credit totals or balances from the Ledger with a view to test the arithmetical accuracy of the books.*

Preparation of Trial Balance

A Trial Balance can be prepared by the following methods:

1. Total Method. In this method the debit and credit totals of each account are shown in the two amount columns against it. This involves showing of both totals against each account. It is not much used in practice.

2. Balance Method. In this method, only the balance of each account is shown against it in the appropriate amount column. As only the balance of each account is shown against it and if an account does not show any balance, it should not be included in the Trial Balance. This method is used in practice, it facilitates the preparation of final statements of accounts.

Trial Balance can be prepared monthly or at the end of a financial year after the accounts have been closed. A specimen is given below:

TRIAL BALANCE AS ON ....

Serial No.	Name of Account	Dr. Balance (or Total) ₹	Cr. Balance (or Total) ₹

Example 4

From the accounts prepared in example 2, prepare a Trial Balance by both methods.

Solution

TRIAL BALANCE AS ON 31ST MARCH, 2021

Sl. No.	Name of Account	Total Method		Balance Method	
		Dr. Total ₹	Cr. Total ₹	Dr. Balance ₹	Cr. Balance ₹
1.	Cash Account	1,30,000	52,000	78,000	—
2.	Capital Account	—	1,00,000	—	1,00,000
3.	Goods Account	55,000	40,000	15,000	—
4.	Shyam	30,000	25,000	5,000	—
5.	Ram	10,000	20,000	—	10,000
6.	Rent Account	2,000	—	2,000	—
7.	Salaries Account	10,000	—	10,000	—
		2,37,000	2,37,000	1,10,000	1,10,000

Note: You see the balance columns and observe that all assets, debtors and expenses have debit balances and all liabilities, creditors and incomes have credit balances.

Example 5

Journalise the following transactions, post them into Ledger and Prepare a Trial Balance in the books of George:

2021

January,

1 Started business with ₹ 10,000, paid into Bank ₹ 5,000.

3 Bought furniture for ₹ 900.

4 Purchased goods from Mohan for ₹ 4,000 for cash.

5 Sold goods for ₹ 1,700.

7 Paid telephone rent for the year ₹ 400.

8 Purchased goods for ₹ 1,000 from Venkat.

10 Paid ₹ 100 for advertisement by cheque.

11 Bought one typewriter for ₹ 750 from Universal Co. on credit.

12 Sold goods to Bedi for ₹ 2,900.

14 Withdraw ₹ 350 from the Bank for private use.

16 Sold goods to Omega for ₹ 650 for cash.

25 Received cash from Bedi ₹ 2,850, discount allowed ₹ 50.

26 Paid into Bank ₹ 2,500.

31 Issued a cheque for ₹ 300 in favour of the landlord for rent for January.

31 Paid salaries of staff ₹ 600.

31 Paid ₹ 950 to Venkat in full settlement of their account.

Solution

JOURNAL ENTRIES

2021				₹	₹
Jan.	1	Cash A/c To Capital A/c (Cash brought in as Capital)	Dr. ...	10,000	 10,000
"	1	Bank A/c To Cash A/c (Cash deposited in the Bank)	Dr. ...	5,000	 5,000
"	3	Furniture A/c To Cash A/c (Furniture purchased)	Dr. ...	900	 900
"	4	Goods A/c To Cash Account (Goods purchased for cash)	Dr. ...	4,000	 4,000
"	5	Cash A/c To Goods A/c (Goods sold for Cash)	Dr. ...	1,700	 1,700
"	7	Telephone Rent A/c To Cash A/c (Paid telephone rent)	Dr. ...	400	 400
"	8	Goods A/c To Venkat (Goods purchased on credit)	Dr. ...	1,000	 1,000
"	10	Advertisement A/c To Bank (Payment of advertisement made by cheque)	Dr. ...	100	 100
"	11	Office Equipment A/c To Universal Co. (Purchased one typewriter on credit)	Dr. ...	750	 750
"	12	Bedi To Goods A/c (Goods sold on credit)	Dr. ...	2,900	 2,900
"	14	Drawings A/c To Bank A/c (Amount withdrawn for personal use)	Dr. ...	350	 350

Date	Particulars		Dr.	Cr.
2021 Jan. 16	Cash A/c To Goods A/c (Goods sold for Cash)	Dr. ...	650	 650
" 25	Cash A/c Discount A/c To Bedi (Cash received & discount allowed)	Dr. Dr. ...	2,850 50	 2,900
" 26	Bank A/c To Cash A/c (Cash deposited)	Dr. ...	2,500	 2,500
" 31	Rent A/c To Bank A/c (Cheque paid for rent)	Dr. ...	300	 300
" 31	Salaries A/c To Cash A/c (Salaries paid)	Dr. ...	600	 600
" 31	Venkat To Cash A/c To Discount A/c (Cash paid in full settlement)	Dr.	1,000	 950 50
	Total	₹	35,050	35,050

Note: In big business firms goods account is not opened in the ledger. Instead sales and purchases accounts are opened. The procedure is to have a sales and purchases Journal (book) separately. The sales and purchases are totalled for Journal entry. In that case purchases and sales are debited and credited instead of goods account. There is no particular ruling of these Journals. It may contain date, particulars of goods and parties and amount.

LEDGER

CASH A/C

Dr. Cr.

2021		₹	2021		₹
Jan. 1	To Capital A/c	10,000	Jan. 1	By Bank	5,000
" 5	" Goods A/c	1,700	" 3	" Furniture A/c	900
" 16	" Goods A/c	650	" 4	" Goods A/c	4,000
" 25	" Bedi & Co.	2,850	" 7	" Telephone Rent A/c	400
			" 26	" Bank A/c	2,500
			" 31	" Salaries A/c	600
			" 31	" Bir & Co.	950
			" 31	" Balance c/d	850
		15,200			15,200
Feb. 1	To Balance b/d	850			

CAPITAL A/C

Dr. Cr.

2021		₹	2021		₹
Jan. 31	To Balance c/d	10,000	Jan. 1	By Cash A/c	10,000
			Feb. 1	By Balance b/d	10,000

BANK A/C

Dr. Cr.

2021		₹	2021		₹
Jan. 1	To Cash A/c	5,000	Jan. 10	By Advertisement A/c	100
" 26	" Cash A/c	2,500	" 14	" Drawings A/c	350
			" 31	" Rent A/c	300
			" 31	" Balance c/d	6,750
		7,500			7,500
Feb. 1	To Balance b/d	6,750			

FURNITURE A/C

Dr. Cr.

2021		₹	2021		₹
Jan. 3	To Cash A/c	900	Jan. 31	By Balance c/d	900
Feb. 1	To Balance b/d	900			

DISCOUNT A/C

Dr. Cr.

2021		₹	2021		₹
Jan. 25	To Bedi & Co.	50	Jan. 31	By Bir & Co.	50

TELEPHONE RENT A/C

Dr. Cr.

2021		₹	2021		₹
Jan. 7	To Cash A/c	400	Jan. 31	By Balance c/d	400
Feb. 1	To Balance b/d	400			

ADVERTISEMENT A/C

Dr. Cr.

2021		₹	2021		₹
Jan. 10	To Bank A/c	100	Jan. 31	By Balance c/d	100
Feb. 1	To Balance b/d	100			

GOODS A/C

Dr. Cr.

2021		₹	2021		₹
Jan. 4	To Cash A/c	4,000	Jan. 5	By Cash A/c	1,700
" 8	" Bir & Co.	1,000	" 12	" Bedi & Co.	2,900
" 31	" Balance c/d	250	" 16	" Cash A/c	650
		5,250			5,250
			Feb. 1	By Balance b/d	250

DRAWINGS A/C

Dr. Cr.

2021		₹	2021		₹
Jan. 14	To Bank	350	Jan. 31	By Balance c/d	350
	To Balance b/d	350			

RENT A/C

Dr. Cr.

2021		₹	2021		₹
Jan. 31	To Bank	300		By Balance c/d	300
Feb. 1	To Balance b/d	300			

SALARIES A/C

Dr. Cr.

2021		₹	2021		₹
Jan. 31	To Cash	600		By Balance c/d	600
Feb. 1	To Balance b/d	600			

VENKAT

Dr. Cr.

2021		₹	2021		₹
Jan. 31	To Cash A/c	950	Jan. 8	By Goods A/c	1,000
" 31	" Discount A/c	50			
		1,000			1,000

OFFICE EQUIPMENT A/C

Dr. Cr.

2021		₹	2021		₹
Jan. 11	To Universal Typewriter Co.	750	Jan. 31	By Balance c/d	750
Feb. 1	To Balance b/d	750			

UNIVERSAL CO.

Dr.					Cr.
2021		₹	2021		₹
Jan. 31	To Balance c/d	750	Jan. 11	By Office Eq. A/c	750
			Feb. 1	By Balance b/d	750

BEDI

Dr.					Cr.
2021		₹	2021		₹
Jan. 12	To Goods A/c	2,900	Jan. 25	By Cash A/c	2,850
			" 25	" Discount A/c	50
		2,900			2,900

TRIAL BALANCE
as on 31st January, 2021

Name of Account	Dr. Amount ₹	Cr. Amount ₹
Cash Account	850	
Capital Account		10,000
Bank Account	6750	
Furniture Account	900	
Advertisement Account	100	
Telephone Account	400	
Goods Account		250
Office equipment Account	750	
Universal Co.		750
Drawings Account	350	
Rent Account	300	
Salaries Account	600	
	11,000	11,000

Posting of Opening Entry

Opening entry is an entry made at the end of financial year from the balance sheet. The assets are debited and liabilities are credited. More shall we tell you about this entry in the next chapter. Just at present you should know how it is posted in Ledger next year. The entry is posted only by writing "To balance b/d" or "By balance b/d" on debit and credit sides respectively. Example follows:

Furniture A/c	Dr.	₹ 2,000	
Cash A/c	"	₹ 5,000	
Debtors A/c	"	₹ 500	
Goods A/c	"	₹ 1,000	
To Creditors A/c			400
To Capital A/c			8,100

(Various assets and liabilities brought to new financial year)

LEDGER

FURNITURE ACCOUNT

Date		₹			
2021 Jan. 1	To Balance b/d	2,000			

CASH A/C

		₹			
	To Balance b/d	5,000			

DEBTORS A/C

		₹			
	To Balance b/d	500			

GOODS A/C

		₹			
	To Balance b/d	1,000			

CREDITORS A/C

					₹
				By Balance b/d	400

CAPITAL A/C

					₹
				By Balance b/d	81,000

QUESTIONS

1. What are the Rules of Journal under British system and under American system?
2. What is (a) narration (b) L.F. (c) Opening entry (d) Compound entry (e) Debit balance (f) Accounting equation (g) b/d and c/d (h) Three column Cash Book?
3. Fill in the blanks:
   (a) Trial Balance is prepared by ______ methods. They are ______.
   (b) If there is an increase in asset, it is to be ____________.

(c) If there is an increase in liability, it is to be ____________.

(d) If there is an increase in expenses, it is to be ____________.

(e) Under British system if any transaction involves a personal account and other real account the rules are:

(i) __________.

(ii) __________.

(f) Trade discount is a discount __________.

(g) Use of Journal in practice is made only for those transactions that __________.

4. Give the American terms for the following:

(i) Goods __________.

(ii) Bills Receivable __________.

(iii) Creditors __________.

(iv) Capital __________.

(v) Closing Stock __________.

(vi) Profit and Loss account __________.

(vii) Drawings __________.

EXERCISES

1. Journalise the following transactions, post them to Ledger and prepare a Trial Balance:

1. Year 2021 Dec. 1. Mohd. Ahmed started business ₹ 4,00,000
2. Jan. 3 – Deposited into Punjab National Bank ₹ 2,00,000
3. " 5 – Cash purchases ₹ 1,50,000
4. " 8 – Cash sales ₹ 60,000
5. " 10 – Furniture purchased payment by cheque ₹ 50,000
6. " 12 – Sold goods to Rao ₹ 40,000
7. " 14 – Purchased goods from George ₹ 1,00,000
8. " 15 – Return goods to George ₹ 50,000
9. " 16 – Received in full settlement from Rao ₹ 39,600
10. " 18 – Withdrawals goods ₹ 10,000
11. " 20 – Drawings cash ₹ 20,000
12. " 24 – Telephone bill paid ₹ 10,000
13. " 26 – Cash paid to George in full settlement ₹ 49,000
14. " 31 – Paid cash for stationery ₹ 2000, Rent ₹ 500 and Salaries ₹ 20,000
15. " 31 – Free sample of goods distributed ₹ 10,000

2. Correct the following Trial Balance:

Account	Dr. Balance (₹)	Cr. Balance (₹)
Capital	11,100	
Machinery	–	11,000
Stock	–	500
Debtors	400	–
Creditors	–	600
Sales	–	2,000
Purchases	1,400	–
Wages	400	
Sales Returns	–	400
Expenses	600	–
Returns out	200	–
Cash	–	100
Bank Loan	700	–
	14,800	14,800

Answer: Total 14,800

3. Journalise the following as an opening entry from balances taken on 30-6-2021 from books of Rajiv and post them in Ledger. Cash 12,000, Furniture ₹ 1,400, Stock ₹ 22,000, Buildings ₹ 10,000, Debtors ₹ 26,000 and Creditors ₹ 16,000 Capital ₹ 55,400.

4. Continuing the above exercise, the following transactions took place in July 2020—The new accounting year. Journalise them, post into Ledger and prepare a trial balance.

2021		
July	1	Sold goods to Raghavan ₹ 30,000, Philips ₹ 20,000 and Anil ₹ 30,000
"	5	Cash paid old Creditor ₹ 20,000
"	17	Cash received from old Debtor ₹ 57,000
"	19	Expenses incurred ₹ 15,000
"	20	Goods sold to Martin ₹ 5000
"	25	Paid Rent ₹ 500, Salaries ₹ 1,000.

4

Financial Statements

The last phase of accounting cycle is the preparation of financial statements. Financial statements are Profit and Loss Account (income statement) and the Balance Sheet (position statement). They are prepared at the end of the accounting year. For companies their format is prescribed under Indian Companies Act, 2013 (Schedule II). They can be presented in two ways: (a) T form i.e. account form and (b) Vertical or report form. Income statement under American system in vertical form may be also single step or multiple step (classified form). The Profit and Loss Account in T form is subdivided under British system in (a) Trading Account, (b) Profit and Loss Account. The various format are given below:

T Form of Profit and Loss Account (British System)

Trading A/c

For the year ending...............

Dr. Cr.

	₹		₹
To Opening Stock		By Sales	
" Purchases		*Less* Returns in	
Less Returns out		" Closing Stock	
" Direct Expenses:		" P & L A/c	
(a) Wages		(Gross Loss) c/d	
(b) Carriage in			
(c) Factory Lighting			
(d) " Motive Power			
(e) " Rent			
(f) Manufacturing Expenses			
(g) Factory insurance			
(h) Consumable stores			
" P&L A/c (Gross Profit) c/d			

Profit & Loss A/c

For the year ending ....

Dr.	₹		Cr. ₹
To Trading A/c (Gross Loss)		By Trading A/c (Gross Loss)	
" Office and Administrative expenses:		" Interest	
(a) Rent, Rates and Taxes		" Discount	
(b) Office Salaries		" Commission	
(c) Postage and Stationery		" Income from investments	
(d) Telephone		" Dividend	
(e) Insurance		" Difference in exchange	
(f) Audit fee		" Net Loss transferred to Capital A/c	
" Selling and Distribution expenses:			
(a) Advertisement			
(b) Salesman's salary and commission			
(c) Carriage out			
(d) Bad Debt			
" Financial Expenses:			
(a) Interest on Loan and Capital			
(b) Discount allowed			
(c) Discount on Bills			
" Depreciation and Maintenance expenses			
" Extra Ordinary expenses e.g. Loss by fire			
" Net Profit transferred to Capital A/c			

Single Step Income Statement (American Vertical Form)

For the year ended ....

	₹	₹
Revenues:		
Net sales		1,63,774
Other income		1,200
Total Revenues		1,64,974
Expenses:		
Cost of Merchandise sold	1,01,305	
Selling Expenses	25,834	
General Expenses	10,672	
Financial Expenses	585	
Total Expenses		1,38,396
Net Income		26,578

Multiple Step Income Statement
(American system Vertical form)

		₹	₹
Revenue from Sales:			
Sales		1,67,736	
Less sales returns	2,140		
Sales discount	1,822	3,962	
Net Sales			1,63,774
Cost of merchandise sold:			
Merchandise Inventory Jan. 1, year X		19,700	
Purchases	1,05,280		
Less returns and discount	1,525		
Net purchases		1,03,755	
Merchandise available for sale		1,23,455	
Less Merchandise Inventory Dec. 31, year X		22,150	
Cost of Merchandise sold			1,01,305
Gross Profit (Loss) on sales			62,469
Operating Expenses:			
Selling Expenses:			
Sales Salaries	20,044		
Advertisement	3,460		
Depreciation	1,100		
Insurance	580		
Other Expenses	230		
Total Selling Expenses		25,834	
General Expenses:			
Office Salaries	6,032		
Taxation	1,810		
Depreciation Office	1,990		
Office Supplies	530		
Miscellaneous Expenses	310		
Total General Expenses		10,672	
Total Operating Expenses			36,506
			25,963
Income from operations:			
Other Income: Rent	1,200		
Other Expenses: Interest	585		615
Net Income			26,578

Note: Figures are imaginary.

T Form Balance Sheet

As on December ....

Liabilities		Assets
Capital —		*Fixed Assets:*
Add Net Profit		Goodwill
Reserves and Surplus:		Land
Loans (Secured and unsecured)		Building
		Plant and Machinery
Current Liabilities:		Furniture
Bills payable		Livestock
Sundry Creditors		Vehicles
Provision for Tax		*Investments:*
Outstanding Expenses		Current Assets:
		Stock in hand
		Sundry Debtors
		Cash in hand
		Cash at bank
		Loans and Advances:
		Loans
		Bills Receivables
		Advances
		Miscellaneous Expenditure
		Preliminary Expenses
		Discount on issue of Securities

The above Balance Sheet shows assets and liabilities in horizontal form and in their permanency order. If order of assets and liabilities are in reverse order, it shows them in liquidity order. Arrangement of assets in any order is called 'Marshalling of Assets'. *See* how dates are written on the heading of P&L A/c and Balance Sheet. Former is for the period and the latter is on a particular day.

Report Form of Balance Sheet (Vertical)

		Amount ₹
1. Cash in Hand		
2. Cash at Bank		
3. Bills Receivable		
4. Book Debts		
Total Liquid Assets	(A)	—

			Amount ₹
5.	Inventories Closing		
6.	Prepaid Expenses		
	Current Assets	(B)	—
7.	Bills Payable		
8.	Trade Creditors		
9.	Outstanding Expenses		
10.	Bank Overdraft		
	Total Current Liabilities	(C)	—
11.	Provision for Tax		
12.	Proposed Dividend		
13.	Other Provisions		
	Total Provisions	(D)	—
	Total Current Liabilities and Provisions	(E)	—
	Net Working Capital (B – E)	(F)	—
	Fixed Assets	—	
14.	Machinery and Plant		
15.	Land and Building		
16.	Goodwill		
17.	Furniture and Fixtures		
18.	Patents and Copy Rights		
	Total Fixed Assets	(G)	
	Capital Employed (F + G)	(H)	—
19.	Other Assets	(I)	
	Total Net Assets (H + I)	(J)	—
20.	Long term loans	(K)	
	Shareholders net worth (J – K)	(L)	
21.	Preference Share Capital	(M)	
	Equity Shareholder's net worth (L – M)	—	
	(a) Represented by		
	(b) Equity share Capital		
	(c) Reserves and Surpluses		
	(d) Forfeited shares		
	Minus: (i) Accumulated Losses		
	(ii) Preliminary Expenses		
	(iii) Discount on issue of securities not written off		

Manufacturing Account

This account is prepared by manufacturing firms before Trading Account. It tells the cost of goods produced. The format of this account that it shows the materials consumed, work in process (progress) and work direct and indirect expenses. It is given below:

Manufacturing Account

Dr.	₹		Cr. ₹
To Materials Consumed:		By Cost of Goods manufactured (Transferred to Trading Account)	
Opening Stock of Materials			
Plus (+) Purchases of *Materials*			
Less Closing Stock of Materials	—		
Total materials used	—		
To Production wages	—		
To Direct expenses	—		
Add work in process (opening)	—		
Less W-I-P (closing)	—		
Total Prime Cost			
To Factory indirect Expenses	—		

In trading Account are shown the closing and opening inventory of finished goods.

☞*Note*: Students should remember the items that appear in manufacturing and trading accounts.

Example 1

From the following particulars, prepare Manufacturing and Trading Account for the half year ending 31 Dec. 2020 in the books of SAFAL manufacturing firm.

	Opening Stock ₹	Closing Inventory ₹
Raw Materials	15,000	10,000
Work in Progress (at prime cost)	3000	2000
Finished Goods	10,800	8000

	₹
Purchase of Raw materials	50,000
Wages	32,000
Indirect Wages	9000
Stores Consumed	3000
Factory Rent	1000
Insurance	2000
Salaries Factory Foremen	2000
Depreciation – Factory Machinery	3000
Sales	1,40,000

Solution

SAFAL Manufacturing Account

For the half year ending 31st Dec., 2020

Dr.		₹		Cr. ₹
To Materials Consumed			By Cost of goods manufactured transferred to Trading A/c	1,08,000
Opening Stock	15,000			
Add Purchases	50,000			
	65,000			
Less Closing Inventory	10,000	55,000		
To Wages		32,000		
		87,000		
Add Opening W-I-P		3000		
		90,000		
Less Closing W-I-P		2000		
Prime Cost		88,000		
To Factory Indirect Expenses:				
Indirect Wages	9000			
Stores Consumed	3000			
Factory Rent	1000			
Salary – Foremen	2000			
Depreciation machinery	3000			
Insurance	2000	20,000		
		1,08,000		1,08,000

SAFAL Trading Account

For the half year ending 31st Dec., 2020

To Cost of finished goods:			By Sales	1,40,000
Opening Stock	10,800			
Add Cost of manufactured goods	1,08,000			
	1,18,800			
Less Closing Stock	8,000	1,10,800		
To Gross Profit to P&L A/c		29,200		
		1,40,000		1,40,000

The items appearing in Trading Account related to cost of goods purchased and sold and the balance left. Opening or closing stock may consist of raw materials, Work in Progress and Finished goods. Goods purchased but in transit do not affect Trading Account. Carriage on purchases is an item of Trading Account, but not Carriage on Sales (Carriage or freight out) as it is a selling expense. Goods sold on consignment or hire purchase are separately recorded and not in Trading Account. Closing stock is *Valued at Market Price or Cost Price, whichever is Lower.* Hence the accountant should take note of it. The Gross profit (loss) is transferred to income statement.

Schedule III of the Companies Act 2013 contains the following format of Balance Sheet and Profit and Loss A/c for a company under Section 129.

PART–I

BALANCE SHEET

Name of the Company_________

Balance Sheet as at________ (₹ in________)

Particulars	Note No.	Figures as at the end of reporting period current	Figures as at the end of previous reporting period
1	2	3	4
I. Equity and Liabilities			
(1) Shareholders' funds			
(a) Share capital			
(b) Reserves and surplus			
(c) Money received against share warrants			
(2) Share application money pending allotment			
(3) Non-current liabilities			
(a) Long-term borrowings			
(b) Deferred tax liabilities (Net)			
(c) Other Long-term liabilities			
(d) Long-term provisions			
(4) Current liabilities			
(a) Short-term borrowings			
(b) Trade payables			
(c) Other current liabilities			
(d) Short-term provisions			
Total			
II. Assets			
(1) Non-current assets			
(a) Fixed assets			
(i) Tangible assets			
(ii) Intangible assets			
(iii) Capital work-in-progress			
(iv) Intangible assets under development			

(b) Non-current investments
(c) Deferred tax assets (net)
(d) Long-term loans and advances
(e) Other non-current assets

(2) Current assests
(a) Current investments
(b) Inventories
(c) Trade receivables
(d) Cash and cash equivalents
(e) Short-term loans and advances
(f) Other current assets

Total

PART–II
STATEMENT OF PROFIT AND LOSS

Name of the Company _______

Profit and loss statement for the year ended _______________ (₹ in________)

Particulars	Note No.	Figures as at the end of reporting period current	Figures as at the end of previous reporting period
1	2	3	4
i. Revenue from operations		×××	×××
ii. Other income		×××	×××
iii. Total Revenue (I + II)		×××	×××
iv. Expenses:			
Cost of materials consumed			
Purchases of Stock-in-Trade		×××	×××
Changes in inventories of finished goods work-in-progress and Stock-in-Trade		×××	×××
Employee benefits expense			
Finance costs			
Depreciation and amortisation expense			
Other expenses			
Total expenses			
v. Profit before exceptional and extraordinary items and tax (iii–iv)		×××	×××
vi. Exceptional items		×××	×××
vii. Profit before extraordinary and items and tax (v-vi)		×××	×××
viii. Extraordinary items		×××	×××
ix. Profit before tax (vii-viii)		×××	×××
x. Tax expense: (1) Current tax (2) Deferred tax		×××	×××
xi. Profit (Loss) for the period from continuing operations (vii-viii)		×××	×××

xii. Profit/(loss) from discontinuing operations	×××	×××
xiii. Tax expense of discontinuing operations	×××	×××
xiv. Profit/(loss) from Discontinuing operations (after tax) (xii-xiii)	×××	×××
xv. Profit (Loss) for the period (xi-xiv)	×××	×××
xvi. Earnings per equity share:		
(1) Basic	×××	×××
(2) Diluted	×××	×××

RULES OF PREPARING P&L ACCOUNT AND BALANCE SHEET

Rule (1). All nominal accounts having Debit balance are transferred to Debit side of Profit and Loss Account and all nominal showing Credit balance are shown on the Credit side of it.

Rule (2). All personal and real accounts having Debit balance (in Trial Balance) are shown in Assets side of the Balance Sheet.

Rule (3). All personal and real accounts showing Credit balance are shown in Liabilities side of the Balance Sheet.

You may notice that all revenue expenses and incomes appear on the debit and credit side of the Profit and Loss Account respectively. All Capital expenditures and incomes are shown on the assets and liabilities of the Balance Sheet.

The expenses of household Income-tax on the personal income and life insurance premium of the proprietor are treated as drawings.

If the item written is salaries and wages in trial balance, it is a Debit side item of profit and loss account. Wages and salaries are shown in trading account. Repairs depreciation and rent of factory are trading account items and of office are shown in income statement.

The order of assets and liabilities, called marshalling of assets and liabilities, may be either in order of liquidity or performance except of a company.

☞ *Note:* Contingent liability is a liability which may become an asset or a liability on the happening of an event (e.g. possible fine, a suit for claim of money) does not appear in Balance Sheet but is shown as a footnote.

Example 2

From the following Trial Balance of Amitab, prepare a Trading and Profit and Loss Account for the year ending 31st December 2020 and Balance Sheet as on that date.

Trial Balance

Particulars	Dr. Balances ₹	Cr. Balances ₹
Opening Inventory	2,74,000	
Sales		40,21,600
Purchases	28,39,500	
Sales Returns and Allowances	20,050	
Purchases Returns		11,500
Accounts payable (Creditors)		6,20,000
Accounts receivable	6,79,000	
Carriage in	87,150	
Wages	5,88,400	
Motive Power	4,28,600	
Manufacturing Expenses	48,400	
Discount		1,100
Capital		5,00,000
General Expenses	48,900	
Office Salaries	43,050	
Rent and Taxes	1,910	
Cash	750	
Bank	47,300	
Withdrawals	30,000	
	51,54,200	51,54,200

Closing Inventory on 31-12-2020 was ₹ 5,38,000.

Solution

Trading and Profit and Loss Account

For the year ending 31st Dec., 2020

Dr.		₹			Cr. ₹
To Opening Inventory		2,74,000	By Sales	40,21,600	
" Purchases	28,39,500		*Less* Returns in	20,050	40,01,550
Less Returns	11,500	28,28,000	By Closing Inventory		5,38,000
" Carriage		87,150			
" Motive Power		4,28,600			
" Wages		5,88,400			
" Mfg. Expenses		48,400			
" Gross Profit c/d		2,85,000			
		45,39,550			45,39,550
To Salaries		43,050	By G/P b/d		2,85,000
" Rent & Taxes		19,100	" Discount		1,100
" General Expenses		48,900			
" N/P Transferred to Capital A/c		1,75,050			
		2,86,100			2,86,100

Balance Sheet of Mr. Amitab
As on 31 December, 2020

Liabilities		₹	Assets	₹
Accounts Payables		6,20,000	Cash	750
Capital	5,00,000		Bank	47,300
Add Net Profit	1,75,050		Accounts Receivables	6,79,000
	6,75,050		Closing Inventory	5,38,000
Less withdrawals	30,000	6,45,050		
		12,65,050		12,65,050

Adjustments

There are some transactions that may not have been recorded after preparation of Trial Balance, but before preparing Profit and Loss Account. For example, the salary for the month of December is paid on 1st January next year. The salary expense becomes due. Depreciation on assets is charged at the end of the year, but does not find any mention in Trial Balance. So, for much transactions adjusting *Journal Entries* are to be passed and then these journal entries are recorded in Financial Statements. Note that these adjustments are given outside the trial balance and effect two accounts. Following are some adjustments: (Amounts from example 3, on page 64)

1. Ending Inventory. Closing Stock is valued either at market price or cost price whichever is lower and the journal entry is:

		₹	₹
Closing Inventory A/c	Dr.	7,000	
To Trading A/c			7,000

Closing Inventory A/c is an asset and hence is shown in Balance Sheet. Trading A/c will be credited. Closing Inventory becomes opening stock next year. If Closing Stock is shown in Trial Balance as debit balance, it will be shown in Balance Sheet as an asset only.

According standard NOAS2 issued by Institute of Chartered Accountant presenter for valuation of Inventories.

2. Outstanding Expenses. These are expenses payable i.e. accrued for payment. Suppose salary ₹ 500, Rent ₹ 100, wages ₹ 300 and a stationery bill ₹ 30 are outstanding on 31 Dec. The journal entry will be:

(a) Trading A/c	Dr.	₹ 300	
To Wages Outstanding			300
(b) Profit and Loss A/c	Dr.	₹ 630	
To Rent outstanding			100
" Stationery outstanding			30
" Salary outstanding			500

All outstanding accounts are personal accounts and they will appear in liabilities side as they have a credit balance. Trading A/c has been debited because wages is an item of Trading account.

3. Prepaid or Paid in Advance or Unexpired expenses. They are payments made in advance, but whose full benefit has not been enjoyed e.g. insurance premium paid in advance. The adjusting journal entry will be:

Prepaid Insurance A/c	Dr.	₹ 300	
To Insurance A/c			₹ 300

Prepaid Insurance A/c is a personal account, having debit balance will appear as an asset in Balance Sheet. Insurance A/c amount will be deducted from Insurance expense appearing in P&L A/c. Note that Insurance A/c has credit balance and should appear on credit side of P&L A/c. But such accounts by convention, is deducted from the related item on debit side of P&L A/c.

4. Accrued Income or Income earned but not received. Suppose Loan was given to Smith of ₹ 5,000 and interest on it at 7% for one year has not been received or interest on investments made for ₹ 3,000 @ 5% for half year has accrued. The adjusting entry will be:

Interest accrued on Investment A/c	Dr.	₹ 75	
Interest accrued on Smith Loan A/c	Dr.	₹ 350	
To Interest A/c			₹ 425

Interest accrued A/c is an asset and interest A/c will be credited to P&L A/c.

5. Income earned in Advance or Unearned income. An apprentice paid three years fees in advance ₹ 1,500 to an institute on 1-1-2015. At the end of the year 2000, the institute will show ₹ 1000 as unearned income. The journal adjusting entry will be:

Apprentice fees A/c	Dr.	₹ 1,000	
To Apprentice fees Received in Advance			₹ 1,000

Apprentice Fees Received in Advance, being a personal account having credit balance will appear as a liability. Students Fees A/c, though having credit balance, but by **convention** its amount of ₹ 1,000 will be deducted from Students Fees A/c of ₹ 2,000 already appearing in P&L A/c credit side as an income.

6. Depreciation. Depreciation is a fall in the value of a fixed asset due to wear and tear or its use. The depreciation is usually charged either as a fixed amount or percentage on its declining value. It is charged against profit like any other expense such as rent, salaries or wages. The adjusting entry is:

Depreciation A/c	Dr.	₹ 3,450	
To Machinery A/c			₹ 450
" Business Premises A/c			₹ 250
" Furniture and Fixture A/c			₹ 2,750

The Depreciation A/c is debited to Profit and Loss Account. The amount of depreciation is deducted from the asset concerned, according to convention, though the asset account in above entry shows a credit balance.

In case of wasting assets like mines, depreciation is provided like other fixed assets. These are the assets which diminish in quantity by use.

7. Interest on Capital. Since owner is separate person and business is separate entity, the interest is allowed on the capital invested by the owner. The adjusting entry is:

Interest on Capital A/c	Dr.	₹ 2,500	
To Capital A/c			₹ 2,500

Interest on Capital A/c is debited to P&L A/c. The interest is added to Capital A/c.

8. Interest on Drawings/Withdrawals. On the basis of same logic as interest on Capital, interest is charged on withdrawals. The adjusting entry is:

Drawings A/c	Dr.	₹ 80	
To Interest on Drawings			₹ 80

Interest on Drawings A/c will be credited to P&L A/c and Drawings A/c will be increased by the amount. But Drawings plus interest will be shown as a deduction from Capital A/c according to convention, even though it shows a credit balance.

9. Bad Debts Irrecoverable. The adjusting entry is:

Bad Debts A/c	Dr.	₹ 500	
To Debtors A/c			₹ 500

Bad Debt A/c to be Debited to P&L A/c and Debtors should be reduced by the amount. It is by CONVENTION, though Debtors A/c has been credited.

10. Provision for Doubtful Debts. The adjusting entry is:

P&L A/c	Dr.
To Provision for Doubtful debts (New)	

The Provision for Doubtful debts (New) should be deducted from Debtors. If already such provision appears in Trial Balance, called old Reserve, should be shown on credit side of P&L A/c.

11. Provision for Discount on Debtors. This is calculated on Net Debtors i.e. Debtors less Bad Debts less Provision for Doubtful Debts (New). Adjusting entry is:

P&L A/c Dr.

To Provision for Discount on Debtors

The Provision for Discount on Debtors is shown as a deduction from Debtors.

12. Provision for Discount on Creditors. This is expected discount that may be allowed by creditors for prompt payment. It is to be calculated on the amount of creditors on last day of the year. The adjusting entry is:

Provision for Discount on Creditors A/c Dr.

To P&L A/c

The Provision for Discount on creditors should be shown as a deduction from creditors.

☞ *Note*: Work sheet, as shown below in example 3, be prepared for adjustment.

Example 3

From the following Ledger balances of Martin on 31-12-2020 prepare the Financial Statements with adjusting entries, opening and closing entries and work sheet:

	₹		₹
Martin's Capital		Printing and Stationery	250
On 1-1-2020	50,000	Rates and Taxes	350
Stock opening	8,000	Travelling Expenses	150
Purchases	20,000	Trade Expenses	200
Sales	80,000	Premises	5,500
Returns in	1,500	Furniture and	
Purchases Returns	400	Fixture	2,500
Carriage in	1,200	Notes Receivable	3,500
Carriage out	2,500	Notes Payable	2,500
Wages	3,300	Debtors	20,000
Salaries	5,500	Creditors	15,800
Rent	1,100	Machinery	4,500
Freight	2,400	Lal's Loan (Dr.)	5,000
Insurance Premium	900	Investments	3,000
Bad Debts	2,100	Cash	250
Discount (Dr.)	500	Bank	3,500
Apprentice fees (Cr.)	1,500	Withdrawals	3,000

Adjustments

(1) Closing Inventory ₹ 7,000.

(2) Wages outstanding 300, Salaries 500, Rent ₹ 100.

(3) Insurance Premium ₹ 600 for this year only.

(4) Apprentice fees for three years in advance received.

(5) Stationery bill unrecorded ₹ 30.

WORK SHEET (Martin) Showing Adjustments

Sl. No.	Account	Dr.	Cr.	Plus	Minus	Trading and P&L Account Dr.	Trading and P&L Account Cr.	Balance Sheet Liabilities	Balance Sheet Assets
(1)	Closing Inventory	7,000	—	—	—	—	—	—	7,000
	Trading A/c	—	7,000	—	—	—	7,000	—	—
(2)	Wages A/c	300	—	3,300+300	—	3,600	—	—	—
	Wages Outstanding	—	300	—	—	—	—	300	—
(3)	Salaries A/c	500	—	5,500+500	—	6,000	—	—	—
	Salaries Outstanding	—	500	—	—	—	—	500	—
(4)	Rent A/c	100	—	1,100+100	—	1,200	—	—	—
	Rent Outstanding	—	100	—	—	—	—	100	—
(5)	Prepaid Insurance	300	—	—	—	—	—	—	300
	Insurance	—	300	—	900 – 300	600	—	—	—
(6)	Stationery	30	—	250+30	—	280	—	—	—
	Stationery Outstanding	—	30	—	—	—	—	30	—
(7)	Prentice Premium	1,000	—	—	1,500–1,000	—	500	—	—
	P.P. in Advance	—	1,000	—	—	—	—	1,000	—
(8)	Depreciation	3,450	—	—	—	3,450	—	—	—
	Premises	—	2,750	—	55,000–2,750	—	—	—	52,250
	Furniture	—	250	—	2,500–250	—	—	—	2,250
	Machinery	—	450	—	4,500–450	—	—	—	4,050
(9)	Accrued Interest	425	—	3,000+75 5,000+350	—	—	—	—	[3,075 [5,350
	Interest Loan	—	350	—	—	—	—	—	—
	” Investments	—	75	75+350	—	—	425	—	—
(10)	Interest on Capital	2,500	—	—	—	2,500	—	—	—
	Capital	—	2,500	50,000+2,500	—	—	—	52,500	—
(11)	Drawings	80	—	3,000+80	—	—	—	3,080	—
	Interest on Drawings	—	80	—	—	—	80	—	—

Note: Adjusting Journal entries have been given above in the explanation with amount.

(6) Depreciation on Premises @ 5%; Furniture @ 10% and Machinery 10%.
(7) Interest on Lal's loan for one year accrued 7%.
(8) Interest on investment @ 5% for half year accrued.
(9) Interest on capital allowed @ 5% P.A.
(10) Interest on withdrawals ₹ 80.

Closing Entries

As the name suggests, these entries are made for closing income and expenses accounts. They are made after adjustments. Following are Journal Entries:

			₹	₹
(1)	Trading A/c	Dr.	46,700	
	To Opening Stock			8,000
	" Sales Returns			1,500
	" Purchases			20,000
	" Carriage in			1,200
	" Wages			3,600
	" Freight			2,400
	(For balances transferred to Trading Account)			
(2)	Sales Account	Dr.	80,000	
	Purchases Returns	Dr.	400	
	Closing Stock	Dr.	7,000	
	To Trading Account			87,400
	(For balances transferred to Trading Account)			
(3)	Trading A/c	Dr.	50,700	
	To P & L A/c			50,700
	(For transfer of gross profit)			
(4)	P & L A/c	Dr.	17,880	
	To Carriage out			2,500
	" Salaries			6,000
	" Rent			1,200
	" Insurance			600
	" Bad Debts			2,100
	" Discount			500
	" Stationery			280
	" Rates & Taxes			350
	" Travelling expenses			150
	" Sundry expenses			200
	" Depreciation			3,450
	" Interest on Capital			2,500
	(For transfer of P & L A/c)			

			₹	₹
(5)	Apprentice Premium A/c	Dr.	500	
	Interest on Lal's Loan A/c	Dr.	250	
	Interest on Investment A/c	Dr.	75	
	Interest on Drawings A/c	Dr.	80	
	To P & L A/c			905
	(For transfer to P & L A/c)			
(6)	P & L A/c	Dr.	31,875	
	To Capital A/c			31,875
	(For transfer of net Profit to Capital A/c)			

Opening Entries

These entries are made from Balance Sheet. The balances are carried to next period and the opening balances are made "To balance b/d" for assets and "By balance b/d" for liabilities. They are not posted to ledger, but are incorporated in new books of accounts.

Cash A/c	Dr.	250	
Bank A/c	Dr.	3,250	
Investment A/c	Dr.	3,075	
Debtors A/c	Dr.	20,000	
Notes Receivable A/c	Dr.	3,500	
Prepaid Insurance A/c	Dr.	300	
Lal's Loan A/c	Dr.	5,350	
Machinery A/c	Dr.	4,050	
Furniture A/c	Dr.	2,250	
Business Premises A/c	Dr.	52,250	
To Creditors			15,800
" Notes payable			2,500
" Outstanding			930
(wages, salaries, rent and stationery)			
" Prepaid Premium			1,000
" Capital			81,295

Example: Next year the posting will be as follows:

Dr. Cash A/c Cr.

To balance b/d			250	

Dr. Creditors A/c Cr.

By balance b/d				

Trading and P & L Account of Martin

For the year ended 31-12-2020

		₹			₹
To Opening Stock		8,000	By Sales	80,000	
" Purchases	20,000		*Less* Returns in	1,500	78,500
Less returns out	400	19,600	" Closing Inventory		7,000
" Carriage in		1,200			
" Wages	3,300				
Add outstanding	300	3,600			
" Freight		2,400			
" Gross Profit c/d		50,700			
		85,500			85,500
To Carriage out		2,500	By G/P b/d		50,700
" Salaries	5,500		" Apprentice Premium	1,500	
Add outstanding	500	6,000	*Less* Advance	1,000	500
" Rent	1,100		" Interest on Lal's Loan		350
Add outstanding	100	1,200	" Interest accrued on investments		75
" Insurance	900		" Interest on withdrawals		80
Less Prepaid	300	600			
" Bad Debts		2,100			
" Stationery	250				
Add outstanding	30	280			
" Rates		350			
" Travelling Expenses		150			
" Sundry Expenses		200			
" Depreciation on:					
Premises		2,750			
Furniture		250			
Machinery		450			
" Interest on Capital		2,500			
" Net Profit Transferred to Capital A/c		31,875			
		51,705			51,705

Balance Sheet

as on 31st December, 2020

Liabilities	₹	Assets		₹
Creditors	15,800	Cash		250
Notes payable	2,500	Bank		3,250
Outstanding:		Investment	3,000	
Wages	300	Plus accrued Interest	75	3,075
Salaries	500	Debtors		20,000
Rent	100	Notes Receivable		3,500
Stationery	30	Closing Inventory		7,000

Liabilities			₹	Assets		₹
Apprentice Premium prepaid			1,000	Prepaid Insurance		300
Martin's Capital:	50,000			Lal's Loan	5,000	
Add Interest on Capital	2,500			*Add* Accrued Interest	350	5,350
Add Net Profit	31,875			Machinery	4,500	
	84,375			*Less* Depreciation	450	4,050
				Furniture	2,500	
Less Withdrawals 3,000				*Less* Depreciation	250	2,250
Less Interest on				Premises	55,000	
Withdrawals	80	3,080	81,295	*Less* Depreciation	2,750	52,250
			1,01,525			1,01,525

Note: A company by law has to show last year balances also in Financial Statement.

Example 4

From the following Trial Balance of Shri Ram, as at 31st December, 2020, you are required to prepare a Trading and Profit and Loss Account for the year ended 31st December, 2020 and a Balance Sheet as at that date, after making the necessary adjustments:

Trial Balance

	₹	₹
Shri Ram's Capital Account		80,000
Shri Ram's Drawings Account	6,000	
Plant and Machinery (balance on 1st Jan., 2020)	20,000	
Plant and Machinery (additions on 1st July, 2020)	5,000	
Stock on 1-1-2020	15,000	
Purchases	82,000	
Returns Inwards	2,000	
Sundry Debtors	20,600	
Furniture & Fixtures	5,000	
Freight & Duty	2,000	
Carriage outwards	500	
Rent, Rates and Taxes	4,600	
Printing & Stationery	800	
Trade Expenses	400	
Sundry Creditors		10,000
Sales		1,20,000
Return outwards		1,000
Postage & Telegrams	800	
Provision for Doubtful Debts		400
Discounts		800
Rent of premises sublet for the year to 30th June, 2021		1,200
Insurance charges	700	
Salaries and Wages	21,300	
Cash in Hand	6,200	
Cash at Bank	25,500	
Reserve Fund		5,000
	2,18,400	2,18,400

Adjustments

1. Stock on 31st December, 2020 was valued at ₹ 14,600.
2. Write off ₹ 600 as Bad Debts.
3. The Provision for Doubtful Debts is to be maintained at 5 per cent on Sundry Debtors.
4. Create a Provision for Discounts on Debtors and on Creditors at 2 per cent.
5. Provide for Depreciation on Furniture and Fixtures at 5 per cent per annum and on Plant and Machinery at 20 per cent per annum.
6. Insurance prepaid was ₹ 100.
7. A fire occurred on 25th December, 2020 in the godown and stock of the value of ₹ 5,000 was destroyed. It was fully insured and the Insurance Company admitted the claim in full.
8. ₹ 2,000 is to be transferred to Reserve Fund out of profits, if any.

Solution

Trading and Profit and Loss Account of Shri Ram

For the year ended 31st December, 2020

	₹	₹		₹	₹
To Opening Stock		15,000	By Sales	1,20,000	
" Purchases	82,000		*Less* Sales Returns	2,000	1,18,000
Less Purchase Returns	1,000	81,000	" Closing Stock	14,600	
" Freight & Duty		2,000	*Add* Loss of Stock	5,000	19,600
" Gross Profit c/d		39,600			
		1,37,600			1,37,600
To Carriage outward		500	By Gross Profit b/d		39,600
" Rent, Rates & Taxes		4,600	" Rent	1,200	
" Printing & Stationery		800	*Less* Received in advance	600	600
" Trade Expenses		400	" Discount		800
" Postage & Telegram		800	" Provision for Discount on creditors		200
" Insurance	700				
Less Prepaid	100	600			
" Salaries & Wages		21,300			
" Bad Debts	600				
Add New Provision	1,000				
	1,600				
Less Old Provision	400	1,200			
" Provision for Discount on Debtors		380			
" Depreciation on: Plant and Machinery (₹ 4,000 + ₹ 500)		4,500			
Furniture & Fixtures		250			
" Net Profit transferred to:					
Reserve Fund	2,000				
Capital A/c	3,870	5,870			
		41,200			41,200

Balance Sheet of Shri Ram

As on 31st December, 2020

	₹	₹		₹	₹
Sundry Creditors	10,000		Cash in Hand		6,200
Less Provision for			Cash at Bank		25,500
Discount on creditors	200		Sundry Debtors	20,600	
		9,800	*Less* Bad Debts	600	
Rent Received in Advance		600		20,000	
Reserve Fund:			*Less* New Provision		
Previous Balance	5,000		for D/D	1,000	
Addition this year	2,000	7,000		19,000	
Shri Ram Capital	80,000		*Less* Provision for		
Add Net profit	3,870		Discount on Debtors	380	18,620
	83,870		Closing Stock		14,600
Less Drawings	6,000	77,870	Prepaid Insurance		100
			Insurance Co.		5,000
			Furniture & Fixtures	5,000	
			Less Depreciation	250	4,750
			Plant & Machinery	20,000	
			Add Additions	5,000	
				25,000	
			Less Depreciation	4,500	20,500
		95,270			95,270

QUESTIONS

1. Fill in the blanks:
   (a) The two forms of presenting financial statements are ______.
   (b) The income statement may be prepared by any of the two steps. They are ______.
   (c) Closing Stock of raw materials and W-I-P appear in ______.
   (d) All nominal accounts having debit balance are shown in _____.
   (e) The assets side of the Balance Sheet shows ______ expenditures.

2. Explain the following:
   (a) Marshalling of assets
   (b) Valuation of Closing Stock
   (c) Opening and Closing entries
   (d) Adjusting entries
   (e) Unearned income
   (f) Contingent Liabilities
   (g) Wasting Asset

EXERCISES

1. Following is a Trial Balance of Krishna on 31-12-2020.

	Dr. ₹	Cr. ₹
Purchases	1,50,000	—
Debtors	2,00,000	—
Salaries	30,000	—
Wages	20,000	—
Rent	15,000	—
Sales Returns	10,000	—
Purchases Returns	—	5,000
Bad Debts written off	7,000	—
Creditors	—	1,20,000
Capital	—	1,00,000
Drawings	24,000	—
Provision for Bad Debts	—	6,000
Printing and Stationery	8,000	—
Interest earned	—	4,000
Insurance	12,000	—
Opening Stock	50,000	—
Office Expenses	12,000	—
Furniture and Fittings	20,000	—
Provision for Depreciation	—	4,000
Prepaid Insurance on 1-1-2020	2,000	—
Sales	—	3,21,000
	5,60,000	5,60,000

Prepare a Trading and Profit and Loss Account for the year ended December 31, 2020 and also the Balance Sheet on that date after making the following adjustments:

(a) Depreciate Furniture and Fittings by 10% on original cost.
(b) Make a Provision for Doubtful Debts equal to 5% of Debtors.
(c) Salaries for the month of December amounting to ₹ 3,000 were unpaid which must be provided for. The balance in the account includes ₹ 2,000 paid in advance.
(d) Insurance is prepaid to the extent of ₹ 4,000.
(e) Provide ₹ 8,000 for office expenses.
(f) Stock valued at ₹ 6,000 was put up by Krishna to his personal use, the cost of which has not been adjusted in the books of account.
(g) Closing stock was valued at ₹ 60,000.

2. The Following is the Trial Balance of X on 31st December, 2020, and it is desired to prepare final statements of accounts showing the results of the transactions of the year:

	Debit ₹	Credit ₹
Capital Account		40,000
Plant and Machinery	50,000	—
Office Furniture and Fittings	2,600	—
Stock, 1st January, 2020	48,000	—
Motor Vans	12,000	—
Sundry Debtors	45,700	—
Cash in Hand	400	—
Cash at Bank	6,500	—
Wages: Factory	1,50,000	—
Office	14,000	—
Purchases	2,13,500	—
Sales	—	4,80,000
Bills Receivable	7,200	—
Bills Payable	—	5,600
Sundry Creditors	—	52,000
Returns Inwards	9,300	—
Provision for Doubtful Debts	—	2,500
Drawings	7,000	—
Returns Outwards	—	5,500
Rent	6,000	—
Factory Lighting and Heating	800	—
Telephone	350	—
Insurance	300	—
Advertising	5,650	—
General Expenses	1,000	—
Bad Debts	2,500	—
Discount Allowed	6,500	—
Discount Received	—	3,700
	5,89,300	5,89,300

The following adjustments are to be made:

(i) Stock 31st December, 2020 ₹ 52,000.

(ii) Rent due, but not paid 31st December, 2020 ₹ 2,000.

(iii) 3 months factory lighting and heating due but not paid ₹ 300.

(iv) Insurance paid in advance ₹ 100.

(v) 10 per cent depreciation to be written off plant and machinery.
(vi) 5 per cent depreciation to be written off furniture.
(vii) 25 per cent depreciation to be written off motor vans.
(viii) Write off further bad debts ₹ 700.
(ix) The provision for doubtful debts to be increased to ₹ 3,000.
(x) Discounts of 2½ per cent on debtors and creditors are to be anticipated.
(xi) Bills Receivable ₹ 1,000, not yet due, were discounted on 31st December, 2020.

3. Maleshwari submitted to you the following Trial Balance, which she has not been able to agree. Rewrite the Trial Balance, correcting the mistakes committed by him and prepare a Profit and Loss Account for the year ended 31st December, 2020 and Balance Sheet as on that date, after giving effect to the undermentioned adjustments:

	₹	₹
Capital	—	1,50,000
Drawings	32,500	—
Stock (1-1-2020)	1,74,450	
Returns Inwards	—	5,540
Carriage Inwards	12,400	—
Deposit with Anand Gupta	—	13,750
Returns Outwards	8,400	—
Carriage Outwards	—	7,250
Loan to Ashok @ 5% given on 1-1-2020	—	10,000
Interest on the above	—	250
Rent	8,200	—
Rent Outstanding	1,300	—
Stock (31-12-2020)	—	1,87,920
Purchases	1,29,700	—
Debtors	40,000	—
Goodwill	17,300	—
Creditors	—	30,000
Advertisement Expenses	9,540	—
Provision for Doubtful Debts	—	12,000
Bad Debts	4,000	—
Patents & Patterns	5,000	—
Cash	620	—
Sales	—	2,79,140
Discount allowed	—	3,300
Wages	7,540	—
	4,50,950	6,99,150

Adjustments

1. The manager of Maleshwari is entitled to a commission of 10% of the Net Profit calculated after charging such Commission.
2. Increase Bad Debts by ₹ 6,000 provide for doubtful debts 10% and provision for Discount on Debtors 5%.
3. Stock valued at ₹ 15,000 destroyed by fire on 25-12-2020 but the Insurance Co., admitted a claim for ₹ 9,500 only and paid it in 2020.
4. ₹ 2,000 out of the Advertisement Expenses are to be carried forward to the next year.

4. The Trial Balance of Mr. Girish on 31-12-2020 is given below. Prepare final accounts:

	Dr. ₹	Cr. ₹
Capital		10,80,900
Stock on 1st January, 2020	4,68,000	
Sales and Sales Returns	86,000	28,96,000
Purchases and Returns	24,31,000	58,000
Freight & Carriage	1,86,000	
Rent & Taxes	57,000	
Salaries & Wages	93,000	
Sundry Debtors and Creditors	2,40,000	1,48,000
Bank Loan at 6%		2,00,000
Bank Interest	9,000	
Printing & Advertisement	1,46,000	
Income from Investments		2,500
Cash at Bank	80,000	
Discount received		41,900
Investments	50,000	
Furniture and Fittings	18,000	
Discount paid	75,400	
General expenses	39,100	
Audit fee	7,000	
Insurance	6,000	
Travelling expenses	23,300	
Postage & Telegrams	8,700	
Cash in Hand	3,800	
Deposit with Sugandha	3,00,000	
Drawings Account	1,00,000	
	44,27,300	44,27,300

Stock on 31st December, 2020 was ₹ 7,86,000. Make the following adjustments:

(a) Included amongst the Debtors is ₹ 30,000 from Umesh and included amongst the creditors ₹ 10,000 due to him.

(b) The effect of Advertising being not yet expired and a quarter of the amount "Printing & Advertising" is to be carried forward to the next year.

(c) Provide 2 per cent for discount on debtors and create provision for Doubtful debts at 5 per cent.

(d) A Depreciation of 10% is to be written off Furniture and Fittings.

(e) Wages and Salaries owing on 31st December, 2020 is ₹ 8,000 and Carriage owing ₹ 1,000.

(f) Insurance paid in advance on 31st December, 2020 is ₹ 800.

(g) Furniture which stood at ₹ 6,000 in the books on 1st January, 2020 was disposed of at ₹ 2,900 on 30th June in part exchange for new furniture costing ₹ 5,200. A net invoice at ₹ 2,300 was passed through the Purchases Day Book.

(h) Purchase Invoice amounting to ₹ 4,000 had been omitted from the books.

(i) A new Sign costing ₹ 1,000 is included in Advertising.

(j) Two dishonoured cheques for ₹ 2,000 and ₹ 3,000 respectively have not been entered in the Cash Book. The first for ₹ 2,000 is known to be bad. In the case of the second cheque for ₹ 3,000 it is expected that the Debtor would be in a position to pay dividend of 75 P. in the rupee.

(k) Private Purchases amounting to ₹ 6,000 had been included in the Purchases Day Book.

(l) Charge full year Interest on Deposit with Sugandha at 7% p.a.

(m) Provide for interest on Bank Loan for the amount due.

5. The following balances are extracted from the Ledger of Mr. Bedi for the year ended 31st December, 2020:

	₹
Capital Account	20,00,000
Drawings Account (Dr.)	1,50,000
Purchases *less* Returns	1,65,02,600
Rates and Taxes	25,000
Salaries	3,52,400
Lighting (Office)	62,100
Office Rent	60,000
Electric Power	2,56,000
Reserve Account	1,25,000
Travelling Expenses	22,200

	₹
Insurance (Fire)	15,000
Advertisement Expenses	3,77,500
Sales *Less* Returns	1,83,52,000
Bad Debts written off	90,500
Discounts (Debit Balance)	44,450
General Expenses	1,12,650
Postage and Telegrams	32,000
Carriage Inwards	51,200
Stock-in-Trade (1-1-2020)	4,02,000
Wages	3,22,120
Land and Buildings	2,56,400
Plant and Machinery	5,02,500
Sundry Creditors	3,54,200
Furniture and Fixtures	3,12,000
Sundry Debtors	6,50,000
Cash in Hand	12,180
Cash at Bank	2,20,400

You are required to make out the Trading and Profit and Loss Account and Balance Sheet after taking into account the additional information given below:

(1) The Stock-in-trade on 31st December, 2020 was ₹ 2,41,000.

(2) Provide Depreciation at 10 per cent on Plant and Machinery, 5 per cent on Furniture and Fixtures and 2½ per cent on Land and Buildings.

(3) Provide 2 per cent for Discounts on Debtors and create provision at 10 per cent for Bad Debts.

(4) Sundry Creditors include an amount of ₹ 20,000 realised from Y whose account has been written off two years back.

(5) Prepaid Insurance ₹ 5,000.

(6) One machine whose value in books as at 1st January, 2020 stood at ₹ 1,20,000 was disposed of on 30th September, 2020 for ₹ 87,500 in part exchange for a new machine costing ₹ 1,90,000 and an invoice for the net amount of ₹ 1,02,500 was entered in the books. No depreciation provided on disposed machine.

(7) Outstanding expenses: Audit fees ₹ 12,000, Salaries ₹ 30,000, Electric Power ₹ 25,000, Advertisement ₹ 18,000.

(8) A deposit received from one Debtor wrongly credited to his personal account of ₹ 50,000.

5

Depreciation

In the last chapter, depreciation was shown as an adjustment. Here we shall examine it under four heads: (1) Meaning of depreciation and its bases, (2) Depreciation methods, (3) Depreciation and management decisions, and (4) Depreciation standards.

MEANING

Prof. Henry Rand Hatfield, who gives classic description of the nature of depreciation as "All machinery is on an irresistible march to Junk heap, and its progress, while it may be delayed, cannot be prevented by repairs." Depreciation is a term most often employed to indicate that tangible assets have declined in service potential. This decline may be loss of efficiency or rising maintenance costs, due to ageing, wear and tear, and exposure to the elements or damage commonly sustained during use. An asset may decline in market value through causes external to itself, called as obsolescence. It may be technical or economic obsolescence. Where natural resources, like timber, oil and coal, are involved the term depletion is used. The term 'amortisation' is used for expiration of intangible assets like goodwill, lease, patents.

International Accounting Standard[1] defines depreciation as "the allocation of the depreciable among of an asset over its estimated useful life". To accountants, therefore, depreciation is not a matter of valuation but a means of cost allocation. Assets are not depreciated on the basis of a decline in their fair market value, but on the basis of a systematic charges of cost to income. They charge the cost of the asset to depreciation expense over its estimated life, making no attempts at valuation of the asset between acquisition and disposition.

The Accounting Standards Committee of U.K. in SSAP No. 12[2] also holds a similar view. It says that depreciation is "a measure of wearing out consumption or other loss of value of a fixed asset whether arising from use, effluxion of time or obsolescence through technology and market

1. Standard No. 4 (1976).
2. (1977).

changes. It should be allocated to accounting periods so as to charge a fair proportion to each period during the expected useful life of the asset."

FACTORS INVOLVED

The estimate of periodic depreciation is dependent on three basic questions:

1. Establishing the depreciation base.
2. Estimating assets useful or service life.
3. Choosing the method of cost apportionment (commonly called methods of depreciation).

Depreciation Base: The base or depreciable cost established for depreciation is a function of two factors: The original cost and salvage or disposal value. Salvage value is the estimated amount that will be received at the time the asset is sold or removed from service. It is this value that the asset must be written down or depreciated during its useful life. From practical point, salvage value is often considered to be zero because the valuation is small. Some fixed assets like buildings have substantial residual value. Theoretically, removal cost of buildings or heavy machinery should be estimated and included in the depreciation base. In practice, removal costs are either ignored or netted against the estimated salvage value of the asset. The formula for arriving at the depreciation base this becomes:

Depreciation base = Acquisition cost – estimated net salvage value

In case of resale the depreciation is the difference between cost and resale value.

Estimating Useful or Service Life

The service life of an asset is the total units of service expected to be derived from that asset. It is commonly measured in terms of time e.g. months or years. It may be expressed also in terms of output or activity e.g. kilos, gallons, machine hours, kilometer. The service life of a car may be estimated as 10-year or 1,000,000 miles. The unit of service to be determined depends upon the factors that limit the service life of any asset.

There are two causes of decrease in asset service life:

(a) Physical causes or casualties and (b) Functional or economic factors. They are inadequacy, obsolescence and supersession. Physical deterioration results largely from wear and tear. Useful events such as accidents, floods, earthquakes also serve to terminate or reduce asset usefulness. Functional or economic factors may render an asset in good physical condition no longer useful because it is not economical to keep it in service. Obsolescence refers to the effect of innovations and technical improvements on the economic service life of existing assets. Inadequacy refers to the effect of growth and changes in the scale of a firm's operation in terminating the service life of assets e.g. a warehouse may be small to accommodate more goods. It can be done only by adding a new building. In general sense, any asset whose capacity is such that it cannot be operated with optimum results or which does not fit the requirements of the business is inadequate. Supersession is the replacement of one asset with another more efficient and economical asset e.g. replacement of an aircraft.

In a highly developed society functional causes of depreciation have a greater influence on service lives than physical wear and tear. The problem of choosing an appropriate unit of service life also calls for search for causes of depreciation. The objective is to choose the unit most closely related to the cause of service exhaustion. No estimate of service life can be made with high precision.

DEPRECIATION METHODS

There are two major considerations in deciding a method of depreciation (a) the quantity of service used may be equal or may vary during each period of service life and (b) the cost of various units of service may be equal or may differ per unit during each period of service life. There is high degree of uncertainty about the estimates of service life and service use, the distinction between these two factors may become blurred. For example if a machine costs ₹ 3,300 and salvage value is ₹ 300. Its service life is estimated, 1,00,000 hours. The average depreciation will be 3,300/1,00,000 = 3 paise per hour. If the machine is used 20,000 hours in first year and 30,000 hours in second year, there is a variation in the quantity of service used and depreciation of ₹ 600 in first year and ₹ 900 in second year will recognise this fact. But if machine is used 20,000 hours in each of five years there may be a difference in the cost of hours of service in each of these five years. Therefore, an assumption that each service hour bears the same depreciation amount may not be reasonable. It is better to calculate say 5 paise per hour depreciation for first 20,000 hours, 4 paise for next 20,000 and so on.

Following are the methods of depreciation that attempt to recognise these factors in a varying degree:

1. Straight line or equal (fixed) instalment method.
2. Accelerated or decreasing charge methods.
   (a) Fixed percentage of declining (diminishing or reducing) balance method.
   (b) Double rate declining balance method.
   (c) Sum of year digits methods.
3. Activity or composite provision method.

4. Special depreciation methods:
   (a) Compound interest methods—They are annuity method depreciation fund method, sinking fund method or endowment policy method.
   (b) Retirement of replacement or renewals method.
   (c) Group and composite life method.
   (d) Inventory method.

To illustrate, Hazaribagh Coal Company purchase Bulldozer and relevant data is as under:

Cost of Bulldozer	₹ 5,00,000
Estimated useful life	5 years
Estimated salvage life	₹ 50,000
Productive life in hours	30,000 hours

1. Straight Line or Equal (Fixed) Instalment Method

The method, simple and widely used, is based on function of time. The depreciation is calculated follows:

$$\text{Depreciation} = \frac{\text{Cost less salvage}}{\text{Estimated service life}} = \frac{500{,}000 - 50{,}000}{5}$$

= ₹ 90,000 per year or ₹ 15 per hour.

The objection to this method is that it assumes that assets' economic usefulness is the same each year, and repair is the same in each period. The rate of return is distorted under this method.

2. Accelerated Rated or Decreasing Charge Methods

A. *Fixed percentage or Reducing Balance or Written Down Value Method:* Under this method a percentage depreciation rate is computed which, when applied to book value of the asset at the beginning of each period, will result in writing the asset down to estimated salvage value at the end of its service life. The amount of depreciation decreases each year. The formula for calculating it is:

$$\text{Depreciation rate} = 1 - n\sqrt{\frac{\text{net salvage value}}{\text{acquisition cost}}}$$

So in our example it is $= 1 - n\sqrt{\dfrac{50{,}000}{500{,}000}} = 36.9\%$.

It may be rounded off 37%. The depreciation in first year is ₹ 1,66,500 and in second year is ₹ 104,895 (i.e. 37% of 4,50,000-1,66,500). This method is more used in U.K. because of some tax advantage. But in U.S.A., for tax purposes it is not allowed. In India, changes in method of depreciation are linked with changes in provisions under Income-tax

Act, and/or Companies Act 2013. Under Section 213 and Schedule II of Companies Act 2013 on acquisition or purchase of assets different rates of depreciation for different lifespan of asset have been prescribed.

B. *Under Double Declining Balance Method:* Under this method, the depreciation rate is twice the straight line approach. In our example the rate will be:

$$\left[\frac{₹\ 90,000}{4,50,000}\times 100 = 20\% \times 2 = 40\%\right]$$

In U.S.A., this method is used only on new assets.

C. *Sum-of-Year Digits Method:* Under this method, the depreciation charge is based on a decreasing fraction of depreciable cost (original cost less salvage value). Each fraction uses the sum of year as a denominator (5 + 4 + 3 + 2 + 1 = 15), in our example and the number of year as a estimated life remaining as at the beginning of the year as a numerator. The numerator decreased year by year and denominator remains constant [5/15, 4/15, 3/15, 1/15]. In formula is:

$$\frac{n(n+1)}{2} = \frac{5(5+1)}{2} = 15.$$

For first year the depreciation in our example will be ₹ 4,50,000 × 5/15 = 1,50,000 and second year ₹ 4,50,000 × 4/15 = 1,20,000 and so on. At the end remains the salvage value.

The argument in favour of all three accelerated methods is that by showing declining amounts of depreciation, the firm offsets rising changes for maintenance, thus levelling our total costs of using the assets from year to year. There is something in this.

But the effect is counterbalanced by increased retention, of founds in early years, so that earnings on these 'secondary' assets no longer offset by rising total costs as under the straight line method. Another advantage of these methods is their ability to "mirror the decline in market values of certain assets", if not to durable assets.

3. Activity Method

This is also called variable charge approach. The depreciation is a function of use or productivity is instead of passage of time. Suppose in our example, the Bulldozer is used for 4,000 hours in first year, the depreciation charge is:

$$\frac{(₹5,00,000 - 50,000)}{30,000}\times 4,000 = ₹\ 60,000$$

This method can be used only for assets where depreciation is a function of activity and not of time. Another problem is that the units of output or service hours received are difficult to estimate.

4. Special Depreciation Systems

The above methods treat all fixed assets as equal to present value. Each asset is expected to earn a rate of return at least equal to cost of capital. The following methods are based on interest. They try to find the annual sum which, accumulated at a compound rate of interest is equal to cost of capital.

Annuity method: Under this the annual charges are calculated by annuity method. The cost of the asset, less the present value of its expected scrap value, is divided by the present value of an annuity of 1. Under the conditions specified, and the result is the annual charge for depreciation. Interest at a specified rate is computed annually on the opening balance of the asset.

In our example we assume 10% interest. The depreciation will be calculated by the following formula:

$$\text{Depreciation} = \frac{\text{Cost of asset less present value of net residual value}}{\text{Present value of ordinary annuity of N rents at specified rate of interest}}$$

$$= \frac{₹\ 500{,}000 - (50{,}000 \times 0.620921)}{3.790787}$$

$$= \frac{500{,}000 - 31046}{3.790787} = ₹\ 123{,}709 \text{ (App.)}$$

Annuity Tables are used to find the annuity value.

The depreciation fund method: Under this method the amount written off as depreciation should be kept aside and is invested in readily salable securities. The securities accumulate. When the life of the asset expires, the securities are sold and a new asset is purchased with the sale proceeds. How much amount is to be invested every year subject a given sum is available at the end of a given period depends on the rate of interest. The formula to calculate is:

$$\text{Depreciation: } \frac{\text{Cost of asset less scrap value}}{\text{Future amount of an ordinary annuity of ₹ 1}}$$

$$= \frac{450{,}000}{6.105100} = 73{,}708.86 = 73{,}709 \text{ (App.)}$$

The sinking fund method: The difference between depreciation fund and sinking fund is that in balance sheet both the fund and secondary assets which represent it are shown under a separate heading. Only the basic quota appears in final accounts, as a sinking fund investment. Income received on secondary asset is directly credited to the fund. The method is not widely used.

Endowment policy method: The basic difference between depreciation fund or sinking fund method and this method is that whereas under the former investments are purchased, under the later an insurance policy for the required sum is taken out. A premium is paid every year. At the end of the given period, the insurance company will pay the agreed sum with which new asset can be purchased. The premium will be the annual depreciation.

Retirement and replacement systems: These methods are used primarily by public utilities and railways. The purpose is to avoid elaborate depreciation schedules for individual assets. The distinction between two systems is that the retirement system charges the cost of retired asset (less salvage value) to depreciation expense. The replacement system charges the cost of units purchased as replacements less salvage value from the units replaced to depreciation expense. In this method the original cost of asset is maintained in the accounts indefinitely. The drawback of these systems is that a proper allocation of costs to all periods does not occur, particularly during early years. To overcome this objection, a special allowance account may be opened in the early years so that an assumed depreciation charge can be provided.

Group and composite systems: In certain circumstances multiple assets and depreciated at on rate e.g. cars, trucks and tractors. The methods i.e. group method and composite method are used. Group refers to a collection of assets that are similar in nature. The term composite refers to a collection of assets that are dissimilar in nature, are heterogeneous and have different lines. The method for both is same; find an average and depreciate on that basis.

The following example classifies it:

Asset	Original cost ₹	Residual value ₹	Depreciation cost ₹	Estimated life	Depreciation straight line ₹
Car	1,45,000	25,000	1,20,000	3	40,000
Truck	44,000	4,000	40,000	4	10,000
Tractor	35,000	5,000	30,000	5	6,000
	2,24,000		1,90,000		56,000

$$\text{Composite rate} = ₹\ \frac{56,000}{2,24,000} = 25\%$$

$$\text{Composite life} = ₹\ \frac{1,90,000}{56,000} = 3.39 \text{ years.}$$

Inventory systems: This method, also called appraisal system, is used to value small tangible assets example tools. An inventory is taken at the beginning and at the end of the year. The value at the beginning inventory plus the cost of new assets acquired for the year less the value of the ending inventory is the amount of depreciation or the year. The method is not systematic and rational. No set of formula is involved.

SPECIAL DEPRECIATION PROBLEMS

Some issues involved in depreciation are:

(1) *Depreciation for partial periods*: In calculating depreciation for partial periods, it is necessary to determine the depreciation for the full year and then to prorate that amount between two periods involved. This is necessary in case an asset is purchased during the year or disposed of. It is normally calculated on the basis of the nearest whole month unless otherwise stipulated.

(2) *Funds for replacement of fixed assets*: A common misconception about depreciation is that it provides funds for the replacement of fixed assets. Depreciation is like any other expense. It does not provide funds for replacement of assets, as they come from revenue. It is a non-cash expense.

(3) *Revision of depreciation rates and method*: If depreciation rates are revised, no changes are to be made in previously reported result. Opening balances are not adjusted. Charges for depreciation in subsequent periods are based on dividing the remaining book value (original cost less accumulated depreciation) by the remaining estimated life. This is the view of Accounting Principles Board opinion No. 28 of U.S.A. and also of SSAP No. 12 (1997) of U.K. The latter states "where there is a revision of the estimated useful life the unamortized cost should be charged over the revised remaining useful life. However, if at any time the unamortized cost is seen to be irrecoverable in full, it should be written down immediately to the estimated recoverable amount, and the latter charged over the remaining useful life." Where there is a change from one method of depreciation to another, the unamortized cost of the asset should be written off over the remaining useful life on a new basis, commencing with the period in which change is made. The effect should be disclosed in the year of change, if material. Where assets are revalued in the financial statements, the depreciation provision should be based on the revalued amount and current estimate of remaining useful life.

DEPRECIATION METHODS AND MANAGEMENT DECISIONS

The importance of depreciation comes from the various management decisions that are affected by it. It is of a particular importance in three management decision areas:

1. Decisions relating to income measurement.
2. Decisions relating to Income-tax determination.
3. Decisions relating to capital investment.

Depreciation and Income Measurement

The purpose of depreciation accounting is to measure the amount that must be recovered from revenue to compensate for the portion of assets cost that has been used up. The idea is to maintain capital intact, which is often used in relation to income measurement.

The straight line method, widely used, has three objections against it, each of which becomes a supporting argument for some other method.

1. It tends to report an increasing rate of return on investment.
2. It does not allow for the fact that productivity of assets may decline with age.
3. It does not take into account variations in the rate of assets used.

1. Increasing Return Argument

To explain this argument we take an example. Suppose one man acquires a bus for ₹ 3,00,000, which he gives on hire. The useful life is estimated four years with salvage value ₹ 60,000. The hire income is ₹ 1,50,000 per year and operating expenses except depreciation are ₹ 54,000 per year. The four year situation is shown below:

1 Year	2 Income ₹	3 Operating Expenses ₹	4 Depreciation ₹	5 Net Income (2 – 3 – 4) ₹	6 Book value ₹	7 Rate earned
1	1,50,000	54,000	60,000	36,000	3,00,000	12%
2	1,50,000	54,000	60,000	36,000	2,40,000	15%
3	1,50,000	54,000	60,000	36,000	1,80,000	20%
4	1,50,000	54,000	60,000	36,000	1,20,000	30%

The idea of an increasing rate of return on investment does not square with an economic reality. Reason suggests that rate of return should remain constant or actually decrease somewhat as an asset becomes old. In above example the straight line method does not take into account the factor of interest that is implicit in lump sum investment to be recovered piecemeal over a long period of time. The increasing rate of return is valid where operation focus on a single depreciable asset e.g. a building. Further the assumptions that hire income and operating expenses will remain the same is not valid.

2. Declining Productivity

Some people suggest that the decline in productivity of many assets is so pronounced that the value (and thus of cost) of asset service in the early stages of service life is materially greater than in later years. If this true, accelerated methods of depreciation may relate costs incurred and revenue realized more closely than the straight line method.

3. Variation in Output

The straight line method makes depreciation a fixed period cost by assumption and thereby fails to allow for the loss of service potential repeated to wear and tear through usage. If an asset is used twice as heavily in one period as another, it may be unrealistic to assume that the amount and cost of the service consumed is the same in both periods. This objection becomes a case for using a measure of output or productivity as the unit of service life, which would make depreciation a variable cost.

Depreciation Policy and Income Taxes

In practice the strongest influence on depreciation policy are tax laws. Depreciation reduced taxable income and Income-tax charge. Income-tax can be postponed by accelerating depreciation deductions. The only possible tax disadvantage to large initial depreciation deductions is that tax rates might increase sufficiently to more than offset the implicit savings. Tax factors encourage the use of minimum estimates of service life and adoption of accelerated depreciation methods. If tax depreciation and accounting depreciation are substantially equal, there is advantage to keep books on tax basis. Tax deduction are based on public policy rather than on sound accounting objectives. Sections 32, 32A, 32(AB, AC), 33, 33AB, 41 and 43 of the **Indian Income-tax Act, 1961** deal with assets eligible for depreciation, conditions for allowing depreciation and types of depreciation allowance. Depreciation is allowed on W.D.V. method at prescribed rates under **Rule 5, of Income-tax Rules 1962**[1] for both tangible and intangible assets.

Depreciation and Capital Investment Decisions

Two important questions relating to the role depreciation in a capital investment decisions are:

(a) Is depreciation a relevant cost in making the decision?

(b) How does depreciation affect the cash flows from the investment?

Two kinds of costs are relevant to the decision to invest capital in productive assets: (i) future costs and (ii) differential costs i.e. costs that will change as the result of the investment decision. Depreciation is referred aptly as a sunk cost. Most managerial decisions depend upon analysis of differential costs and revenue. Depreciation may or may not represent differential or relevant cost in taking those decisions e.g. buying or leasing (or making) or accepting a special order or not. Depreciation on existing assets would be a differential cost only if the use of the assets for specific activity reduces their useful life. Depreciation is a differential cost depends on whether limiting factor in assets life is obsolescence or use and whether the facility in question is now being used to capacity. For this reason depreciation is not generally the relevant figure for management decision.

---

1. For details refer to any book on Income-tax.

Depreciation indirectly generates greater cash flows, a useful concept about investment, from operations by reducing the current Income-tax expense. For this reason, depreciation is universally viewed as a powerful instrument for speeding up cash flows and improving pay back calculations on new investments in plant and equipment (for illustration see Chapter 6).

SELECTION OF DEPRECIATION METHOD

Which method should be selected and why?

The answer depends on many factors such as the equitable distribution of cost of the assets over its effective service life, suitability to management e.g. Income-tax considerations, effects of usage and obsolescence, the pattern of revenue flows, the timing of repair costs, the interest factor and uncertainty of revenue receipts. Conceptually, the selection of a depreciation results in the method that most clearly reflects net income. For example, many companies in India adopt W.D.V. method for tax purposes, but use the straight line method for book purposes. This practice provides the best of both sides: The impact on divided policy or cost of replacement are secondary considerations that the management should consider.

DEPLETION

Natural resources or a wasting asset is in essence a long-term inventory of raw materials that will be removed physically from the property. The basic problem is to determine the cost of the units of services or materials that are consumed during each accounting period. The portion of the cost or other valuation assigned to property containing national resources that is applicable to the units removed from the property is known as depletion.

There are two questions to be answered about depletion:

1. How is the cost basis for write off (depletion) established?
2. What pattern of allocation should be employed?

The cost of natural resources can be divided into three categories:

(1) *Acquisition costs*: The acquisition cost is assigned to the natural resource if the exploration is successful and is written off as a loss if it is unsuccessful.

(2) *Exploration costs*: Some firms treat all such costs as expenses, others capitalize only those costs that are directly related to successful projects and others capitalize all costs whether they are successful or unsuccessful projects.

(3) *Development costs*: These are either related to tangible equipment or intangible development costs. The former are not considered in depletion base and the latter are included in depletion base.

Normally, depletion is computed on the unit of production (activity method), straight line method being of doubtful applicability. The total cost less net residual value is divided by the number of units estimated to be in the resource deposit to obtain a cost of unit of product. This cost per unit is multiplied by the number of units extracted to compute the depletion.

INTERNATIONAL ACCOUNTING STANDARD ON DEPRECIATION ACCOUNTING

Introduction

1. The statement deals with depreciation accounting and applies to all depreciable assets except:

(a) forests and similar regenerative natural resources,

(b) expenditures on the exploration for and extraction of minerals, oil, natural gas and similar non-regenerative resources,

(c) expenditures on research and development, and

(d) goodwill.

Definitions

2. In this statement the following terms are used with the meanings specified.

Depreciation is the allocation of the depreciable amount of an asset over is estimated useful life. Deprecation for accounting period is charged to income either directly or indirectly.

Depreciable assets are assets which:

(a) are expected to be used during more than one accounting period,

(b) have a limited useful life, and

(c) are held by an enterprise for use in the production or supply of goods and services for rental to others, or for administrative purposes.

Useful life is either (a) the period over which a depreciable asset is excepted to be used by the enterprise or (b) number of production or similar expected to be obtained from the asset by the enterprise.

Depreciable amount of a depreciable asset is its historical cost or other amount substituted for historical cost in the financial statements, less the estimated residual value.

This statement does not deal with the difference, which arise when re-evaluations are substituted for historical cost.

Explanation

3. Depreciable assets comprise a significant portion of the assets of many enterprises. Depreciation can therefore have a significant effect in determining and presenting the financial position and results of those enterprises.

4. The view is sometimes expressed that if the value of an asset has increased over the amount at which it is carried in the financial statements,

it is unnecessary to provide for depreciation. It is considered, however, that depreciation should be charged in each accounting period on the basis of the depreciable amount irrespective of an increase in the value of the assets.

Useful Life

5. Estimation of the useful life of a depreciable asset or a group of similar depreciable assets is a matter or judgement ordinarily based on experience with similar types of assets. For an asset using new technology or used in the production of a new product or in the provision of a new service with which there is little experience, estimation of the useful life is more difficult but is nevertheless required.

6. The useful life of depreciable asset for an enterprise may be shorter than its physical life. In addition to physical wear and tear, which depends on operational factors such as the number of shifts for which the asset is to be used and the repair and maintenance programme of the enterprise, other factors need to be taken into consideration. These include obsolescence arising from technological changes or improvements is production, obsolescence arising from a change in the market demand for the product or service output of the asset and legal limits such as the expiry dates of related leases.

Residual Value

7. The residual value of an asset is often insignificant and can be ignored in the calculation of the depreciable amount. If the residual value is likely to be significant, it is estimated at the date of acquisition, or the date of any subsequent revaluation of the asset, on the basis of the realisable value prevailing at the date for similar assets which have reached the end of their useful lives and have operated under conditions similar to those in which the asset will be used. The gross residual value in all cases is reduced by the expected costs of disposal at the end of the useful life of the asset.

Depreciation Methods

8. Depreciable amount are allocated to each accounting period during the useful life of the asset by a variety of systematic methods. Whichever method of depreciation is selected its consistent use is necessary, irrespective of the level of profitability of the enterprise and of taxation considerations, in order to provide comparability of the results of operations of the enterprise from period to period.

Land and Buildings

9. Land normally has an indefinite useful life and it not usually regarded as depreciable asset. However, land which does have a limited useful life for the enterprise is treated as a depreciable asset.

10. Buildings are depreciable assets because they fall within the definition in paragraph 2.

11. Some enterprises have not treated buildings as depreciable assets for the reason that the agreeable value of the building and the land on which it stands does not decline. As land and buildings are separate assets, recognition for accounting purposes of any increased value of the land is a different issue from the determination of the depreciable amount of the buildings.

Disclosure

12. The selection of a location method and the estimation of the useful life of a depreciable asset are matters of judgement. The disclosure of the method adopted and the estimated useful lives or depreciation rates used provides users of financial statements with information which allows them to review the policies selected by managements and enables comparisons to be made with other enterprises. For similar reasons, it is necessary to disclose the depreciable amount allocated in a period and the accumulated depreciation at the end of the period.

13. The depreciable amount of a depreciable asset should be allocated on a systematic basic to each accounting period during the useful life of an asset.

14. The depreciation method selected should be applied consistently from period to period unless altered circumstance justify a change. In an accounting period in which the method is changed, the effect should be quantified and disclosed and the reason for the change should be stated.

15. The useful life of a depreciable asset should be estimated after considering the following factors:

(a) expected physical wear and tear,

(b) obsolescence, and

(c) legal or other limits on the use of the asset.

16. The useful lives of major depreciable assets or classes of depreciable assets should be reviewed periodically and depreciation rates adjusted for the current and future periods if expectations are significantly different from the previous estimates. The effect of the change should be disclosed in the accounting period in which the change takes place.

17. The valuation bases used for determining the amounts at which depreciable assets are stated should be included with the disclosure of other accounting policies—see International Accounting Standard 1, Disclosure of Accounting Policies.

18. The following should be disclosed for each major class of depreciable asset:

(a) The depreciation methods used,

(b) The useful lives or the depreciation rates used,

(c) Total depreciation allocated for the period, and

(d) The gross amount of depreciable assets and the related accumulated depreciation.

19. This International Accounting Standard becomes operative for financial statements covering periods beginning on or after January 1, 1977.

INDIAN ACCOUNTING STANDARD ON DEPRECIATION (AS: 16)

The Institute of Chartered Accountant of India issued the following A.S. on depreciation in September 1994. It has been made mandatory in respect of accounts for periods commencing from 1-4-1995.

1. In standard applies to all depreciable assets except the following items to which special considerations apply:

(a) forests, plantations and similar regenerative natural resources;

(b) wasting assets including expenditure on the exploration for and extraction of minerals oil, natural gas and similar non-regenerative resources;

(c) expenditure on research and development;

(d) goodwill;

(e) livestock; and

(f) land unless it has a limited useful life for the enterprise.

2. The depreciable amount of a depreciable asset should be allocated on systematic basis to each accounting period during the useful life of the asset.

3. The depreciation method selected should be applied consistently from period to period. A change from one method of providing depreciation to another should be made only if the adopting of the new method is required by statute for compliance with an accounting standard or if it is considered that the change would result in a more appropriate preparation or presentation of the financial statement of the enterprise. When such a change in the method of depreciation is made, depreciation should be recalculated in accordance with the new method from the date of the asset coming into use. The deficiency or surplus arising from retrospective recomputation of depreciation in accordance with new method should be adjusted in the accounts in the year in which the method of depreciation is changed. In case the change in the method results in deficiency in depreciation in respect of past years, the deficiency should be charged in the statement of profit and loss. In case the change in the method result in surplus, the surplus should be credited to the statement of profit and loss. Such a change should be treated as a change in accounting policy and its effect should be quantified and disclosed.

4. The useful life of a depreciable asset should be estimated after considering the following factors:

(i) expected physical wear and tear;

(ii) obsolescence; and

(iii) legal or other limits on the use of the asset.

5. The useful lives of major depreciable assets or classes of depreciable assets may be reviewed periodically. Where there is a revision of the estimated useful life of an asset, the unamortised depreciable amount should be charged over the revised remaining useful life.

6. Any addition or extension which becomes an integral part of the existing assets should be depreciated over the remaining useful life of that asset. The depreciation on such addition or extension may also be provided at the rate applied to the existing asset. Where an addition or extension retains a separate identity and is capable of being used after the existing asset is disposed of, depreciation should be provided independently on the basis of an estimate of its own useful life.

7. Where the historical cost of a depreciable asset has undergone a change due to increase or decrease in long-term liability on account of exchange fluctuations, price adjustments, changes in duties or similar factors, the depreciation on the revised unamortised depreciable amount should be provided prospectively over the residual useful life of the asset.

8. Where the depreciable assets are revalued, the provision for depreciation should be based on the revalued amount and on the estimate of the remaining useful lives of such assets. In case the revaluation has a material effect on the amount of depreciation, the same should be disclosed separately in the year in which revaluation is carried out.

9. If any depreciable asset is disposed of, discarded, demolished or destroyed, the net surplus or deficiency, if material should be disposed of separately.

10. The following information should be disclosed in the financial statements:

(i) the historical cost or other amount substituted for historical cost of each class of depreciable assets;

(ii) total depreciation for the period for each class of assets; and

(iii) the related accumulated depreciation.

11. The following information should also be disclosed in the financial statements along with the disclosure of other accounting policies:

(i) Depreciation method used, and

(ii) Depreciation rates or the useful lives of the assets if they are different from the principal rates specified in the statute governing the enterprise.

QUESTIONS

1. (a) Distinguished between depreciation, amortization and depletion.
   (b) What are the three variables in estimating periodic depreciation? Explain the estimated service life of an asset. What are the main causes of decrease in asset service life?
   (c) State three basic objections against time method of depreciation. What is composite depreciation?
2. A machine with an estimated life of five years or 1,00,000 units of output, was acquired on October 4, 2020. The machine sells for ₹ 9,000 and will be paid as follows:

	₹
(a) Cash	15,000
(b) Four instalments, payable at the rate of ₹ 2,000 every six months (includes ₹ 10,000 of interest)	80,000
(c) Old machine accepted as trade in	5,000
Total	1,00,000

   Compute the depreciation for three months in year 2020 and for 2021. The salvage value of the machine is ₹ 15,000. Use each of the following methods:

   1. Straight line, 2. Sum-of-the-years digits, 3. Double declining balance, 4. Unit-of-output 80,000 unit in 2020 and 30,000 units in the year 2021.
3. Messrs. Pirey Lal & Sons owned an old factory building carried in its accounts at a book values of ₹ 2,00,000. Machinery and equipment in the building had a book value of ₹ 3,00,000. In 2020, the company built a new building at a cost of ₹ 12,00,000 and installed a new equipment costing ₹ 6,50,000. Some of the equipment in the old building was replaced and both plants were operated at wear capacity from 2017 to 2021. Depreciation was taken on a straight line basis.

   In 2021, the firm was forced a shut down the old plant because of decline in sales. The Managing Director proposes to stop taking depreciation on the old building and machinery. He says that while the old plant is useful, it is not wearing out. Furthermore, he feels that depreciating the old plant increases costs, overstates inventory, and places the firm in a poor position to bid for business since its costs are high.

   Discuss the validity of arguments put by the Managing Director. What recommendation would you make to the company?
4. Answer the following:
   (a) The rate of return is distorted under _____ method (fill in blank).
   (b) Depreciation fund method and sinking fund method are same (True/false).
   (c) Income-tax allows any amount of depreciation (True/false).

6

Ratio and Funds Flow Analysis

FINANCIAL STATEMENT INTERPRETATION

Interpretation, or drawing of valid conclusions from reported data, is the final formal step in the accounting process. To be of value, accounting data, regardless of how well presented, must be interpreted by and for the user. Sound interpretation consists of:

1. Analysis or taking part of reported data in order to examine critically each element with regard to its effect on a given problem.
2. Integration, or the combining of selected elements of data, frequently in combination with other known elements of information, to form a logical pattern upon which to base deductions.
3. Deductions or the formulation of conclusions regarding the effects of the data being presented.

These factors, when combined and applied to financial statements, make up what is generally known as financial statement analysis. It is the task of the analyst to interpret the statements in a way which will enable owners, management, employers, creditors, and other users of the data to make decisions regarding an organisation and its activities. The users of the data are interested usually in solvency, profitability and stability of an organisation. They, however, do not and should not always rely upon the results of interpretation of financial statements.

The financial statements can be analysed by using (a) basic tools and (b) special tools of financial analysis. The basic tools consist of (i) Percentage analysis, (ii) Ratio analysis, and (iii) Turnover analysis. The special tools are used for (a) trend analysis and (b) special purpose analysis. The trend analysis can be presented by the use of following tools: (i) comparative statements, (ii) financial summaries, and (iii) graphic presentation. The following are representatives of special purpose analysis: (a) Gross Margin analysis, (b) Break-Even analysis, (c) Marginal analysis, (d) Segmental analysis, and (e) Capital Expenditure analysis.

Basic tools of financial statement analysis place more emphasis on single-period statements. Such statements are essentially interim reports on a going concern's continuing activities and therefore may not be fully representative of its long-run solvency, stability or profitability. This is particularly true if abnormally favourable or unfavourable economic conditions prevailed during the period under study. Special tools of financial analysis are mostly based on statements of a number of periods. On occasion more specialized information may be necessary if sound conclusions are to be drawn regarding special facets of an organisation's liquidity, stability and profitability. For that special purpose analysis is made.

PERCENTAGE ANALYSIS

In financial statements analysis, percentage analysis consists of converting the figures of amounts into percentages. Actually percentage analysis is a type of ratio. Percentages are specially useful for comparing successive statements of an individual organisation, or of two or more organisations, or of one organisation with industry percentages. All percentage appearing in the statements are based on a common denominator of 100 per cent. They are usually presented in a separate statement, called common size statements. They are in vertical form.

When percentage analysis is applied to the balance sheet, total assets are ordinarily used as a base or 100 per cent, and all other items appearing on the statement are stated in relation to base. In income statements percentage analysis is applied using net sales as the base or 100 per cent.

Example

	₹		
Total assets	100,000	=	100%
Plant	49,000	=	49%
Net Sales	100,000	=	100%
Gross Margin	58,000	=	58%

The common size statements have limitations that they cannot disclose the reasons behind changes which have taken place in successive periods. They do not reflect actual growth or shrinkage. If each item in a statement changes proportionately the change will not be reflected in the percentage. The use of common size statements to compare different organisations also may be limited because of lack of uniformity in the reported data, e.g., difference in accounts classification or valuation of inventory or methods of depreciation.

TREND ANALYSIS

A trend may be defined as the underlying tendency for something to take a particular direction. If the financial statements for a number of periods are properly analysed, it is possible to obtain information which will indicate the direction in which an organisation is heading. The tools used to know the financial trend are:

(A) Comparative statements
(B) Financial summaries
(C) Graphic presentation

(A) *Comparative Statements:* Comparative financial statements present like data for two or more dates or periods so that similar items may be compared and deductions drawn accordingly. There is no fixed format for such statements. Comparative statements can be prepared by two ways (a) Horizontal Analysis and (b) Vertical Analysis. These statements enhance the usefulness of annual reports and bring out more clearly the nature and trends of current changes effecting the enterprise. Exhibit 6.3 is an example of such horizontal analysis.

EXHIBIT 6.1

Comparative Balance Sheet

	Current year	Last year	Amount	Change Percentage
Assets:	₹	₹	₹	
Current Assets	4,56,000	4,80,000	–24,000	–5.0
Plant & Machinery (net)	5,88,000	4,50,000	+1,38,000	+30.7
Other Assets	1,56,000	70,000	+86,000	+122.9
Total Assets	12,00,000	10,00,000	+2,00,000	+20.0*
Liabilities:				
Current Liabilities	2,04,000	2,80,000	–76,000	–27.1
Long-term debt	3,36,000	1,50,000	+1,86,000	+124.0
Total Liabilities	5,40,000	4,30,000	1,10,000	+25.6
Paid up Capital	4,80,000	3,50,000	+1,30,000	+37.1
Reserves	1,80,000	2,20,000	–40,000	–18.2
Total owners equity	6,60,000	5,70,000	+90,000	+15.8
Total Liabilities and O.E.	12,00,000	10,00,000	+2,00,000	+20.0*

*The totals will not agree, because individual percentages are not weighted.

Comparative Profit and Loss Account

	Current year	Last year	Amount	Percentage
Net sales	20,00,000	15,00,000	+5,00,000	+33.3
Cost of goods sold	–11,60,000	–9,00,000	+2,60,000	+28.9
Gross Profit	8,40,000	6,00,000	+2,40,000	+40
Operating expenses	5,80,000	3,75,000	+2,05,000	+54.7
Operating income	2,60,000	2,25,000	+35,000	+15.6
Income tax	1,00,000	90,000	+10,000	+11.1
Net Profits	1,60,000	1,35,000	+25,00	+18.5

Comparative Profit & Loss (Appropriation) Account

	Current year ₹	Last year ₹	Amount ₹	Percentage
Reserves (Retained earning at beginning)	2,20,000	1,65,000	+55,000	33.3
Net profit for the year	1,60,000	1,35,000	+25,000	+18.5
Total	3,80,000	3,00,000	+80,000	+26.7*
Dividends declared	2,00,000	80,000	+1,20,000	+150
Reserves at the end	1,80,000	2,20,000	–40,000	–18.2*

*The totals will not agree, because individual percentages are not weighted.

The percentage analysis of increase and decreases in corresponding items, as shown above, in comparative financial statements is called "Horizontal Analysis". The amount of each item on the most recent statement is compared with corresponding item on one or more earlier statement. The increase or decrease in the amount of the item is then listed, together with percent increase or decrease. When comparison is made between two statements, the earlier statement is used as a base. The earlier statement used as a base may be of last year or of any other year.

Percentage analysis may also be used to show the relationship of the component part to the total of a single statement. In Balance Sheet, each asset item is stated as a percent of total assets and each liability item is stated as a percent of total liabilities. In P&L A/c, each item is stated as a percent of sales. Such type of analysis is called "Vertical Analysis". For example, the asset side in Exhibit 6.1 will appear as follows:

	Current year	Last year
Current Assets	38%	48%
Plant & Mach.	49%	45%
Other Assets	13%	7%
	100%	100%

"Common Size Statements" are those statements which are prepared to compare percentages of a current period with past periods or to compare individual business with other business or industry. (See net income as a percent of Sales in Exhibit 6.2.)

(B) *Financial Summaries*: Changes or inconsistencies in accounting methods or policies during the periods covered by the statements can result in the misinterpretation of reported trends and changing relationships. For example, change in inventory valuation method or depreciation method can easily destroy the comparability of corresponding items in successive periods. Similarly, material errors and their correction in subsequent periods, and material non-recurring gains or losses can contribute to the misinterpretation of Rupee percentage changes in corresponding items on comparative items on comparative statements. Therefore, financial summaries of 5 to 10 year periods should be prepared. Exhibit 6.4 is an example.

EXHIBIT 6.2

Five Year Financial Summary

Income data	2020 ₹	2019 ₹	2018 ₹	2017 ₹	2016 ₹
Net Sales	20,00,000	15,00,000	12,00,000	13,00,000	10,00,000
Net Profit	1,60,000	1,35,000	84,000	1,04,000	50,000
Net Income as % of sales	8%	9%	7%	8%	5%
Financial Position Data					
Working Capital	2,52,000	2,00,000	1,30,000	60,000	50,000
Long-term loans	3,36,000	1,50,000	1,50,000	1,00,000	1,00,000
Shareholder's capital	6,60,000	5,70,000	4,95,000	4,71,000	4,17,000
Per share Data					
Earning per Share	1.33	1.35	0.84	1.04	0.50
Dividends per share	1.67	0.80	0.60	0.50	0.40
Book value per share	5.50	5.70	4.95	4.71	4.17

(C) *Graphic Presentation*: The accounting data can also be presented in graphic form. The graphic presentation supplements the conventional statements. Following is an illustration: (Exhibit 6.2A)

TREND GRAPH

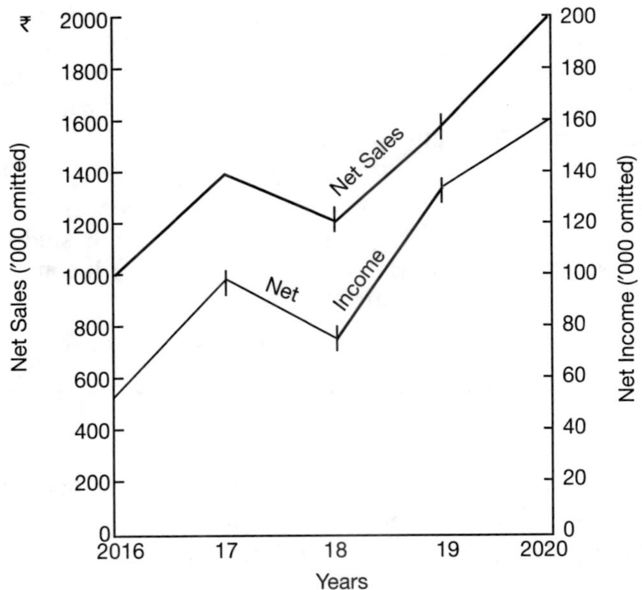

Exhibit 6.2A

The special tools used for special purpose analysis are explained next.

RATIO ANALYSIS

Ratio means a numerical relationship between items or group of items. A ratio may be expressed either as a quotient or a percentage or a rate or times.

Example

Profit = ₹ 8,000 (for year I)

Sales = ₹ 80,000 (year I) and ₹ 100,000 (year II)

Capital employed = 20,000 (End year I)

Cost ₹ 70,000 (year I) and ₹ 80,000 (year II)

The accounting ratio may be expressed in the following forms:

(a) $\text{Quotient} = \dfrac{\text{Sales}}{\text{Capital employed}} = \dfrac{₹\ 80{,}000}{₹\ 20{,}000} = 4{:}1$

(b) $\text{A percentage} = \dfrac{\text{Profit}}{\text{Sales}} \times 100 = \dfrac{₹\ 8{,}000}{80{,}000} \times 100 = 10\%$

(c) A rate times difference in cost is 10,000 and difference in sales is ₹ 20,000 i.e., a variation of ₹ 1 cost for every ₹ 2 sales. OR sales is 4 times than capital employment.

The ratios can be calculated in unlimited number, but to be relevant the items must have *meaningful relationship with one another*. "Ratios are not infallible, though mathematical derivatives, and do not carry the gift of prophecy or the mathematical means of making exact measurement of financial solvency, stability or profitability. They can indicate probabilities and suggest financial strengths or weaknesses."

Financial ratios may be classified in various ways, depending upon the use that is to be made of them. They are divided as (a) Financial Ratios, (b) Profitability Ratios, (c) Turnover Ratios. For study purposes we shall classify them as (1) Balance Sheet ratios, (2) Income statement ratios and (3) Inter-statement ratios.

Balance Sheet Ratios

Balance sheet ratios are indicators or an organisations's financial strength. The important of them are given below:

(A) Liquidity Ratios:

  (i) Current Ratio or Working Capital Ratio or banker's ratio

  (ii) Acid Test Ratio or Quick Ratio.

(B) Capital Structure or Leverage Ratios:

  (i) Debt Ratio

  (ii) Equity Ratio

  (iii) Debt-Equity Ratio.

(C) Others:
   (i) Fixed or Current Assets or Inventories to Total Assets Ratio
   (ii) Fixed Assets to Permanent Liabilities
   (iii) Paid up Capital/Net Worth/Total Borrowings or Bank Borrowings to Net Liabilities
   (iv) Dividends as a percentage of Paid up Capital or Net worth or Equity share earnings
   (v) Earnings per share = Net Income less dividend on preference shares to Total number of equity shares
   (vi) Yield = Equity Dividend per share to Market price per equity share
   (vii) Price Earning Ratio = Market Price of Equity Share to earning per share.

A. Liquidity Ratios or Financial Ratios

Current Ratio: This ratio shows the relationship between current assets and current liabilities. This is sometimes called the working capital ratio because the excess of current assets over current liabilities is often defined as working capital. The formula for this ratio is:

$$\frac{\text{Current assets}}{\text{Current liabilities}}$$

The following data indicate both the working capital positions and current ratios of companies A and B.

	Company A	Company B
Current assets:	₹	₹
Cash	60,000	1,00,000
Debtors (Net)	68,000	2,00,000
Investments	12,000	40,000
Closing stock	2,58,000	4,50,000
Prepaid expenses	2,000	10,000
Total current assets	4,00,000	8,00,000
Current liabilities:	1,00,000	5,00,000
Working capital	3,00,000	3,00,000
Current ratio	4:1	1.6:1

Current assets include prepaid expenses and current liabilities include outstanding expenses.

Both working capital and the current ratio are rough indicators of an organisation's ability to meet its current obligations as they become due. The current ratio can readily be observed in the example is more reliable as an indicator of solvency. The working capital for both companies is same, but the current ratio of Company A is better. The higher the ratio, better it is. Ideal is 2:1.

Acid Test Ratio: Or liquidity ratio the quick or acid test ratio is used to provide an indication of solvency of an organisation. The ratio describes the relationship between quick assets and current liabilities. The term quick or liquid assets excludes closing stock (inventory) prepaid expenses but *includes cash in hand and at bank, debtors and investments*. The formula is:

$$\frac{\text{Liquid or Quick assets}}{\text{Current liabilities}}$$

Applying to above example the acid test ratio for company A is 1.4:1 and for B is 0.68:1. This ratio is used as a supplement to current ratio at times. Ideal is 1:1.

Debt Ratio: This is ratio between total debt, current as well as long term, to total assets. The formula is:

$$\frac{\text{Total debt}}{\text{Total assets}}$$

This ratio helps the unsecured creditors to know the degree of protection given to their claims. Higher the ratio greater is the risk to creditors and *vice versa.*

(B) Leverage Ratios

Equity Ratio: This is the ratio between total amount of owner equity (net worth) and total amount of assets. It is complement to the debt ratio i.e. the sum of two ratios is equal to 100 per cent. This is also called PROPRIETARY RATIO Formula is:

$$\frac{\text{Total owners equity}}{\text{Total assets}}$$

Proprietary funds = Fixed Assets + Working Capital

This ratio indicates long range stability of an organisation.

Debt Equity Ratio: The formula for this ratio is

$$\frac{\text{Total debt}}{\text{Total owners equity}}$$

It expresses the relationship between debt and owners equity. It is an indicator of creditor's risk and of long-run solvency. Preference share capital is sometimes included as debt rather than net worth, because it represents a prior claim.[1] The ratio of debt to equity will vary according to the nature of business, e.g., in electricity companies the debt ratio is higher. Then formula is Fund bearing fixed interest or fixed dividend divided by Total capital employed or Equity shareholders funds. This ratio is also called "Capital Gearing" ratio. Sometimes to know the importance of long-term debt in the capital structure the ratio of long-term debt to

1. *Financial Management and Policy*, J.C. Vanhorn, p. 722.

total capitalization is calculated (total capitalization represents long-term debt and net worth).

Trading on the Equity: Not a ratio as such, but closely related to the balance sheet ratios (particularly the debt and equity ratios) is "trading on the equity" or the favourability of financial leverage, as it is called. It is judged in terms of the effect upon earnings per share to equity shareholders. The relationship between earnings per share and earnings before interest and taxes under various financing alternatives and indifference (or Break-Even) points between these alternatives when a company borrows money for long term, instead of issuing additional shares, with the expectation of increasing its earnings, it is called "trading on equity". If the amount earned on the borrowings is greater than the cost of borrowing money (interest), trading on equity is good, otherwise not. For example, a company buys an asset of ₹ 2,00,000 by borrowing, ₹ 1,00,000 from debenture holders @ 5% P.A., and by issuing ₹ 1,00,000 worth of shares. Suppose also the following:

	₹
Case 1: Annual earnings before interest and tax =	5,000
Case 2: E.B.I.T.	10,000
Case 3: E.B.I.T.	15,000

An analysis of these three cases shows that Case 1 is not favourable, Case 2 is neither favourable nor unfavourable and Case 3 is favourable.

EXHIBIT 6.3

Trading on Equity

	Annual Earnings	*ROI	Case 1 Deb. ₹	Case 1 Shares ₹	Case 2 Deb. ₹	Case 2 Shares ₹	Case 3 Deb. ₹	Case 3 Shares ₹
Case 1:	5,000	2½%[a]	5,000	—	—	—	—	—
Case 2:	10,000	5%[b]	—	—	5,000	5,000	—	—
Case 3:	15,000	7½%[c]	—	—	—	—	5,000	10,000
	ROE[f]	—	—	—	—	5%[d]	—	10%[e]

*Return on investment on total assets

(a) 5,000 ÷ 2,00,000 (b) 10,000 ÷ 2,00,000

(c) 15,000 ÷ 2,00,000 (d) 5,000 ÷ 1,00,000

(e) 10,000 ÷ 1,00,000 (f) Return on owners equity

Suppose the number of shares are 5,000 each in Case 2 and Case 3, Then the

Earning per share in Case 2 will be ₹ 1.

(10,000 – 5,000) = 5,000 ÷ 5,000 and in Case 3 ₹ 2.

(C) Other Ratios

They tell us the pattern of assets or liabilities or both. (See page 112)

Income Statement Ratios

(1) Operating ratio
(2) Profitability ratios
    (a) Net income to sales
    (b) Gross profit to sales
(3) Other ratios

Operating Ratio: It expresses the relationship between total operating expenses and net sales. Total operating expenses means cost of goods sold, and selling and administrative expenses. The formula is:

$$\frac{\text{Total operating expenses}}{\text{Net sales}}$$

The lower operating ratio is better; though high operating ratio does not indicate necessarily a weakness. If the volume of business is so large that the net income increased than the high operating ratio will not indicate weakness.

Net Income to Net sales: It expresses relationship between profit and sales. It shows the rate of return on the sales rupees and is complement of the operating ratio. However, this ratio itself may be meaningless and therefore, consideration must be given to such factors as the volume of sales and the rapidity of turnover of inventory. For example, a low rate of return accompanied by a rapid inventory turnover and a large sales volume may be more profitable than a high rate of return combined with a slow turnover and low sales volume. Net income = Net profit plus non-operating expenses minus non-operating Income. Net Sales means Sales less returns. The formula of this ratio is:

$$\frac{\text{Net income}}{\text{Net sales}}$$

Operating ratio also is 100% minus net income ratio.

Gross Margin Ratio: This ratio expresses the relationship between the gross margin on sales and net sales. This ratio shows the spread or difference between the cost of goods sold and the sales prices change in the ratio may be result of a change in either price or volume or both. The cost of goods sold ratio i.e., the ratio of cost of goods sold and net sales is complement of this ratio. Its formula is:

$$\frac{\text{Gross margin}}{\text{Net sales}}$$

Other Ratio: The other ratios calculated from income statement may be either of the following:

(a) Factory cost or administration cost or selling and distribution cost to net sales.
(b) Value of output to net sales or to raw material consumed or other manufacturing expenses.

Value of output = Sales plus closing stock minus Opening stock.

Inter Statement Ratios

(A) Return on Investment Ratios:
   (i) ROI based on total assets
   (ii) ROI based on total owners equity
   (iii) ROI based on equity shareholders equity

(B) Turnover Analysis:
   (i) Inventory turnover
   (ii) Accounts receivables turnover
   (iii) Accounts payable turnover

(C) Other Ratios:
   (i) Capital turnover ratio (working capital to sales)
   (ii) Average creditors to credit purchases ratio (creditors velocity)
   (iii) Sales to fixed/current assets/working capital
   (iv) Value of output to net worth/total net assets.

Return on Investment Ratios: The rate of return on total assets ratio (also called Rate of Return on Capital employed) expresses relationship between operating income and the total capital employed. It indicates the earning power of any organisation. Interest must be included in the net income. The formula is:

$$\frac{\text{Sales}}{\text{Total Assets}} \times \frac{\text{Profit}}{\text{Sales}} \quad \text{Or} \quad \frac{\text{Net Income after Tax + Interest}}{\text{Average assets employed}}$$

The first formula was developed by "Dupont" company and is known also as "**Dupont system of analysis**"

The rate of return on owner's equity is calculated by Net Income ÷ Average owner's equity. The formula is:

$$\frac{\text{Net income} - \text{Preferred shares dividend}}{\text{Average common stockholder equity}}$$

Or

Net worth – Par value of preferred stock

The Earning per share Ratio: The formula is Net Income after Tax – Preference share dividend ÷ Total ordinary shares.

Turnover Analysis: Turnover means either (i) the number of times an asset is converted into other assets during a period or (ii) the number of days required to "turn" an asset or assets. For example, an asset that turns five times a year, turns, on the average, once every 73 day (365 ÷ 5). Turnover calculations are made in two following cases; and are also known as "**Activity**" Ratios.

Inventory Turnover OR Stock Velocity

It may be calculated either (i) by dividing the cost of goods by the average inventory at cost or (ii) by dividing sales by the average inventory valued at selling price. The formulae are:

(i) $\dfrac{\text{Cost of goods sold}}{\text{Average inventory at cost}}$ (ii) $\dfrac{\text{Sales}}{\text{Average inventory at retail}}$

Average inventory may be either average of closing and opening inventories or inventory taken at different periods during the year. The later gives better results.

Consider the following:

	First year (₹)	Second year (₹)
Cost of goods sold	3,00,000	4,50,000
Average inventory	1,00,000	90,000
Inventory Turnover (Times)	3	5
Inventory Turnover (period)	122	73

Inventory turnover indicates the liquidity of the investment in inventory and efficiency of the organisation. The lower inventory turnover may indicate either of the following probabilities:

1. An excessive amount of funds is tied up in inventories.
2. Excessive quantities of merchandise are being purchased.
3. Slow moving merchandise is being carried.
4. The risk of obsolescence and deterioration has been increased.
5. Excessive facilities are being used for storage.
6. The risk of loss by fire, flood etc., has been increased or excessive insurance premiums are being paid.

Accounts Receivable (*Debtors*) *Turnover*: (Debtors' Velocity)

$$\frac{\text{Net credit sales}}{\text{Average accounts receivables}}$$

This ratio is usually expressed in "Times".

For best results we should use an average that is representative of the balance of the receivables throughout the period e.g., average based on monthly balances is better than one based on opening and closing balances.

Example 1

Given Sales and Receivables

	First year (₹)	Second year (₹)
Net credit sales	6,30,000	7,20,000
Average accounts receivables	70,000	60,000
Accounts receivable turnover	9 times	12 times
Average number of days per turnover	41 days	30 days

This ratio indicates the liquidity of debtors and effectiveness of the organisation's credit and collection procedure.

The effectiveness of credit and collection policy can also be measured in terms of the daily credit sales as reflected in the accounts receivables. Debt collection period ratio is calculated by the following formula:

$$\frac{\text{Accounts receivables at the end}}{\text{Net credit sales for the period}} \times \text{Working days in a year OR } \frac{\text{Days in a year}}{\text{Debtors' Turnover}}$$

Example 2

Working days = 300	First year ₹	Second year ₹
Net credit sales	6,30,000	7,20,000
Receivables at the end	65,000	55,000
No. of days' sales in receivables	31[1]	23[2]

1. $\frac{65,000}{6,30,000} \times 300 = 31$ 2. $\frac{55,000}{7,20,000} \times 300 = 23$

This ratio indicates efficiency in credit and collection policies.

Aging of Accounts Receivables

Aging of receivables means to prepare a summary of due dates of the receivables. An outline is given below:

Customer	Balance	Under 30 days old	31-60 days old	61-90 days old
A	₹ 1,000	1,000	—	—
B	₹ 2,000	—	1,000	1,000
C	₹ 3,000	1,000	—	2,000
D	₹ 4,000	2,000	2,000	—
E	₹ 5,000	—	—	5,000
Total	15,000	4,000	3,000	8,000

Aging Summary

Age	Amount	Percentage
	₹	
Under 30 days	4,000	27 App.
31-60 days	3,000	20
61-90 days	8,000	53 App.
	15,000	1,000

The aging schedule can be used as a basis for estimating the periodic provision for uncollectible (bad and doubtful) accounts. Average percentage rates for each of the age categories established in the analysis may be developed on the basis of past experience and applied to the accounts in the respective categories to determine the amount that should be in the allowance account as of the balance sheet date.

Creditors Turnover or velocity ratio:

Formula : $\dfrac{\text{Credit Purchase}}{\text{Average Accounts Payable}}$

Debt Payment Period Ratio:

Formula : $\dfrac{\text{Average Accounts Payables}}{\text{Credit Purchase}} \times 360$ days (or 12 months)

Limitations: The ratios analysis give a fair idea of the financial stability, liquidity and earning capacity. However, this technique is not an infallible guide and ratios have inherent limitations. A ratio by itself is valueless and a particular ratio used without reference to other appropriate ratios may give a misguiding picture. Likewise ratios extracted from a single set of financial statements are of a limited use and must be read or studied along with corresponding ratios of previous years. This will give a picture of the trend of affairs. "It is not the ratio or ratios, *ipso-facto*", observes R.A. Foulke[1], that means a business concern is out of line. The ratio is a symptom, like the blood pressure, the pulse, or the temperature of an individual. From empirical testing in recent years, it appears that financial ratios can be used to predict certain events successfully, insolvency in particular. However, "**Inflation distorts financial ratio analysis**. Both inter company comparisons and company's financial ratios over time are subject to faulty economic interpretation in period of changing inflation",[2] changes in the reported performance of a company may be due to entirely

1. *Practical Financial Statement Analysis*, R.A. Foulke, 5th Ed. 1961, Tokyo, p. 177.
2. J.C. Vanhorn, *Financial Management & Policy*, 1990, p. 736.

inflation and not the management. To differentiate the causes, the analyst must recompute financial ratios on the basis of replacement cost accounting data as opposed to historical cost data. Hence, ratio must be interpreted in the light of social, political and economic environment of a business enterprise. Exhibit 6.4 gives a ready reference of various ratios.

EXHIBIT 6.4

Ratios Used for Different Purposes

Test for	Test for
1. Pattern of assets and liabilities	a. Net fixed assets/inventories Current assets as a percentage of total net assets. b. Paid up capital/Net worth/Total borrowings (or Bank Borrowings) as a percentage of total net liabilities.
2. Growth	Percentage increase or decrease in net worth, sales, total income, assets and inventories.
3. Solvency and Financial strength:	(Leverage ratios)
(A) Liquidity (short-term obligation)	a. Current Ratio. b. Quick or acid test ratio.
(B) Long-term stability	a. Debt equity ratio or total outsider's liability as % of net worth.
Financial Risk Credit worthiness, leverage or capital structure	b. Equity ratio (also called proprietary ratio). c. Debt to total assets.
4. Financial Management:	
(A) Over trading	Current ratio or Inventory turnover or proprietary ratio.
(B) Over investment in receivables	Receivables turnover (also called Debt Collection ratio).
5. Efficiency in the use of funds	a. Value[1] of production as a percentage of net worth. b. Value of production as a percentage of net assets.
6. (A) Cost Structure	a. Raw materials consumed and other manufacturing expenses or total expenses as a % of value of production. b. Operating ratio. c. Factory cost or administrative cost or selling cost to sales.
(B) Productivity	Sales as a % of net fixed assets or net assets or working capital.
(C) Operating efficiency	Operating ratio.

1. It means sales plus closing stock minus opening stock.

7. Profitability and Rate of Return	a. Gross or net margin ratio. b. R.O.I. ratios. c. Dividends as a % net worth or paid up capital. d. Earning per share. e. Dividend per share/Market price.
8. Turnover Analysis	a. Inventory Turnover. b. Debtors or Creditors Turnover. c. Assets Turnover (Sales/total assets). d. Capital employed as a % sales.

Example 3

The following are the summarized Profit and Loss Account of Triplex Industries Limited for the year ended 31st December, 2020 and a Balance Sheet of the company as on that date.

Profit and Loss A/c

Dr. Cr.

Particulars	₹	Particulars	₹
To Opening Stock	9,950	By Sales	85,000
To Purchases	54,525	By Closing Stock	14,900
To Carriage Inwards	1,425		
To Gross Profit	34,000		
	99,900		99,900
Particulars	**₹**	**Particulars**	**₹**
To Office Expenses	15,000	By Gross Profit	34,000
To Selling Expenses	3,000	By Profit on Sale of Shares	600
To Financial Expenses	1,500	By Interest on Investments	300
To Loss on Sale of an Asset	400		
To Net Profit	15,000		
	34,900		34,900

Balance Sheet

Liabilities	₹	Assets	₹
Share Capital:		Land and Buildings	15,000
2,000 Equity Shares		Plant	8,000
of ₹ 10 each	20,000	Stock	14,000
Reserves	9,000	Debtors	7,000
Profit and Loss Account	6,000	Bill Receivable	1,000
Bank Overdraft	3,000	Cash and Bank Balance	3,000
Sundry Creditors	8,000		
Outstanding Expenses	2,000		
	48,000		48,000

Calculate the following ratios:

(i) Gross Profit Ratio (ii) Debt Equity Ratio

(iii) Liquid Ratio (iv) Fixed Assets Turnover.

Ans. (i) Gross Profit ratio $= \dfrac{\text{Gross Profit} \times 100}{\text{Net Sales}}$

$= \dfrac{34{,}000 \times 100}{85{,}000} = 40\%.$

(ii) Debt-Equity ratio $= \dfrac{\text{Outsider's Liabilities}}{\text{Shareholder's Funds}}$

$= \dfrac{13{,}000}{35{,}000} = 13 : 35$ or .4 times.

Note: Outsider's Liabilities = Overdraft + Creditors + Outstanding Expenses
= 3,000 + 8,000 + 2,000 = 13,000

Shareholder's Funds = Capital + Reserve + Profit
= 20,000 + 9,000 + 6,000 = 35,000.

(iii) Liquid ratio $= \dfrac{\text{Liquid Assets}}{\text{Current Liabilities}} = \dfrac{\text{Current Assets} - \text{Stock}}{\text{Current Liabilities}}$

$= \dfrac{11{,}000}{13{,}000} = .85$ times.

Working Notes

1. Liquid Assets = Debtors + B/R + Cash at Bank
= 7,000 + 1,000 + 3000 = 11,000.
2. Current Liabilities = Bank overdraft + Creditors + Outstanding Exp.
= 3,000 + 8,000 + 2,000 = 13,000.

(iv) Fixed Assets turnover ratio $= \dfrac{\text{Sales}}{\text{Fixed Assets}}$

$= \dfrac{85{,}000}{23{,}000} = 3.7$ times.

Working Notes

Fixed Assets = Land and Building + Plant = 15,000 + 8,000 = 23,000.

Example 4

Following is the balance sheet of XYZ Limited as on 31st December, 2015:

Liabilities	₹	Assets	₹
Equity Share Capital:		Machinery and Equipment	45,000
2,400 shares of ₹ 10 each		Stock	12,000
(Fully paid).....	24,000	Sundry Debtors	9,000

Profit and Loss A/c	6,000	Cash at Bank	2,280
10% Debentures	15,000	Prepaid Expenses	720
Sundry Creditors	23,400		
Provision for Taxation	600		
	69,000		69,000

Calculate the following ratios:

(i) Current Ratio

(ii) Liquidity Ratio.

What conclusions do you draw about the company on the basis of these ratios?

Ans. (i) Current ratio $= \dfrac{\text{Current Assets}}{\text{Current Liabilities}} = \dfrac{24,000}{24,000} = 1.$

(ii) Liquidity ratio $= \dfrac{\text{Liquid Assets}}{\text{Current Liabilities}}$

$$= \frac{11,280}{24,000} = \frac{141}{300} = 0.47 \text{ times or } 141:300.$$

Working Notes

Liquid Assets = Debtor + Cash at Bank

= 9,000 + 2,280 = 11,280

Or = Current Assets – (Stock + Prepaid Exp.)

= 24,000 – (12,000 + 720) = 24,000 – 12,720 = 11,280.

Conclusion. Short-term financial position of the company is not sound. The standard ratio of current assets to current liabilities should be 2:1 and liquid assets to current liabilities 1:1. In both the cases the actual ratio is lesser.

Example 5

From the following data, calculate:

(a) Gross profit ratio;

(b) Net profit ratio;

(c) Inventory turnover ratio;

(d) Current ratio.

	₹		₹
Sales	25,20,000	Fixed Assets	14,40,000
Cost of Sales	19,20,000	Net Worth	15,00,000
Net Profit	3,60,000	Debt (Long-term)	9,00,000
Average Inventory	8,00,000	Current Liabilities	6,00,000
Other Current Assets	7,60,000		

Ans. (a) $\text{Gross Profit Ratio} = \dfrac{\text{Gross Profit} \times 100}{\text{Net sales}}$

$$= \frac{6,00,000 \times 100}{25,20,000}$$

$$= 23.8\%.$$

Note: Gross Profit = Sales – Cost of Sales = 2,52,000 – 19,20,000 = 6,00,000.

(b) $\text{Net Profit ratio} = \dfrac{\text{Net Profit} \times 100}{\text{Net sales}}$

$$= \frac{3,60,000 \times 100}{25,20,000} = 14.3\%.$$

(c) $\text{Inventory turnover ratio} = \dfrac{\text{Cost of goods sold}}{\text{Average stock}}$

$$= \frac{19,20,000}{8,00,000} = 2.4 \text{ times.}$$

(d) $\text{Current ratio} = \dfrac{\text{Current Assets}}{\text{Current Liabilities}}$

$$= \frac{15,60,000}{6,00,000} = 2.6 \text{ times.}$$

Working Note

Current Assets = Other Current Assets + Stock
= 7,60,000 + 8,00,000 = 15,60,000.

Example 6

From the following calculate the Current Ratio:

XYZ Company Limited
Balance Sheet as at 31st December, 2020

Liabilities	₹	Assets	₹
Share Capital	21,000	Fixed Assets (Net)	17,000
Reserves	1,500	Stock	6,200
Annual Profits	2,500	Debtors	3,200
Bank Overdraft	2,000	Cash	6,600
S. Creditors	6,000		
	33,000		33,000

Ans. $\text{Current ratio} = \dfrac{\text{Current Assets}}{\text{Current Liabilities}}$

$$= \frac{16,000}{8,000} = 2 \text{ times}$$

Current Assets = Stock + Debtors + Cash

= 6,200 + 3,200 + 6,600 = 16,000

Current Liabilities = Sundry Creditors + Bank overdraft

= 6,000 + 2,000 = 8,000.

Example 7

The following are the summarised Profit and Loss A/c for the year ending and the Balance Sheet as that date:

Trading and Profit and Loss A/c

Particulars	₹	Particulars	₹
To Opening Stock	10,000	By Sales	1,00,000
,, Purchases	50,000	,, Closing Stock	15,000
,, Direct Expenses	5,000		
,, Gross Profit	50,000		
	1,15,000		1,15,000

Particulars	₹	Particulars	₹
To Administrative Expenses	15,000	By Gross Profit	50,000
,, Interest	3,000		
,, Selling Expenses	12,000		
,, Net Profit	20,000		
	50,000		50,000

Balance Sheet

Liabilities	₹	Assets	₹
Capital	1,00,000	Land and Building	50,000
Current Liabilities	40,000	Plant & Machinery	30,000
Profit and Loss A/c	20,000	Stock	15,000
		Sundry Debtors	15,000
		Bills Receivable	12,500
		Cash in hand and at Bank	17,500
		Furniture	20,000
	1,60,000		1,60,000

From the above, calculate:

(i) Gross Profit Ratio
(ii) Current Ratio
(iii) Acid test Ratio
(iv) Stock turnover Ratio
(v) Fixed Assets turnover Ratio.

Ans. (i) Gross Profit ratio $= \frac{\text{Gross Profit} \times 100}{\text{Net sales}}$

$$= \frac{50,000 \times 100}{1,00,000} = 50\%$$

(ii) Current Ratio $= \frac{\text{Current Assets}}{\text{Current Liabilities}}$

$$= \frac{60,000}{40,000} = 1.5 \text{ times}$$

Note. Current Assets = Stock + Debtors + B/R + Cash at Bank
= 15,000 + 15,000 + 12,500 + 17,500
= 60,000.

(iii) Acid Test Ratio $= \frac{\text{Liquid or Quick Assets}}{\text{Current Liabilities}}$

$$= \frac{45,000}{40,000} = 1.13 \text{ times or } 9:8$$

Note. Liquid Assets = Current Assets – Stock
= 60,000 – 15,000 = 45,000.

(iv) Stock Turn Over Ratio $= \frac{\text{Cost of goods Sold}}{\text{Average Stock}}$

$$= \frac{50,000}{12,500} = 4 \text{ times.}$$

Working Notes

Cost of goods sold = Sales – Gross Profit
= 1,00,000 – 50,000 = 50,000

$$\text{Average Stock} = \frac{\text{Opening Stock} + \text{Closing Stock}}{2}$$

$$= \frac{10,000 + 15,000}{2} = \frac{25,000}{2} = 12,500$$

(v) Fixed Assets Turnover Ratio $= \frac{\text{Net Sales}}{\text{Fixed Assets}}$

$$= \frac{1,00,000}{1,00,000} = 1:1.$$

Note. Fixed Assets = Land and Building + Plant + Furniture
= 50,000 + 30,000 + 20,000 = 1,00,000.

Example 8

(a) Current liabilities of a company are ₹ 1,50,000. Its current ratio is 3:1 and acid test ratio (liquid ratio) is 1:1. Calculate the values of current assets, liquid assets and stock.

(b) From the following particulars, determine debtors turnover ratio and average collection period:

	₹
Total Sales	10,00,000
Credit Sales	8,00,000
Debtors	1,00,000

(c) The current ratio of a company is 2.5:1. Which of the following suggestions would improve, reduce and not change it:

(i) Payment to trade creditors

(ii) Sell machinery for cash

(iii) Purchase goods for cash

(iv) Issue of equity shares

Ans. (a) $\text{Current ratio} = \frac{\text{Current Assets}}{\text{Current Liabilities}} = 3{:}1$

Current Liabilities = 1,50,000 (given)

Current Assets will be 3 times of current liabilities

= 1,50,000 × 3 = 4,50,000

$\text{Acid Test (Liquid) ratio} = \frac{\text{Liquid Assets}}{\text{Current Liabilities}} = 1{:}1$

Liquid Assets is equal to current liabilities = 1,50,000

Stock = Current Assets – Liquid Assets

= 4,50,000 – 1,50,000 = 3,00,000

(b) $\text{Debtors Turnover ratio} = \frac{\text{Credit sales}}{\text{Debtors}}$

$= \frac{8{,}00{,}000}{1{,}00{,}000} = 8 \text{ times.}$

$\text{Average Collection Period} = \frac{\text{Months in the year}}{\text{Debtors Turnover}}$

$= \frac{12}{8} = 1.5 \text{ months.}$

or $\frac{\text{Days in year}}{\text{Debtors Turnover}} = \frac{360}{8} = 45 \text{ days.}$

(c) (i) **Payment to creditors.** It will reduce the cash a current assets and creditors a current liability with the same amounts to the current ratio will improve. For example, if the current assets of the firm is ₹ 10,000 and creditors ₹ 5,000 the current ratio will be $\frac{10{,}000}{5{,}000} = 2$ times. If creditors amounting to ₹ 2,000 are paid the current assets will decrease to ₹ 8,000 and the creditors to ₹ 3,000 and thus the current ratio will be:

$$\frac{8,000}{3,000} = 2.67 \text{ times.}$$

(ii) **Sell machinery for cash.** It will increase cash a current assets and reduce the machinery a non-current assets so increase in current assets will increase current ratio. As current liability is not changing and the increase only in current assets will improve current ratio.

(iii) **Purchase of goods for cash.** This will increase stock, a current assets and decrease cash, also a current assets and as such there will be no change in the current assets and thus the current ratio will remain unchanged.

(iv) **Issue of equity shares.** This will increase cash a current assets and capital a non-current liability. There will be no change in the current liability and the increase only in current assets will improve current ratio.

Example 9

The following is the Balance Sheet of Arvind Mills Ltd., as on 31st December, 2020.

Liabilities	₹	Assets		₹
Sundry Creditors	60,000	Bank		50,000
Bills Payable	1,00,000	Investments		1,50,000
Tax Provision	1,30,000	Book Debts		2,00,000
Outstanding expenses	10,000	Stock		3,00,000
6% Debentures	7,00,000			
8% Preference shares	1,00,000	Fixed Assets	18,00,000	
Equity shares	5,00,000	Less Depreciation	5,00,000	13,00,000
Reserve Fund	4,00,000			
	20,00,000			20,00,000

Other information supplied is as follows:

	₹
(a) Net Sales	30,00,000
(b) Cost of goods sold	25,80,000
(c) Net income before tax	2,00,000
(d) Net income after tax	1,00,000

You are required to calculate:

(i) Liquidity Ratio

(ii) Proprietary Ratio

(iii) Current Ratio

(iv) Gross Profit Ratio

(v) Net Profit Ratio.

Ans. (i) Liquidity ratio $= \dfrac{\text{Liquid Assets}}{\text{Current Liabilities}}$

$$= \frac{4,00,000}{3,00,000} = 1.33 \text{ times or } 4:3$$

Note. Liquid Assets = Bank + Book Debts + Investment
= 50,000 + 2,00,000 + 1,50,000 = 4,00,000

Current liabilities = Creditors + B/P + Outstanding Expenses + Tax Provision
= 60,000 + 1,00,000 + 10,000 + 1,30,000 = 3,00,000

Note. 1. Investment has been assumed to be short term investment and thus a liquid assets.

2. Provision for taxes has to be paid within a year and thus a current liabilities.

(ii) Proprietary ratio $= \dfrac{\text{Proprietors funds}}{\text{Total assets}} \times 100$

$$= \frac{10,00,000 \times 100}{20,00,000} = 50\%$$

Note. Proprietors funds = Preference and Equity share capital + Reserve
= 6,00,000 + 4,00,000 = 10,00,000

Total assets = Total of the assets side of Balance Sheet
= 20,00,000

(iii) Current Ratio $= \dfrac{\text{Current assets}}{\text{Current liabilities}} = \dfrac{7,00,000}{3,00,000} = 7:3$

Note. 1. As fixed assets are separately given so the remaining assets will be current assets

i.e., 7,00,000 = (20,00,000 – 13,00,000)

2. Current liabilities = Creditors + Bills payable + Tax provision + Outstanding Expenses
= 60,000 + 1,00,000 + 1,30,000 + 10,000 = 300,000

(iv) Gross profit ratio $= \dfrac{\text{Gross profit} \times 100}{\text{Net sales}}$

$$= \frac{4,20,000 \times 100}{30,00,000} = 14\%$$

Note. Gross Profit = Net sales – Cost of goods sold

= 30,00,000 – 25,00,000 = 4,20,000

(v) Net profit ratio $= \dfrac{\text{Net profit before tax} \times 100}{\text{Net sales}}$

$= \dfrac{2,00,000 \times 100}{30,00,000} = 6.67\%$

Note. Net profit ratio is calculated on the basis of operating net profit before tax.

Example 10

Attempt the following:

(a) A firm has a current ratio of 3:1. Its net working capital is ₹ 2,00,000. You are required to determine (i) current assets, (ii) current liabilities, and (iii) liquid assets assuming inventory of ₹ 2,20,000.

(b) A firm normally has debtors equal to two months' credit sales. During the coming year it expects credit sales of ₹ 7,20,000 spread over evenly over the year (12 months). What is the estimated amount of debtors at the end of the year?

Ans. (a) Current ratio = 3:1

Working Capital = Current Assets – Current Liabilities

= 3 – 1 = 2 = 2,00,000 (given)

If working capital is 2 current assets = 3

If working capital is 1 current assets = 3/2

If working capital is 2,00,000 current assets $= \dfrac{3}{2} \times 2,00,000 = 3,00,000$

Current liabilities = Current assets – Working capital

= 3,00,000 – 2,00,000 = 1,00,000

Liquid assets = Current assets – Stock

= 3,00,000 – 2,20,000 = 80,000.

(b) Annual sales = 7,20,000 (given)

Monthly sales $= \dfrac{7,20,000}{12} = 60,000$

Debtors at the end of the year

= 60,000 × 2 = 1,20,000.

Note. As the firm normally has debtors equal to two months credit sale the estimated amount of debtors will be equal to two months credit sale.

Example 11

(i) Current Ratio 2.5; Working Capital ₹ 60,000. Calculate the amount of current assets and current liabilities.

(ii) Opening Stock ₹ 29,000; Closing Stock ₹ 31,000; Sales ₹ 3,20,000; Gross profit Ratio 25% on Sales. Calculate Stock Turnover Ratio.

Ans. (i) Current ratio = 2.5 times

If current liabilities = 1

Current Assets = 2.5

Working Capital = 2.5 – 1 = 1.5

If working capital is 1.5 current assets = 2.5

If working capital is 1 current assets = 2.5/1.5

If working capital is 60,000 current assets $= \frac{2.5}{1.5} \times 60,000 = 1,00,000.$

Current liabilities = Current Assets – Working Capital
= 1,00,000 – 60,000 = 40,000

(ii) Gross Profit = 25% on Sales

$$= 3,20,000 \times \frac{25}{100} = 80,000$$

Cost of goods sold = Sales – Gross profit
= 3,20,000 – 80,000 = 2,40,000

$$\text{Average Stock} = \frac{\text{Opening Stock + Closing Stock}}{2}$$

$$= \frac{29,000 + 31,000}{2} = \frac{60,000}{2} = 30,000$$

$$\text{Stock turnover ratio} = \frac{\text{Cost of goods sold}}{\text{Average stock}}$$

$$= \frac{2,40,000}{30,000} = 8 \text{ times.}$$

Example 12

From the following information determine average stock:

Stock turnover : 5 times

Total sales : ₹ 2,00,000

Gross profit : 25% of sales.

If the closing stock is more by ₹ 4,000 than the opening stock, determine the opening and closing stock.

Ans. Gross profit = 25% on sales

$$= 2,00,000 \times \frac{25}{100} = 50,000$$

Costs of goods sold = Sales – Gross profit
= 2,00,000 – 50,000 = 1,50,000

$$\text{Stock turnover ratio} = \frac{\text{Cost of goods sold}}{\text{Average Stock}} = 5 \text{ times}$$

$$\text{Average Stock} = \frac{1}{5}\text{th of cost of goods sold}$$

$$= 1,50,000 \times \frac{1}{5} = 30,000.$$

Total Stock = Average Stock × 2
= 30,000 × 2 = 60,000

Difference between opening and closing stock = 4,000 (given)

Let the opening stock be = x

Closing stock = x + 4,000

Equation, $x + x + 4,000 = 60,000$

or $2x + 4,000 = 60,000$

or $2x = 60,000 - 4,000$

or $2x = 56,000$

or $x = \frac{56,000}{2} = 28,000$

Closing Stock = 28,000 + 4,000 = 32,000.

Example 13

A firm has owner's equity of ₹ 10,00,000. The following ratios are available:

(a) Current debt to total debt 40%
(b) Total debt to owner's equity 60%
(c) Fixed Assets to owner's equity 60%
(d) Total assets turnover 2 Times
(e) Inventory turnover 8 Times

You are required to complete the following Balance Sheet on the basis of above information:

Balance Sheet

Liabilities	₹	Assets	₹
Owner's Equity	—	Cash	—
Long term debt	—	Inventory	—
Current debt	—	Fixed Assets	—
Total	—	Total	—

Solution

Balance Sheet

Liabilities	₹	Assets	₹
Owner's Equity	10,00,000	Cash	6,00,000
Long term debt	3,60,000	Inventory	4,00,000
Current debt	2,40,000	Fixed Assets	6,00,000
Total	16,00,000	Total	1,6,00,000

Hints

(1) Total debt 60% of ₹ 10,00,000 = ₹ 6,00,000

(2) Fixed Assets 60% of ₹ 10,00,000 = ₹ 6,00,000

(3) Total Capital or total Assets = ₹ 6,00,000 + ₹ 10,00,000 = 16,00,000

(4) First find sales by formula $= \dfrac{\text{Sales}}{\text{Total Assets}} = 2$ i.e. ₹ 32,00,000

then find inventory by dividing 32,00,000 by 8 = ₹ 4,00,000

(5) Current debt = 40% of total debt ₹ 6,00,000 = ₹ 2,40,000

(6) Long-term debt = Total debt – Current debt

(7) Current Assets = Total Assets 16,00,000 – Total Fixed Assets ₹ 6,00,000 = ₹ 2,40,000

Cash = Current Assets – Inventory i.e. ₹ 10,00,000 – ₹ 4,00,000 = ₹ 6,00,000.

Example 14

From the following estimated data, average amount of working capital required is to be found out:

	Figures for the year ₹
(a) Average amount locked up in Stocks:	
Stock of finished goods	5,000
Stock of Stores, raw materials etc.	8,000
(b) Average Credit given:	
Inland Sales	3,12,000
Foreign Sales	78,000
(c) Lags in Payment of wages and other outgoings:	
Wages—1½ weeks	2,60,000
Stores materials etc.—1½ months	48,000
Rent, Royalties etc.—6 months	10,000
Clerical Staff—½ month	62,400
Manager—½ month	4,800
Other Expenses—1½ months	48,000
(d) Payment in Advance:	
Sundry Expenses (Paid quarterly in advance)	8,000

(e) Undrawn Profits on the average throughout the year 11,000

10% is to be provided for contingency to the computed figure.

Solution

Current Assets:

		₹
(A) Inventories (5,000 + 8,000)		13,000
(B) Debtors:		
(i) Inland Sales – 6 weeks sale of ₹ 3,12,000 p.a. 3,12,000 × 6/52	= 36,000	
(ii) Foreign Sales – 1½ weeks sale of ₹ 78,000 p.a. i.e. 78,000 × 1½/52	= 2,250	38,250
(C) Advance Payments		2,000
Total Current Assets		53,250
Less Current Liabilities:		
Lags in Payments		
(1) Wages (2,60,000 × 1½/52)	= 7,500	
(2) Stores, materials (48,000 × 1½/12)	= 6,000	
(3) Rent, Royalties	= 5,000	
(4) Clerical Staff	= 2,600	
(5) Manager	= 200	
(6) Other Expenses	= 6,000	27,300
Net W.C.		25,950
Add 10% Contingency		2,595
Average W.C. required		28,545

Note. Undrawn profit does not affect the working capital required.

Example 15

The financial statements of ONGC Ltd. for the year 2020 revealed the following information:

Ratio of current assets to current liabilities	1.75 to 1.0
Liquidity ratio (debtors and bank balances to current liabilities)	1.25 to 1.0
Issued capital in equity shares of ₹ 10 each	₹ 1,20,000
Net current assets (as over current liabilities)	₹ 60,000
Fixed assets (net block)—Percentage of share-holders' equity as on the closing date	60%
Gross profit—Percentage of turnover	20%
Annual rate of turnover of Stock (based on cost on 31-12-2020)	5.26 times
Average age of outstanding debtors for the year 2020	2 months
Net profit—Percentage on issued Share capital	16%

On 31st December, 2020, current assets consisted of stock, debtors and bank balances.

You are required to reconstruct, in as much detail as possible:

(1) The Balance Sheet as on 31st Dec., 2020 and

(2) The Trading and Profit and Loss accounts for the year ended 31st Dec., 2020.

(Working should be clearly shown)

Solution

Trading and Profit and Loss A/c

For the year ending 31st Dec., 2020

Particulars	₹	Particulars	₹
To Cost of goods sold	2,12,504	By Sales	2,65,630
To Gross Profit c/d (20% of sales)	53,126		
	2,65,630		2,65,630
To Operating Expenses (balancing figure)	33,926	By Gross Profit b/d	53,126
To Net Profit (16% of ₹ 1,20,000)	19,200		
	53,126		53,126

Balance Sheet as on 31st Dec., 2020

Liabilities	₹	Assets	₹
Share Capital:		Fixed Assets:	
12,000 equity shares		(Net Block)	90,900
of ₹ 10 each	1,20,000	Current Assets:	
		Bank Balance	56,728
Reserves & Surplus:		Sundry Debtors	44,272
Profit & Loss A/c	31,500	Stock	40,400
Current Liabilities	80,800		
	2,32,300		2,32,300

Notes:

(1) Net current assets = ₹ 60,600

i.e. Current assets – Current liabilities = ₹ 60,600 ...(i)

Also, $\dfrac{\text{Current assets}}{\text{Current liabilities}} = 1.75$

i.e. Current assets – 1.75 Current liabilities = 0 ...(ii)

Subtract equation (ii) from equation (i).

Then, we have

0.75 × Current liabilities = ₹ 60,600

$$\text{Or, Current liabilities} = \frac{₹\ 60,000}{0.75}$$

= ₹ 80,800

Current assets = ₹ 60,600 + ₹ 80,800
= ₹ 1,41,400.

(2) Liquidity ratio is 1.25

$$\text{i.e. } \frac{\text{Liquid assets}}{\text{Current liabilities}} = 1.25$$

Or Liquid assets = 1.25 × ₹ 80,800
= ₹ 1,01,000.

(3) Stock as on 31st Dec., 1997
= Current assets – Liquid assets
= ₹ 1,41,400 – ₹ 1,01,000
= ₹ 40,400.

(4) Stock turnover = 5.26

$$\text{i.e. } \frac{\text{Cost of goods sold}}{\text{Stock}} = 5.26$$

Or, Cost of goods sold = 5.26 × ₹ 40,400
= ₹ 2,12,504.

(5) Gross profit = 20% of turnover (sales)
So, cost of goods sold = 80% of sales
Or, 80% of sales = ₹ 2,12,504

$$\text{i.e. Sales} = \frac{₹\ 2,12,504}{.80}$$

= ₹ 2,65,630.

(6) Net fixed assets = 60% of shareholders' equity
Therefore, Net current assets = 40% of shareholders' equity
Net current assets = ₹ 60,600

$$\frac{\text{Net fixed assets}}{.60} = \frac{\text{Net current assets}}{.40}$$

$$\text{Or} \quad \text{Net fixed assets} = \frac{₹\ 60,600}{.40} \times .60$$

= ₹ 60,600 × 3/2
= ₹ 90,900.

(7) Shareholders' equity
= Fixed assets + Net current assets

= ₹ 90,900 + ₹ 60,600
= ₹ 1,51,500

Reserves and Surplus
= Shareholders' equity – Share Capital
= 1,51,500 – ₹ 1,20,000
= ₹ 31,500.

(8) Average age of outstanding debtors
(i.e. Average Collection Period) = 2 months
So, Debtors' turnover = 12/2 = 6
All sales may be assumed to be credit sales.

$$\text{Then, } \frac{\text{Credit sales}}{\text{Debtors}} = 6$$

$$\text{Or Debtors} = \frac{\text{Credit sales}}{6}$$

$$= \frac{₹\ 2,65,630}{6} = ₹\ 44,272.$$

(9) Bank Balance = Liquid Assets – Debtors
₹ 1,01,000 – ₹ 44,272 = ₹ 56,728.

Example 16

From the following information, prepare a Balance Sheet. Show the workings.

	₹		₹
1. Working Capital	75,000	5. Liquid Ratio	1.15
2. Reserves and Surphus	1,00,000	6. Fixed Assets to Proprietors' Funds	0.75
3. Bank Overdraft	60,000		
4. Current Ratio	1.75	7. Long-term Liabilities	Nil

Solution:

Let Current Liabilities be 'x'

The current assets will be $1.75x$.

Working Capital is ₹ 75,000

Therefore, Current Assets – Current Liabilities = ₹ 75,000

or $1.75x - x =$ ₹ 75,000

or $.75x =$ 75,000

or $x = \frac{75,000}{75} =$ ₹ 1,00,000

Current Liabilities are ₹ 1,00,000.

Therefore, Current Assets will be ₹ 1,75,000.

Liquid Ratio $= \dfrac{\text{Liquid Assets}}{\text{Current Liabilities}}$

Suppose Liquid Assets are 'x'

$$\frac{x}{1,00,000} = 1.15 \text{ or, } x = ₹\ 1,15,000$$

Stock = Current Assets – Liquid Assets

= ₹ 1,75,000 – ₹ 1,15,000 = ₹ 60,000

Sundry Creditors = Current Liabilities – Bank Overdraft

= 1,00,000 – 60,000 = ₹ 40,000

Proprietors' Funds = Fixed Assets + Working Capital

Presuming the amount of Fixed assets as 'x',

$$\frac{x}{x + 75,000} = \frac{3}{4}$$

or $4x = 3x + 2,25,000$

or x (i.e. Fixed Assets) = 2,25,000

Proprietors' Funds = Fixed Assets + Working Capital

= 2,25,000 + 75,000 = ₹ 3,00,000

Share Capital = 3,00,000 – 1,00,000 = ₹ 2,00,000

The Balance Sheet will now finally appear as follows:

Balance Sheet As on............

Liabilities	₹	Assets	₹
Share Capital	2,00,000	Fixed Assets	2,25,000
Reserves and Surplus	1,00,000	Current Assets:	
Current Liabilities:		Stock	60,000
Sundry Creditors	40,000	Liquid Assets	1,15,000
Bank Overdraft	60,000		
	4,00,000		4,00,000

Example 17

From the following figures and ratios, draw out Balance Sheet and Trading and Profit and Loss Account:

	₹
Share Capital	1,80,000
Working Capital	63,000
Bank Overdraft	10,000

There is no fictitious. In current assets there is no asset other than stock, debtors and cash. Closing stock is 20% higher than the opening stock.

Current Ratio : 2.5
Proprietary Ratio : 0.7
Stock Velocity : 4
Net Profit Ratio : 10% (to average capital employed)
Quick Ratio : 1.5
Gross Profit Ratio : 20% to sales
Debtors Velocity : 36.5 years

Solution:

Current Ratio is 2.5

Presuming Current Liabilities as x.

Current Assets – Current Liabilities = Working Capital

$$2.5x - x = 63,000$$

or $$x = 42,000$$

Current Assets = 1,05,000

Current Liabilities = 42,000

Quick Ratio (i.e., Quick Assets/Current Liabilities) is 1.5

It means Quick Assets are ₹ 63,000

Closing Stock (₹ 1,50,000 – 63,000) = 42,000

Closing Stock is 20% higher than Opening Stock

$$\text{Opening Stock} = \frac{42{,}000 \times 100}{120} = ₹\ 35{,}000$$

$$\text{Average stock} = \frac{42{,}000 + 35{,}000}{2} = ₹\ 38{,}500$$

Stock Velocity (Cost of Sales/Average Stock) is 4

Cost of sales = 38,500 × 4 = ₹ 1,54,000

Sales = Cost of Sales + Gross Profit
= 1,54,000 + 38,500 = 1,92,500

$$\text{Debtors} = \frac{1{,}92{,}000 \times 36.5}{365}$$

= ₹ 19,250

Average Capital Employed = ₹ 1,80,000 + 63,000 – (1/2 of 7,000)
= ₹ 2,39,500

Net Profit = ₹ 23,950

Operating Expenses = Gross Profit – Net Profit
= ₹ 38,500 – 23,950
= ₹ 14,550

Trading and Profit and Loss Account

Particulars	₹	Particulars	₹
To Opening Stock	35,000	By Sales	1,92,500
To Purchases	1,61,000	By Closing Stock	42,000
(1,54,000 + 42,000 – 35,000)			
To Gross Profit	38,500		
	2,34,500		2,34,500
To Operating Expenses	14,550	By Gross Profit	38,500
To Net Profit	23,950		
	38,500		38,500

Balance Sheet

Particulars	₹	Particulars	₹
Share Capital	1,80,000	Fixed Assets (Balancing Figure)	1,17,000
Current Liabilities:		Current Assets:	
Sundry Creditors	32,000	Cash	43,750
Bank Overdraft	10,000	Debtors	19,250
		Closing Stock	42,000
	2,22,000		2,22,000

FUND FLOW ANALYSIS

The Balanced Sheet and Profit and Loss Account do not present all the valuable information included in the accounts. The Balance Sheet shows the financial condition of an organisation as of a moment of time and income statement summarizes the results of operations for a period of time. They do not disclose important information like (i) how much cash was generated by operations, (ii) how the acquisition of new assets were financed or (iii) how the redemption of a debenture was done. For this reason various special statements are prepared. The three important statements are: (a) statement of source and disposition of working capital, (b) statement of source and disposition of cash, and (c) statement of sources and application of funds.

The term funds is used in various senses. From the standpoint of funds flow analysis, funds are generally defined in one of the following three ways:

1. In terms of cash.
2. In terms of working capital.
3. In terms of all financial resources resulting from transactions with parties external to the organisation.

In terms of cash, funds mean only cash receipts and payment. In terms of working capital, it includes current assets and current liabilities i.e., transactions which affect them. In terms of all funds, it considers all financial transactions. We may classify it with an example. Suppose a company buys a machine for ₹ 1,00,000. It pays (a) ₹ 30,000 in cash, (b) ₹ 20,000 by a bills of exchange and (c) ₹ 50,000 by mortgage for five years of land. Under the cash approach only ₹ 30,000 cash paid is called funds. Under working capital approach, both ₹ 30,000 and bill for ₹ 20,000 are funds. Under the last approach all financial resources are funds i.e., including mortgage. However, each concept has its usefulness under appropriate circumstances.

Sources and Disposition of Working Capital

The assets and liabilities of an organisation, from financial point of view fall into two categories: Current and non-current. Current assets and liabilities are those which are constantly changing form or "working", whereas non-current assets and liabilities are more or less permanent. The excess of current assets over current liabilities is called working (or net working) capital. Inadequate working capital is one of the indications of financial disaster. It may be shown, in its financial position form, separately in following form:

Current assets – Current liabilities = Working capital

Working capital + Non-current assets – Non-current liabilities = Net assets or owner's equity.

The financial statements should be supplemented by a schedule reflecting the net changes in various working capital elements and a statement summarizing how these changes came about. A specimen is given in Exhibit 6.5.

Exhibit 6.5

Schedule of Net Changes in Working Capital

For the year ending 31-12-2020

Current Assets	2020	2019	Working capital	
			Increase	Decrease
	₹	₹	₹	₹
Cash	44,000	30,000	14,000	—
Investments	20,000	25,000	—	5,000
Debtors (Net)	60,000	39,500	20,500	—
Bill Receivables	10,000	10,500	—	500
Closing Stock	1,35,000	1,00,000	35,000	—
Prepaid Insurance	1,000	1,000	—	—
Total current assets	2,70,000	2,06,000	—	—
Current Liabilities:				
Accrued wages payable	2,500	2,500	—	—
Creditors	1,32,000	80,000	—	52,000
Bills payable	50,000	50,500	500	—

Income-tax outstanding	60,000	53,000	—	7,000
Dividends outstanding	7,500	10,000	2,500	—
Total current liabilities	2,52,000	1,96,000	—	—
Working capital (C.A. – C.I.)	18,000	10,000	—	—
Net increase in working capital		3,000		8,000
			72,500	72,500

The prepaid insurance and accrued wages have not changed. This does not mean that no change has taken place in them during the period. A net change of zero in an account in itself means nothing. An increase in current asset increases working capital and decrease in current asset decreases working capital. Similarly, an increase in current liability decreases working capital and decreases in current liability increases working capital.

The schedule or summary of working capital does not show the source and disposition of all the working capital that management has at its disposal during the period. They also do not give causes of these changes. So "a statement of source and disposition of working capital" is prepared for this purpose. Before we discuss it is important to know that all transactions in business may be divided in following three categories:

(a) transactions that affect only working capital accounts.
(b) transactions that affect only non-working capital accounts.
(c) transactions that affect both working capital and non-working capital accounts.

Transactions that take place wholly within the working capital accounts do not affect the amount of working capital and, as a result, they are not reflected as individual transactions in the statement of source and disposition of working capital. For example, the collection of a customer's account causes an increase in one working capital account (cash) and a decrease in another (debtors). Since these accounts normally have like balance, an increase in one with an equal decrease in the other has the net result of no change in the amount of working capital. Likewise, the payment of a creditor's account results in decreases in two working capital accounts (creditors and cash). These accounts normally have opposite balances, an equal decrease in each results in no change in the amount of working capital. Although transactions which affect only working capital accounts are not reflected as individual transactions in the statement of source and disposition of working capital. They are, of course, summarized in schedule of working capital changes.

Transactions which take place entirely outside the working capital accounts do not affect the amount of working capital and, as a result, they are not reflected as individual transactions in the statement of source and disposition of working capital. For example, purchase of land or redemption of a debenture by issue of a company's previously unissued capital would have no effect on working capital. Other examples are appropriation of profits, issue of bonus shares or acquiring a fixed asset by use of debentures.

Only those transactions that affect both working capital, and non-working capital accounts result in change in the amount of working capital. These transactions are relevant for the statement of source and disposition of working capital.

During any period the working capital may be increased or decreased by the following typical sources or uses:

Typical Sources	Typical Uses
1. Income from operations	1. Loss from operations
2. Sale of non-current asset	2. Purchase of non-current assets
3. Increase in long-term debt	3. Decrease in long-term debt
4. Sale of additional shares	4. Redemption of redeemable preferences shares
	5. Dividends on shares

Working Capital and the Results of Operations

The income-producing activities of any organisation affect the working capital either by increase in net income or it is decreased by net loss. The amount of the effect, however, is usually not the same as the amount of reported net income or net loss. There are certain debits (changes) to income and expenses accounts that reduce the reported net income or increase the reported net loss without affecting working capital. Similarly, some credits that increase the reported net income or decrease the reported net loss but do not affect the working capital. For example, the depreciation debited to profit and loss account has no effect on working capital. Writing off goodwill has no effect on working capital. Therefore, to find the actual amount of working capital, the such charges must be added back and deduct credits which were made to profit and loss account that did not affect working capital. Typical items of such type are: Depreciation on fixed assets, depletion of wasting assets, writing off intangible assets and writing off debenture or shares discount or premium.

Working Capital and Gains or Losses on Sale of Fixed Assets: Under all income statement approach any gain or loss on sale of fixed asset is shown in the profit and loss account.[1] In such case the amount of cash received is associated with working capital. Therefore, when a gain is involved, it is included in the reported net profit and this gain element must be deducted from the amount of sale or from the amount of net profit provided by operations. This is done in order to avoid double counting. Take the following example:

1. Under current operating performance approach such items are shown in the profit and loss (appropriation) account.

A machine's book value = ₹ 40,000; sale price = ₹ 50,000; Capital gain = ₹ 10,000.

₹ 50,000 the sale proceeds, should be shown in statement of working capital and ₹ 10,000 gain should be deducted from net income (and added to reported net loss) provided by operations. If the machine is sold for ₹ 35,000 then there is a loss of ₹ 5,000. In that case, the amount of ₹ 35,000 should be shown as sale proceeds in working capital statement and ₹ 5,000 would be added to reported net income from operations (deducted from reported net loss). Following is a chart of typical non-working capital items that are to be adjusted. Remember that the net profit or net loss shown in profit and loss account must be adjusted for all transactions shown therein which do not affect working capital.

Chart

	Reported net profit	Reported net loss
1. Depreciation on fixed assets	Add back	Deduct
2. Depletion of wasting assets	-do-	-do-
3. Writing off intangible assets (Goodwill, Preliminary expenses)	-do-	-do-
4. Gain on sale of fixed assets	Deduct	Add back
5. Loss on sale of fixed assets	Add back	Deduct
6. Amortization (writing off) share/debenture discount	-do-	-do-
7. Amortization of premium on shares or debentures	Deduct	Add back

Preparation of Statement

The statement is prepared from data derived from a comparison of balance sheets as of the beginning and end of a period besides, additional information is taken from analysis of specific accounts like a net increase in the reserves (retained earnings). This may be the result of net profit only or net profit minus corrections of previous years' earnings or net profit minus dividends. Similarly, the net increase in a fixed asset may be the result of one or more purchases or sales or both. The following steps are suggested to prepare the statement:

First step: Prepare a schedule of changes in working capital.

Second step: Analyses the net changes in non-current accounts to determine the individual elements of the change and their effects on working capital.

Third step: Prepare the statement.

Fourth step: Prove the statement by following formula:

(i) Increase in working capital = W.C. provided minus W.C. used

or

(ii) Decrease in working capital = W.C. used minus W.C. provided.

Example 18

Following is Balance Sheet (summarised) of A.B. Co. Ltd. for two years:

	Dec. 2020	Dec. 2019	Dr.	Cr.
Assets:	₹	₹	₹	₹
Current assets	10,00,000	9,00,000	1,00,000	
Non-current assets	30,00,000	30,00,000		
	40,00,000	39,00,000		
Liabilities:				
Current liabilities	6,00,000	6,50,000	50,000	
Non-current liabilities	10,00,000	10,00,000		
Share Capital	10,00,000	10,00,000		
Reserves	14,00,000	12,50,000		1,50,000
	40,00,000	39,00,000	1,50,000	1,50,000

We solve the above example, under different assumptions.

(A) *Effect of Dividends*: Suppose a dividend of ₹ 50,000 was declared in 2020.

Change in working capital:

Current assets – Current liabilities = Increase or decrease in W.C.
2020 (10,00,000 – 6,00,000) = 4,00,000
2019 (9,00,000 – 6,50,000) = 2,50,000 = 1,50,000 increase in W.C.
Statement of Source and Disposition of Working Capital

Working Capital provided by operations	20,000[1]
Working Capital used for:	
Cash Dividend declared	5,000
Increases in W.C. (see above)	15,000

(B) *Effect of Depreciation*: Suppose further the current assets of 2020 are ₹ 10,20,000 and net non-current assets are ₹ 29,80,000. Other figures remain the same. Then the change in working capital will appear as under:

	2020 ₹	2019 ₹	W.C. Increase ₹
Current assets	10,20,000	9,00,000	1,20,000
Current liabilities	6,00,000	6,50,000	50,000
Net increase in W.C.			1,70,000

1. ₹ 1,50,000 changes in reserves plus dividend.

If we assume that there were no changes in the non-current liability accounts, that the only change in the non-current account was for the amount of depreciation taken during the period, and the only change in the reserves, except for the declaration of cash dividend, resulted for operations, the statement of source and disposition would appear as follows:

	₹	₹
Working capital provided by:		
Operation:		
Reported net profit	2,00,000[1]	
Add Depreciation	20,000[2]	2,20,000
Working capital used for:		
Declaration of cash dividend		50,000
Increase in working capital (see above)		1,70,000

(C) *Purchase of Fixed Assets*: To illustrate the effect of purchase of fixed assets (or non-current assets), we assume that in the summarized Balance Sheets, the current assets are ₹ 9,20,000 and non-current assets (net) are ₹ 30,80,000 for the year 2020. Other figures remain the same. The working capital changes would be shown as under:

	2020 ₹	2019 ₹	W.C. increase or (decrease) ₹
Current assets	9,20,000	9,00,000	20,000
Current liabilities	6,00,000	6,50,000	50,000
Net increase in W.C.			70,000

Let us assume that there was no changes in the non-current liability accounts, that the change in the non-current asset accounts was due to (i) periodic depreciation entry, (ii) the purchase of machinery for ₹ 1,00,000 cash and that the only change in reserves was the result of operations, except for the declaration of cash dividends of ₹ 50,000. The statement of source and disposition of working capital would appear as follows:

	₹	₹
Working Capital provided by:		
Operations:		
Reported net profits	2,00,000	
Add: Depreciation	+20,000	2,20,000
Working capital used for:		
Purchase of machinery	1,00,000	
Declaration of cash dividend	50,000	–1,50,000
Increase in W.C. (see above)		70,000

(D) *Sale of Fixed Asset*: Assume that in the Summarized Balance Sheet, the current assets are ₹ 12,20,000 and non-current assets (net) are

1. ₹ 1,50,000 changes in reserves plus dividend.
2. Decrease in net non-current assets.

₹ 27,80,000 for the year 2020. The other figures remain unchanged. Then the working capital changes shall appear as follows:

	2020	2019	Working Capital (increase or decrease)
	₹	₹	₹
Current assets	12,20,000	9,00,000	3,20,000
Current liabilities	6,00,000	6,50,000	50,000
Net increase in W.C.			3,70,000

If we assume that there were no changes in non-current liabilities, that the change in non-current assets was due to (i) periodic depreciation entry, (ii) sale of machinery with a book value of ₹ 2,00,000 for ₹ 1,20,000 cash and that cash dividend in 2020 was declared. The reserves changed because of change in income from operations. The statement of sources and disposition of working capital would appear as follows:

	₹	₹
Working Capital provided by:		
Operations:		
Reported net profits	2,00,000	
Add Depreciation	20,000	
Loss on sale of machinery	80,000[1]	3,00,000
Sale of machinery		1,20,000
		4,20,000
Working Capital used for:		
Declaration of cash dividend		50,000
Increase in W.C. (see above)		3,70,000

Example 19

Following are the comparative Balance Sheet of P & A Co. Ltd. for two years.

	30-6-2020	30-6-2019	Differences Dr.	Differences Cr.
	₹	₹	₹	₹
Assets:				
Cash	65,000	39,000	26,000	
Debtors (net) (account receivables)	25,000	30,000		5,000
Stock (inventories)	21,300	20,000	1,300	
Prepaid expenses	700	1,000		300
Plant and machinery (Net)	2,88,000	3,00,000	12,000	
Total	4,00,000	3,90,000		
Liabilities:				
Creditors (accounts payable)	55,000	63,000	8,000	
Income tax payable	3,750	2,000		1,750
Dividend payable	1,250			1,250
Debentures (redeemable)	80,000	1,00,000	20,000	

1. ₹ 20,000 – 12,000 = 8,000.

Share capital (capital stock)	1,20,000	1,00,000		20,000
Reserves (retained earnings)	1,40,000	1,25,000		15,000
Total	4,00,000	3,90,000	55,300	55,300

Additional Information

1. The dividends for 2020 were declared of ₹ 5,000.
2. The depreciation of ₹ 10,000 was provided during 2020.
3. An asset with a book value of ₹ 30,000 (cost 45,000 and accumulated depreciation of ₹ 15,000) was sold for ₹ 22,000.
4. A new machinery costing 28,000 was purchased, by paying ₹ 13,000 in cash; ₹ 5,000 by issue of share and ₹ 10,000 by issue of debentures.
5. Debenture of ₹ 10,000 were sold for cash. Debentures of ₹ 40,000 were redeemed, ₹ 35,000 in cash and balance in shares.

Solution

	2020 ₹	2019 ₹	W.C. increase or (decrease) ₹
Cash	65,000	39,000	26,000
Debtors (Net)	25,000	30,000	(5,000)
Stock	21,300	20,000	1,300
Prepaid expenses	700	1,000	(300)
Creditors	55,000	63,000	8,000
Income-tax payable	3,750	2,000	(1,750)
Dividends payable	1,250		(1,250)
Net increase in W.C.			27,000

Statement of Sources and Disposition of Working Capital

	₹	₹
Working Capital provided by:		
Operations:		
Reported net profit*	20,000	
Add: Depreciation	10,000	
Loss on sale of plant and machinery	8,000	38,000
Sale of machinery		22,000
Issue of debentures		10,000
Issue of share capital		10,000
		80,000
Working Capital used for:		
Purchase of machinery	13,000	
Redemption of debentures	35,000	
Declaration of cash dividends	5,000	
		53,000
Increase in working capital		27,000

* Difference of Reserves ₹ 15,000 + Dividend ₹ 5,000.

Notes: (1) Depreciation is not a "source of funds" in strict sense. It saves funds and does not generate funds. However, depreciation reduces tax liability. Then they are not shown in the "Funds Statement".

(2) If provision for Tax and proposed dividend are treated as "current liability", then deduct them from current assets to find working capital. They are not shown in fund flow Statement. Alternatively, if you treat them as "non-current liability", add them back to net Profits and show as a source. However, the actual tax and dividend paid, are shown as uses in case of such treatment as well.

Funds Flow Statement

This statement is known by various names:

(a) statement of funds or funds statement.

(b) statement of sources and application (or sources) of funds.

(c) statement of resources provided and applied.

(d) where-got, where gone statement.

This statement is prepared in the same way as the statement of source and disposition of working capital, except that this statement includes all the results of all transactions. The decrease in working capital is classified as sources of funds and increase in working capital as uses of funds. First take sources and then uses (given on page 135) by deducting the item of last period from item of current period.

Hidden Information

Sometimes information about any item may be hidden in the problem. Students have to find it. For example, machinery purchased amount may have to be found out. Then prepare machinery account and provision for depreciation on machinery account.

Example 20

If we are to prepare funds flow statement, based on data of Example No. 19 above, it shall appear as follows:

Statement of Sources and Uses of Funds

Funds provided by		
Operations:	₹	₹
Reported net profits	20,000	
Add Depreciation	10,000	
	30,000	
Loss on sale of machinery	8,000	38,000
Sale of Machinery		22,000
[1]Issue of debentures		20,000
[2]Issue of share capital		20,000
Total		1,00,000

1. For cash ₹ 10,000 + for machinery ₹ 10,000.
2. For cash ₹ 10,000 + for machinery ₹ 5,000 + for debenture ₹ 5,000.

Funds used for:	
[1]Purchase of machinery	28,000
[2]Redemption of debentures	40,000
Declaration of cash dividends	5,000
Increase in W.C.	27,000
Total	1,00,000

Note: The funds from operations are found by adding or subtracting items given on page 136 in the chart to or from the amount of net profits.

Cash Flow Statement

This statement is a statement that spotlights for a particular period those factors which caused the net change in the cash account during the period. This statement is based essentially on the same logic as that underlying the working capital statement. The steps for analysing transactions relating to the two statements is also fundamentally the same except that changes in current liabilities, are treated separately under this statement. The main difference in the preparation of two statements is related to finding the amount of resources provided by operations. In the statement of source and disposition of working capital, the amount of working capital provided by operations is based on income determined on the accrual basis. In the cash flow statement the amount of cash provided by operations is based on cash basis.

Institute of Chartered Accountant has issued an accounting standard AS-7, called 'Cash flow statements' w.e.f. 1.1.2004. It is mandatory for some companies like banks, insurance companies, financial institution and comparison whose shares are listed in stock exchange companies are required also by stock exchanges under clause 32 of listing agreement to prepare cash flow statement. AS-3 does not provide any format lays down the break up of major items into three heads.

The cash flow statement can be prepared by two ways: (1) Direct Method and (2) Indirect Method. Under direct method cash receipts and payment from operations are presented in cash flow statement under indirect method. The net profit (loss) is used as a base and convert it to net cash provided by operating activities. It adjusts net profit for items affected net profit but did not affect cash. Non-cash and non-operating charges in P&L account are added back to profit while non-cash and non-operating credits are deducted to calculate operating profit before working capital changers.

1. For cash ₹ 13,000 + ₹ 10,000 in debenture + ₹ 5,000 in shares.
2. Cash ₹ 35,000 + ₹ 5,000 in shares.

Under both methods cash flows are classified under three heads: (1) Cash flow from operating activities, (2) Cash flow from investing activities, (3) Cash flows from financing activities.

Note: The difference under both methods is only in showing cash flow from operations. A widely accepted format under both methods is given below.

Cash Flow Statement (Direct Method)

A. ***Cash flows from operating activities***

- Cash receipts from customers
- Cash paid to suppliers and employees
- Cash generated from operations
- Income taxes paid
- Cash flow before extraordinary item
- Proceeds from earthquake disaster settlement

  Net Cash from Operating Activities

B. ***Cash flows from investing activities***

- Purchase of fixed assets
- Proceeds from sale of equipment
- Interest received
- Dividend received

  Net Cash from Investing Activities

C. ***Cash flows from financial activities***

- Proceeds from issuance of share capital
- Proceeds from long-term borrowings
- Repayments of long-term borrowings
- Interest paid
- Dividend paid

  Net Cash from Financing Activities

- Net Increase (Decrease) in Cash and Cash Equivalents (A + B + C)
- Cash and Cash Equivalents at Beginning of Period
- Cash and Cash Equivalents at End of Period

Cash Flow Statement (Indirect Method)

A. ***Cash flows from operating activities***

Net profit before tax and extraordinary items

Adjustments for:

- Depreciation
- Foreign exchange
- Investments
- Gain or loss on sale of fixed assets

- Interest/dividend
- Operating profit before working capital changes.

Adjustments for:

- Trade and other receivables
- Inventories

Cash generation from operations:

- Interest paid
- Direct taxes
- Cash before extraordinary items
- Deferred revenue

Net Cash from Operating Activities.

B. ***Cash flows from investing activities***

- Purchase of fixed assets
- Sale of fixed assets
- Sale of investments
- Purchase of investments
- Interest received
- Dividend received
- Loans to subsidiaries

Net Cash from Investing Activities

C. ***Cash flows from financing activities***

- Proceeds from issue of share capital
- Proceeds from long-term borrowings
- Repayment to finance/lease liabilities
- Dividend paid

Net Cash from Financing Activities

- Net Increase (Decrease) in Cash and Cash Equivalents (A + B + C)
- Cash and Cash Equivalents at the Beginning of the Period
- Cash and Cash Equivalents at the End of the Period.

Alternatively the Cash Flows from Operating Activities (Indirect Method) may be summarised as below:

Net profit before tax and extraordinary items.

Adjustments for non-cash and non-operating items

- (+) Depreciation
- (+) Amortization of intangible assets, preliminary expenses, debenture discount and the like
- (+) or (–) Other non-cash and non-operating items included in net profit.

Adjustments for gains and losses on sale of fixed assets and investments

- (–) Gains on sale of fixed assets and investments
- (+) Loss on sale of fixed assets and investments.

Adjustments for changes in current assets and current liabilities

- (–) Increases in current assets
- (+) Decreases in current assets
- (+) Increases in current liabilities
- (–) Decreases in current liabilities
- (–) Income-tax paid
- (–) Extraordinary items

Net Cash Flows from Operating Activities.

Advantages of Cash Flow Statement

The purpose of case flow statement is to provide information about the cash flows associated with the periods of operations and also about the entity's investing and financing activities during the period. This information is important to shareholders, part of whole investment return (dividends) is dependent on cash flows and to lenders, whose interest payment and principal repayment require the use of cash. The welfare of other constituents of a company including its employees, its suppliers, and the local bodies that may levy taxes on it, depends to varying degrees on the company's activity to generate adequate cash flows to fulfil its financial obligations. The usefulness of cash flow statement can be summarised as follows:

1. *Show the relationship of net income to changes in the business cash*: Usually cash and net income move together. High levels of income tend to lead to increase in cash and *vice versa*. However, a company's cash balance can decrease when its net income is high, and cash can increase when income is low. The users want to know the difference between the net profit and net cash provided by operations. The net profit shows the progress of the business during the year while cash flow relates more to the liquidity of the business. The users can assess the reliability of net profit with the help of cash flow statement.
2. *Determine the ability to pay dividends and other commitments*: A cash flow statement indicates the sources and uses of cash under suitable headings such as operating, investing and financing activities. Shareholders are interested in receiving dividends on their investments in the shares. Creditors want to receive their interest and principal amount on time. The statement of cash flows helps investors and creditors to predict whether the business can make these payments.
3. *Predict future cash flows*: The cash flow statement makes it possible to predict the amounts, timing and uncertainty of future cash flows

on the basis of what has happened in the past. This approach is better than accrual basis data presented by profit and loss account and the balance sheet.

4. *Discloses success or failure of cash planning*: A success or failure of cash planning can be known by comparing the projected cash flow statement with the actual cash flow statement and necessary remedial measures can be taken. Moreover it provides a better measure for inter-period and inter-firm comparison.
5. *Evaluate management decisions*: The statement of cash flows reports the companies' investing and financing activities and thus gives the investors and creditors about cash flow information for evaluating managers' decisions.
6. *Discloses the movement cash*: A comparison of cash flow statement for the previous year with the budget for that year would indicate to what extent the resources of the enterprise were raised and applied. A comparison of the original forecast with actual result may highlight tend of movement that might otherwise undetected.
7. *Efficiency in cash management*: Cash flow analysis helps in evaluating financial policies and cash position. It facilitates the management to plan and coordinate the financial operations properly. The management can estimate how much funds are needed, from which source they will be derived, how much can be generated internally and how much should be arranged from outside.

Example

From the information as contained in the income statement and the balance sheet of Anurag & Co., you are required to prepare a cash flow statement using (i) Direct Method and (ii) Indirect Method.

A. *Income Statement for the year ended 31.3.2021*

		₹
Net Sales		25,20,000
Less: Cost of sales	19,80,000	
Depreciation	60,000	
Salaries and wages	2,40,000	
Operating expenses	80,000	
Provision for taxation	88,000	24,48,000
Net Operating profit		72,000
Profit on sale of equipment		12,000
		84,000
Retained earnings		1,51,800
		2,35,800
Dividend declared and paid during the year		72,000
Profit and Loss account balance as on 31.3.2021		1,63,800

B. ***Comparative Balance Sheets***

	As at 31.3.2020 ₹	As at 31.3.2021 ₹
Fixed assets		
Land	48,000	96,000
Building and equipments	3,60,000	5,76,000
Current assets		
Cash	60,000	72,000
Debtors	1,68,000	1,86,000
Stock	2,64,000	96,000
Advances	7,800	9,000
	9,07,800	10,35,000
Capital	3,60,000	4,44,000
Surplus in Profit and Loss A/c	1,51,800	1,63,800
Sundry creditors	2,40,000	2,34,000
Outstanding expenses	24,000	48,000
Income tax payable	12,000	13,200
Accumulated depreciation on building and equipments	1,20,000	1,32,000
	9,07,800	10,35,00

Cost of equipment sold was ₹ 72,000.

Solution:

Direct Method

ANURAG & CO.

Cash Flow Statement for the year ended 31.3.2021

	₹	₹
Cash Flows from Operating Activities:		
Cash receipts from customers	25,02,000	
Cash paid to supplier and employees	21,15,200	
Cash generated from operations	3,86,800	
Income tax paid	(86,800)	
Net Cash from Operating Activities		3,00,000
Cash Flows from Investing Activities:		
Purchase of land	(48,000)	
Purchase of building and equipment	(2,88,000)	
Sale of equipment	36,000	
Net Cash used in Investing Activities		(3,00,000)
Cash Flows from Financing Activities:		
Issue of share capital	84,000	
Dividend paid	(72,000)	
Net Cash from Financing Activities		12,000

Net Increase in Cash and Cash Equivalents	12,000
Cash and Cash Equivalents at the beginning	60,000
Cash and Cash Equivalents at the end	72,000

Working Notes:

	₹	₹
(1) *Cash paid to suppliers and employees:*		
Cost of goods sold		19,80,000
Add: Operating expenses		80,000
Salaries and wages		2,40,000
		23,00,000
Add: Creditors at the beginning	2,40,000	
Stock at the end	96,000	
Advances at the end	9,000	
Outstanding expenses at the beginning	24,000	3,69,000
		26,69,000
Less: Creditors at the end	2,34,000	
Stock at the beginning	2,64,000	
Advances at the beginning	7,800	
Outstanding expenses at the end	48,000	5,53,000
		21,15,200
(2) *Cash receipts from customers:*		
Sales revenue		25,20,000
Add: Debtors at the beginning		1,68,000
		26,88,000
Less: Debtors at the end		1,86,000
		25,02,000
(3) *Income tax paid:*		
Tax payable at the beginning		12,000
Add: Provision for taxation		88,000
		1,00,000
Less: Tax payable at the end		13,200
Tax paid during the year		86,800
(4) *Purchase of building and equipments:*		
Balance at the beginning		3,60,000
Less: Cost of equipment sold		72,000
Balance		2,88,000
Balance at the end		5,76,000
Purchased during the year		2,88,000
(5) *Sale price of equipment:*		
Cost Price	72,000	
Less: Accumulated depreciation		48,000
		24,000
Add: Profit on sale	12,000	36,000

(6) *Accumulated depreciation written off on equipments (sold):*	
Accumulated depreciation at the beginning	1,20,000
Add: Depreciation for the year	60,000
	1,80,000
Less: Accumulated depreciation at the end	1,32,000
	48,000

Indirect Method

ANURAG & CO.
Cash Flow Statement for the year ended 31.3.2020

	₹	₹
Cash Flows from Operating Activities:		
Net profit before taxation and extra-ordinary item	1,60,000	
Adjustments for:		
Depreciation	60,000	
Operating profit before working capital changes	2,20,000	
Increase in debtors	(18,000)	
Decrease in advances	1,68,000	
Increase in advances	(1,200)	
Decrease in creditors	(6,000)	
Increase in outstanding expenses	24,000	
Cash generated from operation	3,86,800	
Income tax paid (See No. 3)	(86,800)	
Net Cash from Operating Activities		3,00,000
Cash Flows from Investing Activities:		
Purchase of land	(48,000)	
Purchase of building and equipments (See No. 4)	(2,88,000)	
Sale of equipment (See No. 5)	36,000	
Net Cash Used in Investing Activities		(3,00,000)
Cash Flows from Financing Activities:		
Issue of share capital	84,000	
Dividend paid	(72,000)	
Net Cash from Financing Activities		12,000
Net Increase in Cash and Cash Equivalents		12,000
Cash and Cash Equivalents at the beginning		60,000
Cash and Cash Equivalent at the end		72,000

Note: In the above example, under direct method, if we prepare funds flow statement only difference will be in flows from operations. This amount will be—Profit ₹ 72,000 + Depreciation ₹ 60,000 = ₹ 1,32,000. Decrease in working capital will be shown as sources. In calculating working capital cash, debtors, stock, advances, creditors, outstanding expenses and income tax payable shall be included.

Conversion of Accrual Basis to Cash Basis of Income

In accrual basis of accounting revenue is recognized in the period in which sale is made or the service is rendered, and costs and expenses are recognized in the period in which they contribute to revenue. It does not matter when cash is received or paid. In cash basis of accounting is a method of accounting whereby revenue is recognized only when cash is received and costs and expenses are recognized only when cash is paid out. Therefore, to convert accrual basis income to cash basis income, we have to adjust net profits for all non-cash charges and credits reflected therein. An adjustment is necessary because:

(a) A non-cash gain or loss on the disposal of a non-current asset is included in reported net profits.
(b) A non-cash charge, e.g., depreciation on fixed assets or amortization on an intangible asset (like goodwill) is included in net income.
(c) A non-cash charge or credit accrual, deferral, sale, purchase or change in stock (inventory) account is included in reported net income. Items that fall in (a) or (b) are treated exactly in the same way as in case of two statements described earlier. In other words, add back losses, deduct gains, and add back depreciation.

The (c) above includes items that affect working capital. The accounts involved include debtors (receivables), creditors (payables), stock (inventories), prepaid income and prepaid expenses. We take an example to explain each.

(A) *Effect of change in debtors account on reported net profits:* Suppose cash sales are ₹ 1,00,000, credit sales ₹ 50,000; Debtors at the beginning of period ₹ 10,000 and at the end ₹ 15,000. Under accrual basis a revenue of ₹ 1,50,000 plus ₹ 50,000 will be recognized whereas under cash basis only ₹ 1,45,000 would be recognized [₹ 1,00,000 + cash received from debtors ₹ 45,000 (i.e., ₹ 10,000 + 50,000 – 15,000)]. Thus, to convert accrual income to cash, we must deduct on increase in debtors account from net profits and a decrease.

(B) *Effect of a change in creditors and stock account:* Suppose cash purchases ₹ 2,00,000, Credit purchases ₹ 1,00,000, Beginning stock ₹ 50,000, Ending stock ₹ 60,000, Creditors at start ₹ 20,000, Creditors at end ₹ 15,000. The cost of goods sold under accrual basis would be computed as ₹ 2,90,000 (₹ 50,000 + ₹ 3,00,000 – ₹ 60,000). Under cash basis it would be ₹ 3,05,000 (₹ 20,000 + ₹ 2,00,000 – ₹ 15,000 + ₹ 1,00,000). The difference of ₹ 15,000 between two basis is equal to the difference between creditors at state and at the end plus the difference between stock at the beginning and at the end. Thus, to convert accrual basis in cash basis, we must deduct increases in inventory and decrease in creditors from net profits. Decreases in inventory are added, whereas increases in creditors account are added.

(C) *Effect of change in a prepaid account on net profits:* Let us assume:

	₹
Prepaid insurance at the beginning	1,000
Cash premium paid during the year	200
Prepaid insurance at the end	900

Under accrual basis, insurance expenses would be ₹ 300 (₹ 1,000 – 900 + 200) and under cash basis ₹ 200. To change this we would add 100 to the net profits. So the amount of a decrease in prepaid expenses should be added to the net profits and the increase in amount should be deducted. The prepaid income is treated in opposite way i.e., in case of increase, the difference in amount to be added and in case of decrease the amount (the difference) to be deducted from net profits.

(D) *Effect of change in outstanding expenses:* The decrease in outstanding expenses should be deducted from net profit and increase in them should be added to net profits. The change in tax liability should also be treated like the change in outstanding expenses. We summarise below the above items.

Account	Change in Account	Correction Needed
(A) Debtors	Increase	Deduct
	Decrease	Add
(B) Creditors	Increase	Add
	Decrease	Deduct
(C) Stock	Increase	Deduct
	Decrease	Add
(D) Prepaid Expenses	Increase	Deduct
	Decrease	Add
(E) Prepaid Incomes	Increase	Add
	Decrease	Deduct
(F) Outstanding Expenses	Increase	Add
	Decrease	Deduct

The cash flow statement contains following sources and uses:

Sources of Cash

1. Profit from operations.
2. Decrease in any asset (except cash).
3. Increase in any liability.
4. Sale proceed from share issue.

Uses of Cash

1. The loss from operations.
2. Increase in any asset (except cash).
3. Decrease in any liability.
4. Cash dividends paid.
5. Redemption of shares in cash.

The changes in current assets (except marketable securities) and current liabilities (except items as tax liability, dividends payable) are not usually shown separately as sources or uses of cash. They are rather adjusted in net profits to determine the net cash flow from operations.

Example 20A

Using the data of Example 19 we can prepare the statement of sources and uses of cash as under:

	₹	₹
Cash provided by:		
Operations		35,750*
Sale of Machinery	22,000	
Issue of debentures	10,000	
Issue of share	10,000	77,750
Cash used for:		
Purchase of machinery	13,000	
Redemption of debentures	35,000	
Payment of dividends	3,750 e[1]	51,750
Increase in cash		26,000

* Net Profit ₹ 20,000 + Depreciation ₹ 10,000 + loss on sale of machinery 8,000 + decrease in debtors ₹ 5,000 + decrease in prepaid expenses ₹ 300 + increase in income tax payable ₹ 1,750 = ₹ 45,050 deduct increase in stock ₹ 1,300, increase in creditors ₹ 8,000 total ₹ 9,300 = ₹ 35,750.

e[1] Only ₹ 3,750 have been paid (5000 – 1250).

Example 21

Calculate funds from operations from the following Profit and Loss account:

Profit and Loss A/c

Particulars	₹	Particulars	₹
To Depreciation	9,000	By Gross Profit	85,000
,, Discount (written off)	2,000	,, Profit on Sale of Plant	40,000
,, Loss on Sale of Machine	4,000		
,, Goodwill (written off)	22,000		
,, Preliminary Expenses	6,500		
,, Sundry Expenses	25,000		
,, Net Profit	56,500		
	12,50,000		1,25,000

Ans.

Funds from Operation

Net Profit as per P/L A/c		56,500
(+) Non-operating expenses:		
Depreciation	9,000	
Goodwill written off	22,000	
Preliminary expenses written off	6,500	
Discount on Issue of Shares	2,000	
Loss on Sale of Machine	4,000	
		43,500
		1,00,000

(–) Non-operating income:	
Profit on sale of Plant	40,000
Funds from operation	60,000

Alternatively

Adjusted P/L A/c

Particulars	₹	Particulars	₹
To Sundry expenses	25,000	By Gross Profit	85,000
,, Funds from operation (Balancing Figure)	60,000		
	85,000		85,000

Example 22

Calculate funds from operations from the following details:

Profit and Loss A/c

Particulars	₹	Particulars	₹
To Salaries	3,00,000	By Gross Profit	8,00,000
,, Sundry expenses	1,00,000	,, Profit on sale of machinery	1,00,000
,, Loss on sale of Furniture	55,000	,, Rent received	50,000
,, Discount allowed	15,000		
,, Goodwill	80,000		
,, Preliminary Expenses written off	20,000		
,, Depreciation	1,30,000		
,, Net Profit	2,50,000		
	9,50,000		9,50,000

Ans.

Funds from Operations

Net Profit		2,50,000
Add: Non-Operating expenses:		
Loss on sale of furniture	55,000	
Goodwill	80,000	
Preliminary Expenses written off	20,000	
Depreciation	1,30,000	2,80,500
		5,30,500
Less: Non-operating income:		
Profit on sale of machinery	1,00,000	
Rent received	50,000	1,50,000
Funds from operation		3,85,000

Notes. 1. Discount allowed has been treated as discount allowed to customers as operating expenses as it is not allowed on issue of shares and debentures.

2. Rent received is treated as non-operating income because the business does not seem to be involved in house property dealings.

Example 23

From the following Profit and Loss account of a trader, determine the amount of funds from business operations.

Profit and Loss A/c

Particulars	₹	Particulars	₹
To Salaries	50,000	By Gross Profit	3,00,000
,, Expenses	12,000	,, Profit on sale of plant and equipments	12,000
,, Depreciation	30,000	,, Interest received	3,000
,, Loss on sale of furniture	5,000		
,, Net Profit	2,18,000		
	3,15,000		3,15,000

Ans. Funds from Operations

		₹	₹
	Net Profit as per P/L A/c		2,18,000
Add:	Non-Operating Expenses:		
	Depreciation	30,000	
	Loss on Sale of Furniture	5,000	35,000
			2,53,000
Less:	Non-Operating income:		
	Profit on Sale of Plant and Equipments	12,000	
	Interest received	3,000	15,000
	Funds from Operation		2,38,000

Note. Interest received has been treated as non-operating income. The firm does not seem to be involved in financial business so the interest received is not a trading income.

Example 24

From the following balance sheet of 'A Ltd.' you are required to prepare a schedule of changes in working capital and a Statement of Flow of Funds:

Liabilities	December 31, 2019 ₹	December 31, 2020 ₹
Capital and Liabilities	80,000	85,000
Profit and Loss Appropriation Account	14,500	24,500

Creditors	9,000	5,000
Mortgage	—	5,000
Provision for doubtful debts	1,000	1,300
	1,04,500	1,20,800

Assets	₹	₹
Land and Buildings	50,000	50,000
Plant and Machinery	24,000	34,000
Stock	9,000	7,000
Debtors	17,500	20,800
Cash at Bank	4,000	9,000
	1,04,500	1,20,800

Ans.

Schedule of Changes in Working Capital

Particulars	Amount ₹		Change in Working Capital	
	Dec. 31, 2019	Dec. 31, 2020	Increase (Debit)	Decrease (Credit)
Current Assets				
Cash at Bank	4,000	9,000	5,000	—
Debtors (Net)	16,500	19,500	3,000	—
Stock	9,000	7,000	—	2,000
	29,500	35,500		
Current Liabilities				
Creditors	9,000	5,000	4,000	
Working Capital*	20,500	30,500	—	
Increase in Working Capital	10,000	—	—	10,000
	30,500	30,500	12,000	12,000

*Excess of current assets over current liabilities of the year.

Funds Flow Statement

Sources	Amount ₹	Application	Amount ₹
Funds from operation	10,000		
Increase in Capital	5,000	Net Increase in Working Capital	10,000
Increase in Mortgage	5,000	Purchase of Plant	10,000
	20,000		20,000

Working Notes

1. Calculation of funds from operation

   Profit as on Dec. 31, 2020 = 24,500

   (–) ,, ,, ,, Dec. 31, 2019 = 14,500

   10,000

2. Provision for doubtful debts has been adjusted in debtors account i.e. debtors as on 31st Dec., 2019 have been reduced to ₹ 16,500 = (17,500 – 1,000). In the same way debtors as on 31st Dec., 2020 have been ₹ 19,500 = (20,800 – 1,300).

Alternatively

Provision for doubtful debts may be shown as current liability and debtors at their original value in the schedule. The ultimate effect of this treatment will be the same as above i.e., increase in Working Capital to the extent of ₹ 3,000.

Example 25

Balance Sheets of M/s. Ram & Sons on 1st January, 2020 and 31st December, 2020.

Balance Sheet

Liabilities	1-1-2020 ₹	31-12-2020 ₹	Assets	1-1-2020 ₹	31-12-2020 ₹
Creditors	4,00,000	4,40,000	Cash	1,00,000	70,000
M/s. Ram's Loan	2,50,000	—	Debtors	3,00,000	5,00,000
Loan from P.N. Bank	4,00,000	5,00,000	Stock	3,50,000	2,50,000
			Machinery	8,00,000	5,50,000
			Land	4,00,000	5,00,000
Capital	12,50,000	15,30,000	Building	3,50,000	6,00,000
	23,00,000	24,70,000		23,00,000	24,70,000

During the year a machine costing ₹ 1,00,000 (accumulated dep. ₹ 30,000) was sold for ₹ 50,000. The provision for depreciation against machinery as on 1st January, 2020 was ₹ 2,50,000 and on 31st December, 2020, ₹ 4,00,000. Net profit for the year 2020 amounted to ₹ 4,50,000.

You are required to prepare a Funds Flow Statement.

Ans.

Schedule of Changes in Working Capital

Particulars	1-1-2020	31-12-2020	Increase	Decrease
Current Assets				
Cash	1,00,000	70,000	—	30,000
Debtors	3,00,000	5,00,000	2,00,000	—
Stocks	3,50,000	2,50,000	—	1,00,000
	7,50,000	8,20,000		
Current Liabilities				
Sundry Creditors	4,00,000	4,40,000	—	40,000
Working Capital*	3,50,000	3,80,000	—	—
Increase in Working Capital	30,000		—	30,000
	3,80,000	3,80,000	2,00,000	2,00,000

*Excess of Current Assets over Current Liabilities.

Funds Flow Statement as on 31-12-2020

Sources	Amount ₹	Application	Amount ₹
Sale of machine	50,000	Purchase of Land	1,00,000
Loan from P.N. Bank	1,00,000	Purchase of Building	2,50,000
Funds from operations	6,50,000	Repayment of M/s. Ram's Loan	2,50,000
		Drawings	1,70,000
		Increase in working capital	30,000
	8,00,000		8,00,000

Working Notes

1. Operating Profit

		₹
Net Profit for the year		4,50,000
Add: Non-fund items:		
Loss on sale of machine	20,000	
Provision of depreciation	1,80,000	2,00,000
Funds from operations		6,50,000

2. Machinery Account

	₹		₹
To opening balance	8,00,000	By Cash (Sales)	50,000
		,, Provision for depreciation	1,80,000
		,, Profit and Loss A/c (Loss on sale)	20,000
		,, Closing Balance	5,50,000
	8,00,000		8,00,000

3. Capital Account

	₹		₹
To Drawings (Balancing figure)	1,70,000	By Balance b/d	12,50,000
,, Balance c/d	15,30,000	,, Profit and Loss A/c (Profit)	4,50,000
	17,00,000		17,00,000

Example 26

The following are the summarised Balance Sheets of a company as on 31st December, 2019 and 2020.

	2019 ₹	2020 ₹
Liabilities:		
Share Capital	2,00,000	2,50,000
General Reserve	50,000	60,000
Profit & Loss	30,500	30,600
Bank Loan (Long-term)	70,000	—
Sundry Creditors	1,50,000	1,35,000
Provision for Taxation	30,000	35,000
	5,30,500	5,10,600
Assets:		
Land and Buildings	2,00,000	1,90,000
Machinery	1,50,000	1,69,000
Stock	1,00,000	74,000
Sundry Debtors	80,000	64,200
Cash	500	600
Bank	—	8,000
Goodwill	—	5,000
	5,30,500	5,10,800

Additional information:

During the year ended 31st December, 2020

(1) Dividend of ₹ 23,000 was paid.

(2) Assets of another company were purchased for a consideration of ₹ 50,000 payable in shares.

The following assets were purchased:

(1) Stock ₹ 20,000.

(2) Machinery ₹ 25,000.

(3) Machinery was further purchased for ₹ 8,000.

(4) Depreciation written off on machinery ₹ 12,000.

(5) Income-tax provided during the year ₹ 33,000.

(6) Loss on sale of machinery ₹ 200 was written off to general reserve. You are required to prepare the Cash Flow Statement.

Solution

Cash Flow Statement

For the year ending 31st December, 2020

	₹	₹
Cash Balance as on 1st Jan., 2020		500
Add: Sources of Cash:		
Sale of Machinery	1,800	
Cash from Operations:		
Funds from Operations	88,300	
Add: Decrease in Stock	46,000	
Decrease in Debtors	15,800	
	1,50,100	
Less: Decrease in Creditors	14,800	1,35,300
		1,37,600
Applications of Cash:		
Payment of Dividend	23,000	
Purchase of Machinery	8,000	
Tax Paid (See Note 4)	28,000	
Mortgage Loan repaid	70,000	1,29,000
Closing cash and Bank balances		8,600
(Cash in Hand ₹ 600 + Cash at Bank ₹ 8,000)		

1. Adjusted Profit & Loss A/c

Particulars	₹	Particulars	₹
Dividend	23,000	Balance b/d	30,500
Depreciation on Building	10,000	Funds from Operations	
Provision for Tax	33,000	(Balancing Figure)	88,300
Transfer to General Reserve	10,200		
Depreciation on Machinery	12,000		
Balance c/d	30,600		
	1,18,800		1,18,800

Machinery A/c

Balance b/d	1,50,000	Depreciation	12,000
Share Capital	25,000	General Reserve	200
Bank	8,000	Bank	1,800
		Balance c/d	1,69,000
	1,83,000		1,83,000

General Reserve = 50,000 + 10,200 – 200 = 60,000; Provision for Tax = 30,000 + 33,000 – 28,000 = 35,000; Decrease in Stock = Stock on 31-12-2019 ₹ 1,00,000; Stock at the end 2020 ₹ 54,000 = 46,000 (increase in cash). The figure ₹ 54,000 is after deducting stock purchased by issue of shares.

QUESTIONS

1. How is rate of return computed? How can it be improved? Should it be calculated at the beginning of the year? What adjustments are to be made for its calculation?
2. Explain inventory turnover. What is the significance of gross margin per inventory turnover? Is it a measurement of relative liquidity?
3. Is net working capital by operations be looked upon as a form of income measurement? Can a business increase its net working capital and yet have losses from operations? Is net working capital same as net income?
4. Following are a source of capital or not: (a) decrease in fixed asset (b) increase in shareholders' equity and (c) decrease in non-current liability.
5. Indicate the adjustments that are needed to convert accrual basis income to cash basis income.
6. Give the formula for each of the following: (a) Current ratio, (b) Inventory turnover, (c) Debtors turnover, and (d) Operating ratio.
7. Agro Sales Corporation has in recent prior years maintained the following relationship among the data on its financial statements:

(a)	Rate of gross margin to net sales	4%
(b)	Rate of net income to net sales	10%
(c)	Rate of selling expenses to net sales	20%
(d)	Accounts receivable turnover	8 per year
(e)	Inventory turnover	6 per year
(f)	Acid test ratio	2 to 1
(g)	Current ratio	3 to 1
(h)	Quick asset composition	32% Marketable securities 60% accounts receivable (Debtors)
(i)	Total assets turnover	2 per year
(j)	Ratio of total assets to intangible assets	20 to 1
(k)	Ratio of accumulated depreciation to cost of fixed assets	1 to 3
(l)	Ratio of accounts receivable to accounts payable	1.5 to 1
(m)	Ratio of working capital to shareholder equity	1 to 1.6
(n)	Ratio of total debt to shareholder equity	1 to 2

The corporation had a net income of ₹ 1,20,000 for 2020 which resulted in earnings of ₹ 5.20 per share of ordinary share capital. Authorised capital, issued and outstanding; Equity ₹ 10 per share par value, issued at 10% premium, preference 6% ₹ 100 per share par value, issued at 10% premium. Market value per share of equity on Dec. 31, 2020 ₹ 78, preference dividend paid 2015 ₹ 3,000. Times interest earned 2020 ₹ 33. The amounts of inventory, accounts receivable, 50% Debentures and total shareholders was same at the beginning and at the end of the year.

Prepare a balance sheet and income statement for the year 31-12-2020.

8. From the following information you are required to calculate rate of return on net sales/current assets/owner's equity/and different turnover ratios:

Profit and Loss A/c 30-4-2020

	₹
Net sales	7,40,000
Cost of goods sold	4,50,000
Gross margin	2,90,000
Operating expenses including Depreciation of ₹ 28,000	1,18,000
Net operating income	1,72,000
Income tax	86,000
Net income after taxes	86,000

Balance Sheet 30-4-2020

Liabilities	₹	Assets	₹
Capital	1,50,000	Cash	1,10,000
Reserve	3,74,000	Debtors	1,43,000
Creditors	74,000	Stock	1,12,000
Operating expenses payable	28,000	Fixed Assets (net)	2,73,000
Wages outstanding	12,000		
	6,38,000		6,38,000

A new product line is considered. It is estimated that 20,000 units of new line can be sold in a year at a unit price of ₹ 25. Each unit will cost ₹ 18, operating expenses will increase by ₹ 85,000 a year and income tax is 50%.

Current assets to support the product line will be financed by sale of shares. The additional asset investment has been estimated as follows:

Cash ₹ 43,000, Debtors ₹ 32,000, Stock ₹ 50,000, Total ₹ 125,000. Using 2015 statements, calculate (a) Turnover Ratios, (b) Rate of return on current assets/net sales/owner's equity. Calculate also the turnover and rates of return for the combined operation with new product line included. From your analysis do you think the new product line should be accepted? (Don't average assets or owner's equity.)

9. The comparative Balance Sheets for Reliance Corporation as on 31st December are as follow:

	2020 ₹	2019 ₹
Cash	6,000	4,000
Marketable Securities	2,000	4,000
Accounts Receivable (net)	14,000	10,000
Allowance for uncollectable accounts	(4,000)	(2,000)

Inventory	9,000	7,000
Plant & Equipment	90,000	87,000
Accumulated Depreciation	(23,000)	(20,000)
	94,000	90,000
Account payable	4,000	5,000
Other Liabilities	3,000	1,000
7% long-term notes payable due 2020	20,000	20,000
Preferred stock	5,000	10,000
Common stock ₹ 2 par value	10,000	10,000
Paid in capital in excess of par value	30,000	30,000
Retained Earnings	22,000	14,000
	94,000	94,000

All sales are made on account and amounted to ₹ 1,50,000 in 2020. Gross profit on sales in 42% of sales and net income is 10% of sales. Income tax is 40% of I.B.I.T. Instructions. Compute the following for 2020:

(a) Return (before Income-tax and interest) on total assets
(b) Receivables turnover
(c) Inventory turnover
(d) Current ratio
(e) Quick ratio
(f) Times interest earned (before Income-tax).

10. BOFOR Ltd. gives you following information:

	2020 ₹	2019 ₹	2018 ₹	2017 ₹
Net sales	8,00,000	6,42,000	6,24,000	6,00,000
Cost of goods sold	5,60,000	4,17,300	4,11,840	4,08,000
Gross profit on sales	2,40,000	2,24,700	2,12,160	1,92,000
Net Income (after tax)	56,000	25,680	30,000	34,500
Stock (FIFO) ending	80,000	1,25,000	82,400	1,02,000
Debtors ending	88,000	45,000	50,000	40,000
Industry sales index	110	112	108	100

All sales are made on credit terms of 2/10, n/30. Assume 300 days. Calculate for each year in a tabular form

(1) Gross profit and net income as a percentage of sales
(2) Number of day's sales in stock and debtors
(3) Operating expenses as a percentage of sales
(4) Index of company's sales to Industry sales.

11. The comparative balance sheets on December 31, for Fair Tax Ltd. are as follows:

	Year 2 ₹	Year 1 ₹
Cash	52,500	60,000
Debtors	1,00,000	90,000
Stock	97,500	40,000
Fixed Assets	2,60,000	1,60,000
Less Depreciation	(85,000)	(50,000)
Total Assets	4,25,000	4,25,000
Creditors	70,000	60,000
Paid up Capital	2,80,000	2,00,000
Share Premium	20,000	0
Reserves	55,000	40,000
	4,25,000	4,25,000

On June 15th Year 2, the company issued 8,000 shares in exchange of a fixed asset. There was no sale or retirement of any fixed asset in Year 2. Dividends of ₹ 25,000 were paid to shareholders during Year 2. The reserve for bad and doubtful debts was reduced by ₹ 3,000 during Year 2 as a result of writing off accounts known to be bad, and increased by ₹ 5,000 at the end of the year. You are required to prepare a statement of sources and uses of fund.

12. From the following information, prepare a statement showing the sources and application of funds for the year 2020 (Make reasonable assumptions).

Balance Sheet on Dec. 31

Accounts	2020 ₹	2019 ₹
Current assets	2,00,000	1,50,000
Long lived assets	3,70,000	3,80,000
Patents	30,000	34,000
Unamortized bond discount	9,000	Nil
	6,09,000	5,64,000

1. Long lived assets which cost ₹ 40,000 and which were 75% depreciated were sold during the year for ₹ 6,000.
2. The amortization of Bond discount for the year was ₹ 2,000.
3. Depreciation for the year ₹ 20,000.
4. Cash dividends amounting to ₹ 50,000 were declared and paid during the year.

13. Criticize the following statement, considering its function and content.

Statement showing Causes of Net Change in Working Capital

Funds were obtained from

	₹	₹
Operations (net income transferred to Reserve)		1,79,001.12
Current assets used up in year's operations:		
Cash in hand and at banks	33,427.73	
Postage stamps	20.00	33,447.73
Issue of equity shares		30,000.00
		2,42,448.85
Funds were applied to:		
Payments of cash dividends	35,442.00	
Declaration of share dividends (not yet issued)	27,400.00	
Investment in addition to:		
Trade Debtors	10,004.43	
Bill Receivable	2,500.00	
Stock	1,01,442.21	
Investments	10,440.00	
Surrender value of life insurance	1,141.25	
Fixed assets (net increase)	15,142.50	
Patent	20,000.00	
Prepaid expenses	2,452.03	2,25,964.42
Payments of serial debentures		10,000.00
Reduction in current liabilities		6,484.43
		2,42,448.85

14. The balance sheets of a company as on 31 December are as follows:

Capital Accounts	2020 ₹	2019 ₹
Balance at the beginning	16,000	5,000
Net profit for the year	20,000	15,000
Surplus on revaluation of property	10,000	—
	46,000	20,000
Less withdrawals	16,000	4,000
	30,000	16,000
Loan account	6,000	10,000
Creditors	8,000	11,000
	11,700	Nil
	55,700	37,000
Freehold Property (as revalued)	22,000	12,000
Plant & Machinery cost	5,000	5,000
Plant additions	6,000	
	11,000	

Deduct sale	1,000	
	10,000	
Accumulated depreciation	2,250	7,750
	2,000	3,000
Trade investment at cost	—	7,000
Stock	16,000	11,000
Debtors	9,950	2,700
Cash at bank	55,700	37,000

Investments were sold for ₹ 11,000, the machinery disposal of which had a net book value of ₹ 250, was sold at the beginning of the year for ₹ 350.

All profits on disposal of assets had been passed through the P&L A/c.

You are required to prepared a sources and application of Funds statement for the year ended 2020.

7
Break-even Analysis

Introduction

Managers are constantly faced with decision about selling prices, variable costs and fixed costs. Basically, managers must decide how to acquire and utilize economic resources in the light of some objectives. Unless they can make reasonably accurate predictions about cost and revenue levels, their decisions may yield undesirable or even disastrous results. These decisions are usually short run: How many units should we manufacture? Should we change our prices? How will cost changes affect profit? What profits can be expected on a given sales volume? Should we spend more on advertising? These questions are answered by Break-even analysis. However, long-run decision such as the purchase of plant and machinery also hinge on predictions of the resulting break-even relationships. Most of break-even relationships are examples of deciding among courses of action, often called decision model. Break-even-analysis, sometimes called Cost-Volume-Profit Analysis (C.V.P.), is concerned with determining the optimal level and mix of output to be produced with available resources. Horngren says, "The focus is on the impact upon operating income or net income of various decisions that affect sales and costs."

Break-Even Point

The break-even point is that level of output at which there is no profit or loss. It is that point of activity (sales volume) where total revenues and total expenses are equal. It indicates the possibilities associated with changes in costs and sales. To explain the break-even point, we assume that fixed expenses of the company are ₹ 3,00,000 and variable expenses are ₹ 25 per unit. The sale price is ₹ 40 per unit. The break-even point is 20,000 units, because at this point there is no profit or loss and total revenues are equal to total cost.

The break-even point can be computed or shown by any of these approaches.

(a) Mathematical Computations:
 (i) Equation method
 (ii) Contribution margin method
(b) Graphic Approach—Break-even chart

Example 1

No. of units Produced and Sold	Fixed expenses	Variable Expenses @ ₹ 25	Total cost	Sale Proceeds @ ₹ 40
0	3,00,000	0	3,00,000	0
10,000	3,00,000	2,50,000	5,50,000	4,00,000
20,000	3,00,000	5,00,000	8,00,000	8,00,000
25,000	3,00,000	6,25,000	9,25,000	10,00,000

Equation Method

Every income statement may be expressed in equation form as follows:

Sales – Variable expenses – Fixed expenses = Net profit

Or

Sales = Variable expenses + Fixed expenses + Net profit

In the above example let

x = Number of units to be sold to break-even, where break-even point is determined by zero net profit (or income)

$$₹\ 40x = ₹\ 25x + ₹\ 3{,}00{,}000 + 0$$

$$₹\ 15x = ₹\ 3{,}00{,}000 + 0$$

$$x = ₹\ \frac{300{,}000 + 0}{15} = 20{,}000 \text{ units}$$

x = 20,000 units (or ₹ 8,00,000 total sales @ ₹ 40 per unit)

Contribution Margin Method or Profit Volume Method

The contribution margin or marginal income method is more popular. Contribution margin is equal to sales minus variable expenses. If contribution margin is expressed as a percentage of sales it is called C/M ratio. The break-even point can be computed in terms of units, or in terms of money value (rupees, pounds, dollars, etc.) of sales volume or as a percentage of estimated capacity. Contribution margin ratio is also called profit volume (P/V) ratio.

(a) *In units, the formula*

$$\text{B.E. in sales volume in units} = \frac{\text{Fixed costs + Desired income}}{\text{Contribution margin per unit}}$$

Or

$$\frac{\text{Fixed costs + Desired income}}{\text{Selling price – Variable cost per unit}}$$

In example 1, it will be

$$\frac{3{,}00{,}000 + 0}{₹\ 40 - ₹\ 25} = 20{,}000 \text{ units}$$

[Variable costs are 62½% of sales (₹ 25 out of ₹ 40), then contribution margin will be 37½% of sales, i.e., ₹ 15 out of ₹ 40]

(b) *In Rupees, the formula*

$$\text{B.E. sales in rupees} = \frac{\text{Fixed costs}}{\text{Contribution margin in ratio or P/V ratio}}$$

Or

$$\frac{\text{Fixed costs}}{1 - \dfrac{\text{Variable costs}}{\text{Sales}}}$$

Or

$$\frac{\text{Fixed Costs}}{\text{Cost per Unit}} \times \text{Selling Price per Unit}$$

Or

$$\frac{\text{Total Cost}}{\text{Total Contribution}} \times \text{Total Sales}$$

$$= \frac{₹3,00,000}{1 - \dfrac{₹\,25}{₹\,40}} = \frac{₹\,3,00,000}{\dfrac{15}{40}}$$

$$= \frac{3,00,000 \times 40}{15} = ₹\,8,00,000$$

$$\text{C/M (P/V) Ratio} = \frac{\text{Sales} - \text{V.C.}}{\text{Sales}} \text{ or } 1 - \frac{\text{V.C.}}{\text{Sales}} \text{ or } \frac{\text{F.C.} + \text{Profit}}{\text{Sales}}$$

(c) *As a percentage of capacity*

If sales volume of say ₹ 10,00,000 can be regarded as normal, the percentage of normal at which the firm must operate to break-even is computed as under:

$$\frac{\text{B.E. sales volume in Rupees}}{\text{Normal sales volume in Rupees}} = \frac{8,00,000}{10,00,000} = 80\% \text{ B.E. capacity percentage.}$$

If profits are desired, an activity level higher than break-even capacity percentage must be reached.

Note: When the break-even sales volume in Rupees is determined first, break-even units can be found by dividing rupees sales by unit sales price

$$\frac{\text{B.E. sales volume in Rupees}}{\text{Unit sales price}} = ₹\frac{8,00,000}{40} = 20,000 \text{ units}$$

Conversely, when break-even unit are computed first, break-even sales rupees can be found by:

B.E. sales in unit sales × unit sale price = 20,000 units × ₹ 8,00,000.

Data for break-even analysis can't be taken directly from the conventional or full cost income (Profit & Loss account) statement. Each expense must be analysed to determine its fixed and variable portions. Break-even analysis may be based on historical data, past operations or future sales and costs. In the latter case, the starting point of analysis is the determination of estimated or standard costs for various levels of output with the help of flexible budget. The data in flexible budget can be used directly or without refinement for break-even analysis or can be converted into a break-even chart. Where step costs are involved, the optimal output level will often lie at one of the points just before a new injection of fixed cost becomes necessary. For example, if sales price is ₹ 5 per unit, V.C. ₹ 3 per unit and output levels are units 5,000; 100,00; 15,000; 12,000; 25,000 and step fixed costs are ₹ 10,000; 15,000; 20,000; 25,000 and 35,000. The profit will be ₹ 15,000 both at level of 20,000 and 25,000 units. After that profit will come down.

In case any item is missing, it can be found easily. Following are some examples:

(1) *To find break-even sales in rupees*: If net income, sales and fixed costs are given. Suppose net income is ₹ 75,000, sales ₹ 10,00,000 and fixed costs ₹ 3,00,000 then B.E. sales will be found as under:

Contribution = net income plus fixed costs

So ₹ 75,000 + 3,00,000 = 3,75,000 contribution

₹ 3,75,000 is contribution on sales of ₹ 10,00,000.

At B.E. point contribution is equal to fixed costs. So ₹ 3,75,000 contribution comes from sale of ₹ 10,00,000 and contribution of ₹ 3,00,000 will come from sale

$$= \frac{3,00,000}{3,75,000} \times 10,00,000$$

B.E. sales in amount = ₹ 8,00,000.

(2) *To find net income*: If actual sales, fixed cost and break-even sales are given. Using the above data sales ₹ 10,00,000, fixed costs ₹ 3,00,000 and break-even sales ₹ 8,00,000, are given. Find the net income.

At B.E. point, contribution is equal to fixed costs. So contribution is ₹ 3,00,000 i.e., 37.50% of B.E. Sales ₹ 8,00,000. So contribution on actual sales of ₹ 10,00,000 = ₹ 3,75,000 deduct fixed costs ₹ 3,00,000 the net profit remains ₹ 75,000.

(3) *To find actual sales*: If net income, fixed costs and break-even sales are given. Again assume the above data. Net income ₹ 75,000, fixed costs ₹ 3,00,000, B.E. ₹ 8,00,000. The actual sales will be calculated as follows:

On B.E. sales of ₹ 8,00,000, the contribution is ₹ 3,00,000 so P/V ratio is 37.50% (or 3/8). Therefore, net income of ₹ 75,000 is earned on sale of ₹ 2,00,000. Hence total sales are ₹ 2,00,000 + ₹ 8,00,000 = ₹ 10,00,000.

(4) *To find variable cost, fixed costs*: If sales and profits or two periods are given. Assume the following data:

Example 2

	Sales ₹	Profit ₹
June 2021	50,000	10,000
May 2021	40,000	4,000

Find the fixed and variable costs.

The difference between sale and profit is total cost. Hence total costs for June 2021 are ₹ 40,000 and for May 2021 are ₹ 36,000. The difference between sales, costs and profits for two periods are: Sales ₹ 10,000, Costs ₹ 4,000, Profit ₹ 6,000.

An increase in sales of ₹ 10,000 is an increase in costs of ₹ 4,000 and an increase in profit of ₹ 6,000. This shows that each rupee increase in sales covered its variable costs of ₹ 0.40 and contributed ₹ 0.60 to profit or fixed expenses and profit. The variable cost factor is found by subtracting the C/M ratio from 100 per cent. Since ₹ 6,000 + ₹ 10,000 = 60% (the C/M ratio), the variable cost ratio is 40% or more directly ₹ 4,000 + ₹ 10,000 = 40%. The variable cost and fixed costs can be found now.

	June 2021 ₹	May 2021 ₹
Total cost	40,000	36,000
V.C. (40% of sales)	20,000	16,000
Fixed costs	20,000	20,000

The C/M or P/V ratio helps profit calculation without the necessity of detailed calculations of variable costs. The formula is:

Profit = (Sales × C/M) – Fixed costs

Using above data of June 2021 Profit = ₹ (50,000 × 0.60) – ₹ 20,000 = 30,000 – 20,000 = ₹ 10,000

The same formula helps to find the C/M ratio

Profit = (Sales × C/M) – Fixed costs

₹ 10,000 = (₹ 50,000 × C/M) – ₹ 20,000

₹ 10,000 + ₹ 20,000 = ₹ 50,000 × C/M

$$\frac{₹\ 30{,}000}{₹\ 50{,}000} = C/M$$

60% = C/M

(5) To find the different costs:

Example 3

You are given the following information: (1) Gross profit ₹ 7,00,000 (Sales – Mfg. Costs), (2) B.E. sales ₹ 55,00,000, (3) Sales 50,00,000, (4) Contribution ₹ 10,00,000, (5) Variable manufacturing costs ₹ 3,00,000, (6) Direct materials ₹ 18,00,000, (7) Direct labour ₹ 17,00,000. There is no opening or closing inventory. You are required to calculate (a) fixed manufacturing overhead, (b) variable selling and administration costs, and (c) fixed selling and administration costs.

	₹	₹
(a) Sales during the year		50,00,000
Less: Gross profit		7,00,000
Total manufacturing costs		43,00,000
Materials	18,00,000	
Labour	17,00,000	
Manufacturing overheads	3,00,000	38,00,000
Fixed manufacturing overheads		5,00,000
(b) Sales	50,00,000	
Contribution	10,00,000	
Variable cost of sales	40,00,000	
Variable manufacturing costs	38,00,000	
Variable selling and adm. costs	2,00,000	
(c) Contribution	= ₹ 10,00,000	
P/V ratio	= 20%	
B.E. sales	= ₹ 55,00,000	

Formula: $\dfrac{\text{Fixed costs}}{\text{P/V ratio}} = \text{Break-even Sales}$

Total Fixed Cost i.e., $\dfrac{\text{Fixed costs}}{20\%} = 55{,}00{,}000 = ₹\ 11{,}00{,}000$

Fixed selling and administration costs = 11,00,000 – 5,00,000 = ₹ 6,00,000 Fixed Mfg. Costs.

Example 4

M.M.M. Corporation Ltd. presents the following data of a product:

(i) Material, labour and variable overhead cost per unit ₹ 12

(ii) Fixed manufacturing, administrative and selling costs ₹ 96,000

(A) The corporation wants to know the units they have to sell, if selling price is ₹ 20 per unit, to break-even, to earn a profit of ₹ 32,000 and to make a profit of 20% on sales. (B) Further what selling price they must charge, if the demand of the product is 10,000 units, in order to break-even, to make a desired profit of ₹ 24,000 and to make a profit of 20% on sales.

Solution

(A) (a) Break-Even point $= \dfrac{96,000}{8} = 12,000$ units **(Ans.)**

(b) Sales to earn a profit of ₹ 32,000

$= \dfrac{96,000 + 32,000}{8} = 16,000$ units **(Ans.)**

(c) Profit of 20% on sales:

Suppose the number of units to be sold x, then

Sales = ₹ 20 × x = 20 x Profit = 20% of 20 x = 4x

Sales = V.C. + F.C. + Profit. So average the equation

20 x = 12 x + 96,000 + 4x.

20 x = 16 x + 96,000

4x = 96,000 units

x = 24,000 units. **(Ans.)**

(B) (a) Break-Even point $= \dfrac{\text{F.C.}}{\text{Contribution}}$ i.e. $10,000 = \dfrac{96,000}{C}$

10,000C = 96,000

C = 9.6

Sales – V.C. = Contribution

S – 12 = 9.6

S = ₹ 21.60

(b) Selling price to make a profit of ₹ 24,000. Let x be the price.

Then Sales – V.C. = F.C. + Profit

(10,000 Units × ₹ x) – (10,000 × ₹ 12) = 96,000 + 24,000

10,000 x – 1,20,000 = 12,00,000

10,000 x = 2,40,000

x = ₹ 24 **(Ans.)**

(c) Price to be charged to make a profit of 20% on sales.

Let the price to be charged x, then

Sales = 10,000 units × ₹ x = ₹ 10,000 x

Profit = 20% on Sales i.e., 20% of 10,000 x i.e., 2,000 x.

Apply the formula: Sales – V.C. = F.C. + Profit

= 10,000 x – 1,20,000 + 96,000 + 2000 x

= 10,000 x – 2,000 x = 2,16,000

8,000 x = 2,16,000

x = ₹ 27. **(Ans.)**

Example 5

Manju (P) Ltd. has the following information for the half year ending 30-6-2021. Fixed Expenses ₹ 50,000, Sales ₹ 2,00,000, Profit ₹ 50,000. During the second half of the year the company suffered a loss of ₹ 10,000. You are asked to calculate:

(a) The P/V ratio, B/E point and margin of safety for six month ending 30th June, 2021.

(b) Calculate the net profit and B.E. sales if sales volume is ₹ 3,00,000. Margin of safety is 40% and P/V ratio is 5% and no other information is given.

Solution

(a) Sales – V.C. = C (F.C. + Profit)

3,00,000 – V.C. = 1,50,000 (90,000 + 60,000)

V.C. = 1,50,000

$$\text{P/V ratio} = \frac{1,50,000}{3,00,000} \times 1,000 = 5\%$$

In case of loss contribution will be = 90,000 – 30,000 = 60,000

$$\text{P/V ratio} = \frac{\text{Contribution}}{\text{Sales}} \times 100$$

$$50\% = \frac{60,000}{\text{Sales}} \times 100$$

$$\text{Sales} = \frac{60,000}{50} \times 100 = ₹\ 1,20,000$$

(b)

$$\text{M/S Ratio} = \frac{\text{Margin of safety}}{\text{Sales}} \times 100$$

$$40 = \frac{\text{M.S.}}{3,00,000} \times 100$$

100 M.S. = 1,20,00,000

M.S. = 1,20,000

Break-Even = Sales – M/S

= 3,00,000 – 40% of sales

= 3,00,000 – 1,20,000

B.E. = 1,80,000

$$\text{M.S.} = \frac{\text{Profit}}{\text{P/V ratio}} \quad \text{i.e. } 1,20,000 = \frac{\text{Profit}}{50\%}$$

1,20,000 × 50 = Profit × 100

100 Profit = 60,00,000 OR $\frac{1,20,000 \times 50}{100}$

Profit = 60,000.

Alternatively

Profit percentage = M/S × P/V ratio = 4% × 5% = 20% of sales

Net Profit 3,00,000 × 20% = ₹ 60,000.

Example 6

Following details pertain to a company:

	Period I	Period II
No. of units sold	10,000	30,000
Selling price per unit	₹ 50	₹ 50
Profit (Loss)	(1,00,000)	1,00,000

Calculate the amount of fixed costs and break-even in units, the number of units sold to earn a profit of ₹ 4,00,000.

Solution

	Sales	Profit (Loss)
Period I	5,00,000	(1,00,000)
Period II	15,00,000	1,00,000

$$\text{P/V ratio} = \frac{\text{Change in Profit}}{\text{Change in Sales}} \times 100$$

$$= \frac{2,00,000}{10,00,000} \times 100$$

$$= 20\%$$

Sales – V.C. = Contribution

5,00,000 – 4,00,000 = 1,00,000

(a) Fixed costs = Contribution + loss = ₹ 2,00,000

(b) Break-even point $= \frac{2,00,000}{20\%} =$ ₹ 10,00,000

(c) To earn profit of ₹ 4,00,000, units to be sold will be

$$= \frac{2,00,000 + 4,00,000}{20\%} = \frac{₹\ 30,00,000}{₹\ 50} = 60,000 \text{ units.}$$

Example 7

A firm sells its product per unit @ ₹ 10 and allows 5% trade discount. The variable cost per unit is ₹ 7.00 and Fixed costs ₹ 10,000. Find out:

(a) If sales are 10% above the break-even volume, determine the net profits.

(b) The P/V ratio is 25%. By what percentage must sales be increased to offset 20% reduction in selling price?

Solution

$$\text{Break-Even Point} = \frac{10,000}{(₹\,10 - ₹\,7.50)} = 4,000 \text{ units} \quad \text{i.e. } ₹\,40,000.$$

Note. Even if trade discount is considered not as a variable cost, it will not effect break-even

(a) If sales are 10% above break-even volume, it means sale of 4,400 units. The contribution will be 4,400 × ₹ 2.50 = 11,000 less fixed costs

Profits = 11,000 – 10,000 = ₹ 1,000.

(b) If price is reduced by 20% new price will be ₹ 8. V.C. = ₹ 7.50 contribution 0.50 per unit.

To maintain the same contribution of ₹ 1000, volume of sales will be:

$$\frac{\text{Contribution}}{\text{New Contribution}} \times \text{New Sales}$$

$$= \frac{11,000}{2,200} \times 35,200 = ₹\,1,76,000$$

If selling price is reduced by 20% the volume of sales will have to be increased by ₹ 1,32,000 i.e. by 16,500 units.

Example 8

A hotel has 450 rooms, with a fixed cost of ₹ 3,50,000 per month. Room rates average ₹ 62 per day with variable costs of ₹ 12 per room rented per day. Assume 30 day month.

1. How many rooms must be occupied per day to break-even?
2. How many rooms must be occupied per month to make a profit of ₹ 1,00,000 after tax? Tax rate 60%.

Solution

$$\text{Rooms to break-even: } \frac{\text{F.C.}}{\text{C/M}} = \frac{3,50,000}{50 \times 30}$$

$$= 234 \text{ Rooms per day}$$

Rooms to be rented to earn profit after tax of ₹ 1,00,000

$$\frac{\text{F.C.} + \dfrac{\text{Desired Profit}}{1 - \text{Tax rate}}}{\text{C/M}}$$

$$= \frac{3,50,000 + \dfrac{1,00,000}{1 - 60\%}}{50}$$

$$= \frac{3,50,000 + 2,50,000}{50} = 12,000 \text{ Rooms } ₹\,400 \text{ per day}$$

Example 9

Fill in the missing figures marked ×.

Profit and Loss A/c

For the year ending 30-6-2021

	Total	Per unit	Per cost
Sales (30,000 units)	₹ ×	₹ ×	100%
Less V.C.	×	×	×
C/M	×	₹ ×	× %
Less Fixed costs	×		
Net Income	₹ 27,000		
Break-Even Point			
In units	× units		
In Rupees	₹ 1,80,000		
Margin of safety			
In Rupees	₹ ×		
In percentage	20%		
Degree of operating leverage	5		

Solution

The first step is to compute the sales for the year in both units and rupees. The second step is to determine the total contribution margin for the year

(a) Units sold 30,000

Total sales – B.E. sales = M/S in Rupees

Total sales – ₹ 1,80,000 = M/S in Rupees

$$\frac{\text{M/S in Rupees}}{\text{Total sales}} = \text{M/S percentage (20\%)}$$

If M/S in ₹ is 20% of total sales, then break-even point in Rupees is 80% of total sales. So $\frac{1,80,000}{\text{Total Sales}} = 80\%$ i.e. ₹ 2,25,000.

The selling price per unit is 2,25,000 ÷ 30,000 = ₹ 7.50 per unit.

Total contribution margin for the year = degree of operating leverage multiplied by net income i.e. 5 × ₹ 27,000 = ₹ 1,35,000. Now we can complete the account.

	Total	Per unit	Per cent
Sales (30,000 units)	2,25,000	7.50	100
Less V.C.	90,000	3.00	40
C/M	1,35,000	4.50	60%
Less Fixed costs	1,08,000		
Net Income	27,000		

Break-Even point = 1,08,000 ÷ ₹ 4.50 = 24,000 Units or ₹ 1,80,000

M/S = 2,25,000 – 1,80,000 = 45,000

Margin of Safety

It indicates how much sales may decrease from a budgeted or selected sales figure before the company will break-even i.e., before the company will suffer loss. In Example 1, suppose the budgeted sales are ₹ 10,00,000. The margin of safety is ₹ 2,00,000. The margin of safety expressed as a percentage of sales is called the margin of safety ratio (M/S) and is calculated as follows:

$$\text{Margin of Safety} = \frac{\text{Budgeted Sales} - \text{Break-even Sales}}{\text{Budgeted Sales}}$$

$$= \frac{₹10{,}00{,}000 - ₹\ 80{,}00{,}000}{₹\ 10{,}00{,}000} = 20\%$$

Other related formulas:

Profit	=	CM ratio × M/S ratio
M/S ratio	=	Profit + C/M
C/M ratio	=	Profit + M/S ratio

Applying these formulae to Example 1

$$\text{Profit} = 37.5\% \times 20\% = 7.5\%$$

$$\text{M/S ratio} = \frac{7.5\%}{37.5\%} = 20\%$$

$$\text{C/M ratio} = \frac{7.5\%}{20\%} = 37.5\%$$

Once the firm has reached the break-even point, the difference between sales in excess of break-even sales and variable cost is the firm's profit (V.C. of the additional units after B.E. units is to be taken).

BREAK-EVEN CHART

Break-even calculation can be presented in a break-even chart, or **indifference chart** in which the cost line and the sales line intersect at the break-even point. The information needed to construct this chart is forecast sales and fixed and variable costs. It can be presented in many forms like (a) conventional break-even chart—in which fixed costs are drawn first, (b) alternative chart—in which variable costs are drawn first, and (c) detailed chart—in which costs in the sub-classifications are shown.

A conventional break-even chart, based on Example 1 drawn in Exhibit 7.1.

A horizontal base line, the X-axis, is drawn to represent sales volume. The Y-axis shows costs in rupees. The fixed cost line is parallel to the X-axis. The total cost line is drawn from fixed cost point and sales line is drawn from point O. These lines cut each other at break-even point. The shaded area shows loss. In conventional break-even chart the variable costs are plotted above fixed costs. The "ANGLE OF INCIDENCE" is shown also.

BREAK-EVEN CHART (CONVENTIONAL)

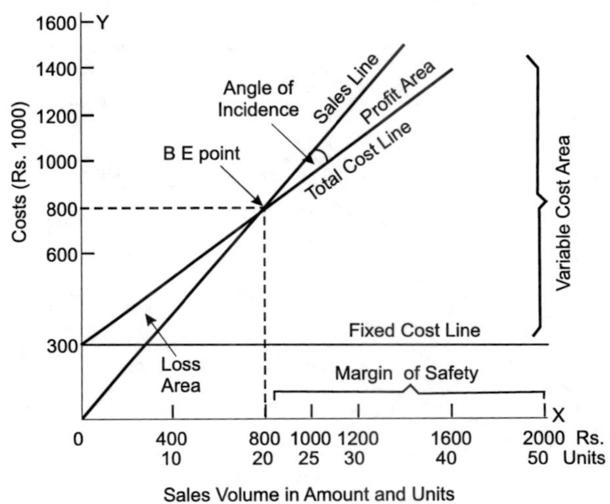

Exhibit 7.1

The alternative chart shown in Exhibit 7.2. It indicates the recovery of fixed costs at various levels of percentage capacity and at rupee sales or unit sales.

The break-even chart, Exhibit 7.3, shows greater details by breaking down fixed and variable cost into sub-classifications. Even the profit wedge may be sub-divided into income-tax, interest, dividends and retained earnings.

BREAK-EVEN CHART SHOWING ALTERNATE APPROACH

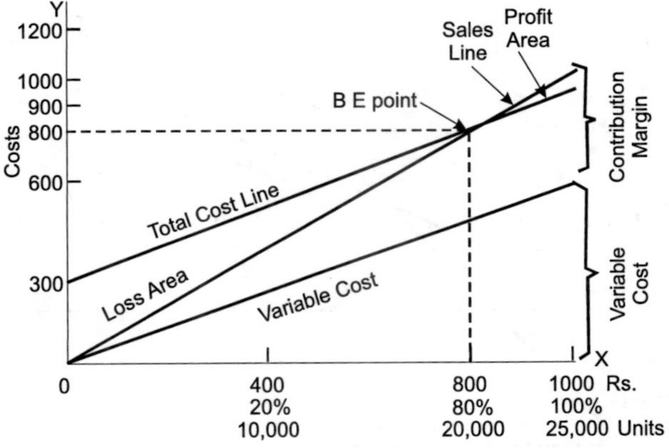

Exhibit 7.2

BREAK-EVEN SHOWING COSTS BREAKUP

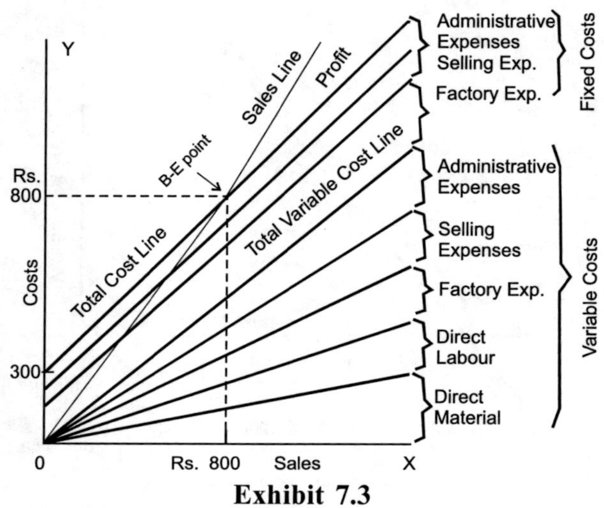

Exhibit 7.3

Break-even Chart for Optimum Output

In the chart below there are two points where the total cost line and sales line intersect. Technically, therefore, there are two break-even points although, clearly, the second—near the maximum output—is not normally treated as the break-even point.

BREAK-EVEN CHART SHOWING OPTIMUM OUTPUT

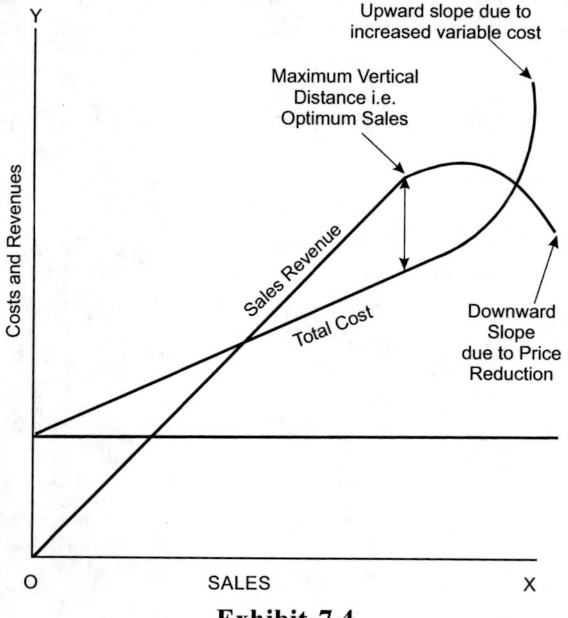

Exhibit 7.4

Selection of the point which gives maximum profit involves the determination of the greatest vertical distance which exists between the sales and total cost lines. In the example, the optimum output is signified by the arrow. This is the point where marginal cost and marginal revenue agree.

Control Break-even Chart

The control break-even chart is useful for comparing budgeted and actual profits, break-even point and sales.

Study the following example and the chart drawn on that basis:

Budgeted fixed costs	=	₹ 15,000
Budgeted variable costs	=	₹ 12,000 (for budgeted, sales)
Budgeted sales	=	₹ 40,000
Actual fixed costs	=	₹ 15,000
Actual variable costs	=	₹ 16,200
Actual sales	=	₹ 45,000

Note: Profits as per budgeted Sales = 13,000

Profits for Actual Sales:	
Budgeted Profits	₹ 16,000
Actual Profits	₹ 13,300
Negative Profit Variance	₹ 2,700

The budgeted cost for the increased sales should be ₹ 13,500, not ₹ 16,200. This apparently disproportionate increase in costs should be explained.

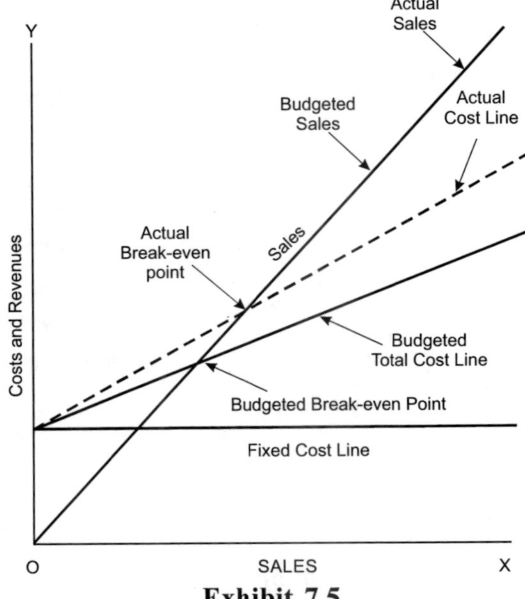

Exhibit 7.5

The Economist's Break-even Chart

There are two differences between the accountant's and economist's break-even charts:

1. The accountant usually assumes a constant unit variable cost instead of a unit variable cost that changes with level of production. In other words, accountant assumes linearity but economist does not. The revenue function will be a curve and curve may rise slowly at the start and then rise steeply as the volume is expanded. One may have two break-even points. (see Exhibit 7.6)
2. The accountant's sale line is drawn under assumption that price does not change with the level of production or sales, but the economist assumes that price changes may be needed to spur sales volume. Therefore, the economist chart is non-linear. An extension of economist's curve would show a second break-even point at a high volume level. Total revenue would begin to fall as unit prices fall. Extension beyond second break-even volume would bring losses. But extension of accountant's lines would add to net profit until maximum attainable volume is reached.

The economist's assumptions are more valid. The chart is shown below:

BREAK-EVEN CHART SHOWING ECONOMIST'S AND ACCOUNTANT'S APPROACH

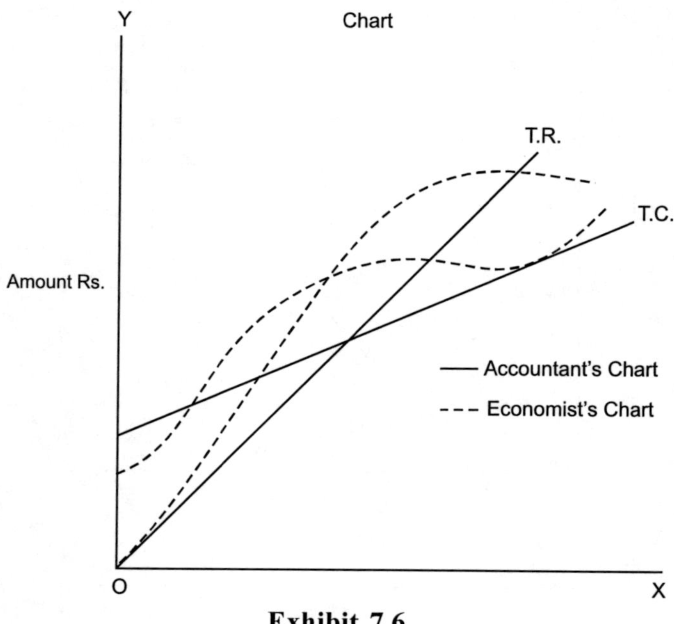

Exhibit 7.6

The difference between the chart is greatest during imperfect market competition. The difference actually relates to their purpose. Economist's chart provides a summary of explanation of profit maximizing behaviour, while accountant's chart is a technique for approaching certain decisions. To be judged on how well it is in those decisions.

THE UNIT PROFIT GRAPH (P/V GRAPH)

The break-even chart is generally prepared on the basis of total revenue and expenses. These rupees sales and expense figures can be translated into a profit per unit graph in order to show more clearly the effect of fixed cost on the cost per unit. Suppose the normal capacity is 100% and total sales ₹ 5,00,000 (5,000 units @ ₹ 100) variable cost ₹ 3,00,000 and fixed cost ₹ 1,50,000. The break-even point is ₹ 3,75,000 (₹ 1,50,000 × 5/2) i.e. 75% of normal capacity (3,75,000/5,00,000). The variable cost is ₹ 60 per unit, fixed cost ₹ 30 per unit if 5000 units are made and sold. As the units produced decrease, the fixed cost per unit increases. The effect can be presented as under:

Example 10

Unit Schedule

	₹	₹	₹	₹	₹
Units	1,000	2,000	3,000	4,000	5,000
Variable cost per unit	60	60	60	60	60
Fixed cost per unit	150	75	50	37.50	30
Total cost per unit	210	135	110	97.50	90
Sale price per unit	100	100	100	100	100
Profit or loss per unit	(110)	(35)	(10)	2.50	10

The break-even point will be at 3,750 units (Fixed cost per unit ₹ 40 + variable cost ₹ 60 i.e., total cost ₹ 100). The above schedule can be presented by a graph as shown in Exhibit 7.7.

The unit profit graph and the schedule help to find out which unit cost should be used in setting sales prices. The unit costs must be judged at all levels of activity. In case of fluctuating activity levels or changing costs, the formula for finding unit cost is

$$\text{Cost per unit} = \frac{F + Vx}{Ux}$$

F = Fixed costs

V = Variable expenses at normal capacity

U = Units of production of normal capacity

x = Level of activity (expressed as a percentage of normal capacity).

Suppose the fixed expenses are ₹ 1,70,000, variable expenses ₹ 2,70,000, units produced 3,700 i.e., 74% of normal capacity units 5,000

$$\text{Cost per unit} = \frac{1,70,000 + 2,70,000\ (0.74)}{5,000\ (0.74)} = ₹\ 100\ (\text{approx.})$$

$$\text{Cost at 90\% capacity will be} = \frac{1,70,000\ + 2,70,000\ (0.90)}{5,000\ (0.90)} = ₹\ 92\ (\text{approx.})$$

If units produced is not given, it can be found as follows:

Variable expenses are ₹ 2,70,000 i.e., ₹ 54 per unit or 54% of sales P.V. ratio is 46%. Hence units produced (and also B.E.) = ₹ 1,70,000 + 46% = 74% capacity i.e., 3,700 units.

BREAK-EVEN SHOWING UNIT SCHEDULE

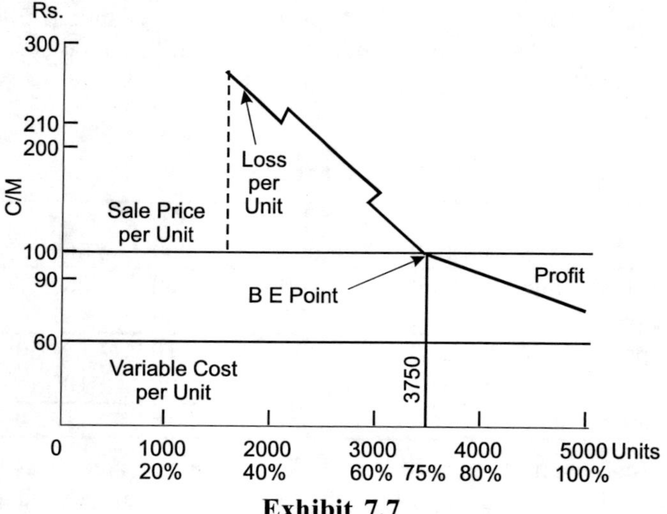

Exhibit 7.7

The effect of price reduction on profits has been shown on P/V graph below. The increase in sales volume required to overcome the effect of a price reduction is proportionately greater when the rate of contribution margin is relatively low at the start. If each unit of product makes only a modest contribution, then a reduction in price makes it all the more difficult to recover the fixed costs and to earn profits.

Though the pricing policy will depend upon the long range and short range objectives of management, in any event, it is important to know what will probably happen if a certain course of action is adopted. Prices may be cut with full knowledge that immediate profits will be reduced, with an idea to establish in the market. But, in the case of a company, whose management is not informed with respect to cost-volume relationships, it may cut prices in an attempt to gain immediate profits; and when the profits do not materialize the management will be surprised.

P/V GRAPH SHOWING THE EFFECT OF CHANGE IN PRICE ON PROFIT

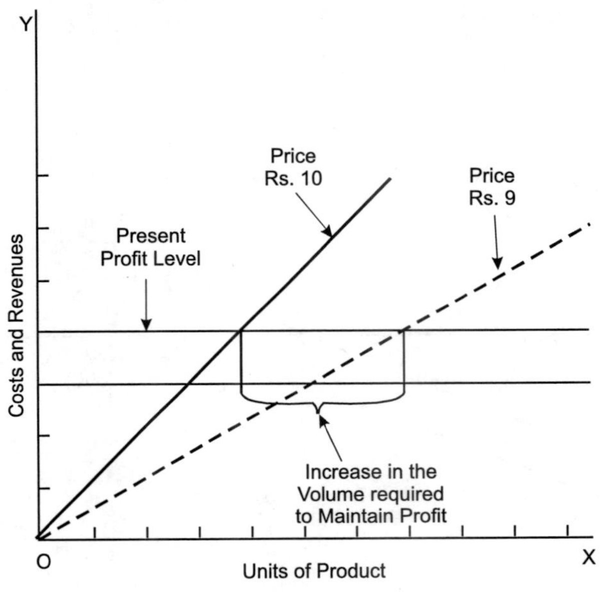

Exhibit 7.8

Even if many products are produced graphic presentation of cost-volume-profit relationship can also be shown. If any product results in loss and contributes no marginal income, its slope would be more downward. Take the following example:

Products	Sales Value of Production ₹	Variable Costs ₹	% of V.C. to Sales	Marginal Income ₹	P/V Ratio
A	60,000	50,000	83%	10,000	17%
B	70,000	30,000	43%	40,000	57%
C	45,000	15,000	33%	30,000	67%
D	25,000	5,000	20%	20,000	80%
Totals	2,00,000	1,00,000	50%	1,00,000	50%
			Less F.C.	80,000	
			Profit	20,000	

This illustration indicates that the P/V ratio varies from 17% for product A to 80% for product D. Viewing the other products' contribution, product A should also give a higher contribution margin. However, unless product A can be replaced by some other product with higher P/V ratio, or unless machinery and plant engaged in manufacture of A can be used to produce more profitable products, product A can be dropped.

P/V CHART SHOWING MARGINAL CONTRIBUTION OF PRODUCTS A, B, C AND D TOWARDS FIXED COSTS AND PROFITS

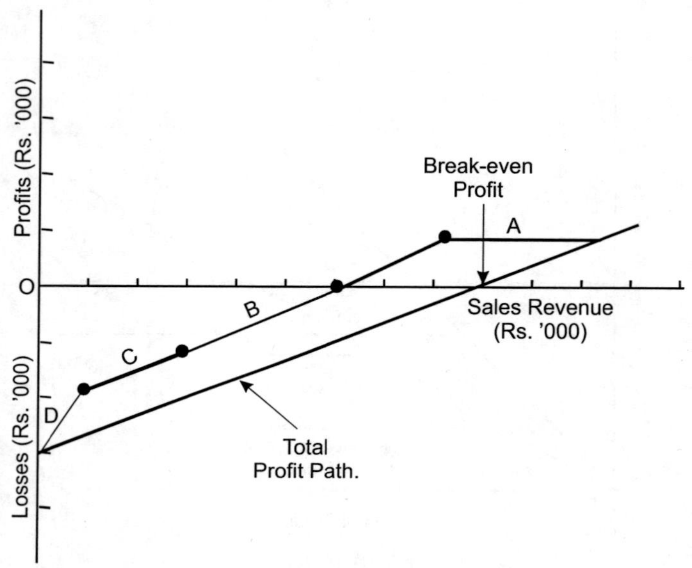

Exhibit 7.9

EFFECT OF CHANGES IN VARIOUS ELEMENTS

Profits may be affected by the changes in any of the following factors:

1. Fixed costs, 2. Variable costs, 3. Price, 4. Volume, 5. Combination of any of them, 6. Sales mix. The effects of these changes can be shown in a chart also, thus adding a dynamic dimension to the analysis.

Effect of Changes in Fixed Costs

Increase or decrease in fixed costs do not change the P/V ratio, but they do change the break-even point. With the same P/V ratio the slope of the fixed cost, recovery line remains the same. The distance between new fixed cost line and break-even is more if fixed costs go up and is short if fixed costs go down. Exhibit 7.10 shows the effect if fixed costs go down.

Increase in fixed costs: If fixed costs are increased, the break-even point is higher; beyond the break-even point profits are lower by the amount of increase and below the break-even point, losses are greater by the amount of increase.

Decrease in fixed costs: If fixed costs are decreased the break-even point is lower. Beyond the break-even point, profits are greater by the amount of the decrease below the break-even point, profits are greater by the amount of the decrease, below the break-even point, losses are smaller by the amount of the decrease.

BREAK-EVEN SHOWING FIXED COSTS CHANGES

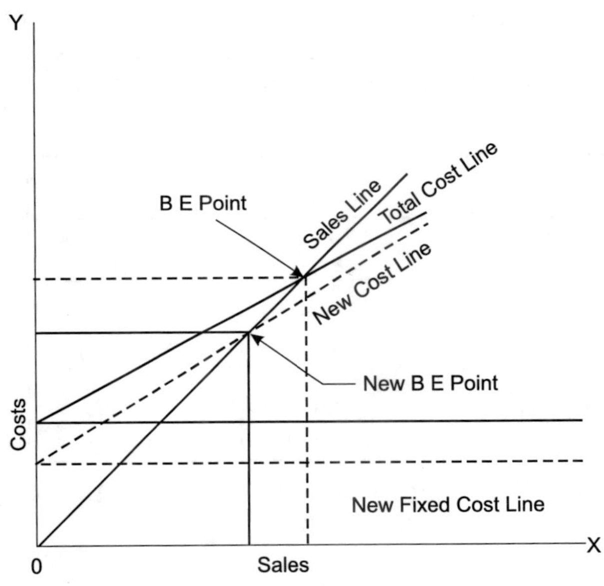

Exhibit 7.10

Suppose a firm has a P/V ratio of 40% and fixed costs ₹ 42,000. The effects of a change in the fixed cost of ₹ 6,000 (more or less) are as follows:

	Decrease ₹	Fixed cost ₹	Increase ₹
Fixed costs	36,000	42,000	48,000
P/V ratio	40%	40%	40%
B-E Point	90,000	1,05,000	1,20,000
Decrease (increase)	– 15,000	0	+15,000

The change in the break-even point is the same in each case and can be determined by dividing the amount of the change (₹ 6,000) by the P/V ratio (40%).

Effect of Changes in Variable Costs

Both the unit contribution margin and break-even point are altered by changes in unit variable costs. Variable costs are subject to various degrees of control at different volumes because of psychological as well as other factors—conventional break-even chart assumes directly proportional fluctuations of variable costs with volume.

Increase in variable costs brings low P/V ratio and higher break-even point. Profits after break-even point are lower and losses before break-even point are higher. Decrease in variable costs results in higher P/V ratio and lower break-even point. The profits beyond break-even point are higher, losses before break-even point are lower. Suppose a firm has selling price of an article ₹ 20 per unit, variable cost ₹ 10 per unit and fixed costs ₹ 48,000. Suppose there is an increase of ₹ 2 or decrease of ₹ 2 unit. As a result the effects are shown below:

Example 11

	Decrease ₹	Present ₹	Increase ₹
Unit sale price	20	20	20
V.C. per unit	8	10	12
Contribution	12	10	8
P/V ratio	60%	50%	40%
Fixed costs	₹ 48,000	₹ 48,000	₹ 48,000
Break-even point:			
(a) Sales in rupees	80,000	96,000	1,20,000
(b) In units	4,000	4,800	6,000

BREAK-EVEN SHOWING EFFECT OF INCREASE IN VARIABLE COSTS

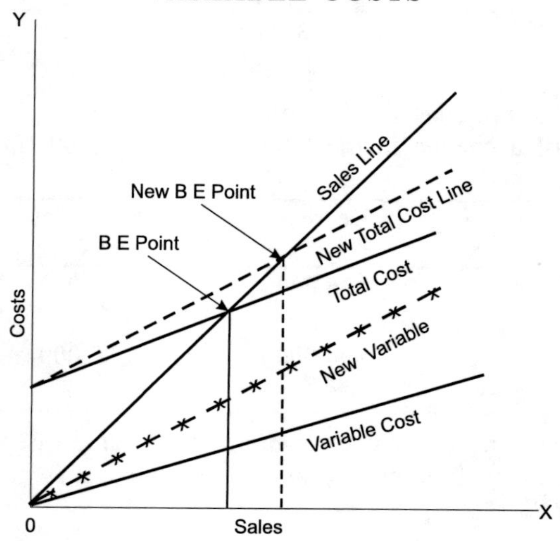

Exhibit 7.11

Effect of Change in Selling Prices

A change in the selling price of a product alters its P/V ratio and break-even point.

An increase in selling price will cause higher contribution and P/V ratio, the break-even point drops. Profits beyond break-even point are higher and losses below the break-even point are lower. If selling price decreases, the P/V ratio is low and break-even point goes up. Profits beyond the break-even point are lower and losses below the break-even point are higher. Suppose the price is ₹ 10 per unit, variable cost ₹ 10 per unit, fixed costs ₹ 36,000. If the price is reduced by 10% (one rupee) or is increased by 10%, the effect on P/V ratio and break-even will be as under:

Example 12

	Increase 10% ₹	Present Price ₹	Decrease 10% ₹
Sale price per unit	11	10	9
Variable cost per unit	6	6	6
Contribution per unit	5	4	3
P/V ratio	45.45%	40%	33-1/3%
Fixed costs	36,000	36,000	36,000
Break-even point:			
In rupees	79,200	90,000	1,08,000
In units	7,200	9,000	12,000

It should be remembered that changes in the profits, as a result of increase or decrease in selling price are far greater than might be first presumed. If in the above example the selling price is ₹ 9 and 15,000 units are sold, the profit will be ₹ 24,000. So, just by decrease in price of 10% brings a fall in profits by 62.5%. Exhibit 7.12 shows the effect of an increase in sale price.

BREAK-EVEN SHOWING EFFECT OF INCREASE IN SELLING PRICE

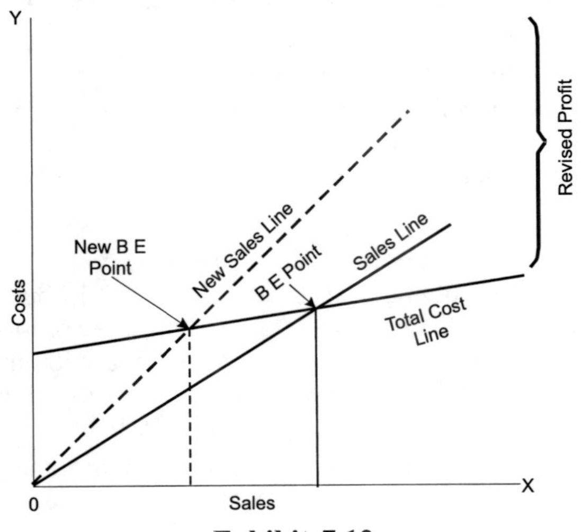

Exhibit 7.12

Effect of Changes in Volume

A change in volume does not affect the P/V ratio and break-even point, unless there is any change in selling price and/or costs. However, the increase or decrease in volume increases or decreases profits respectively. It should be noted that the effect on profits is more of any change in price rather than volume.

Effect of Price and Volume Changes

The common belief is that the sales increase if price is reduced and profits will not be reduced and might even be increased. Such an argument seems quite plausible at first. Price reduction does not necessarily lead to the desired increase in volume. If the increase in volume does occur, it is often not large enough to overcome the effect of the price reduction on total profits. This is particularly the situation if P/V ratio is low. Consider the following table of a firm, fixed costs being ₹ 30,000.

	Present ₹	10% decrease ₹	15% decrease ₹
Selling price per unit	10	9	8.50
Variable cost per unit	7	7	7.00
Contribution per unit	3	2	1.50
Decrease in contribution	–	₹ 1	1.50
% increase in present volume to cover the price decrease	–	50% (₹ 2 + ₹ 1)	100% (₹ 1.50) ₹ 1.50

The percentage of change by which sales would be increased to offset the price reduction can also be found by comparing break-even point. If the selling price is reduced by 10%, the break-even point in units is increased by fifty per cent.

Break-even point after price reduction	= 15,000 units
Break-even point before price reduction	= 10,000 units
Increase in B.E. units	5,000 units

Percentage increase in B.E. = 50%
(5,000 ÷ 10,000)

If the firm's P/V is low, the selling price may be increased, even though a fall in sales volume may be the result. If, in our example, the price is increased by 10% i.e., upto ₹ 11 per unit, the contribution will be ₹ 4 per unit. The break-even will decrease by 25% without any adverse effect on profits. If the fall in sales volume following a 10% decrease were less than 25%, the profit position would be better.

In order to relate profit to volume, profit-volume analysis graph is used. Exhibit 7.13 is based on income statement with imaginary figures.

BREAK-EVEN SHOWING PRICE/VOLUME CHANGES

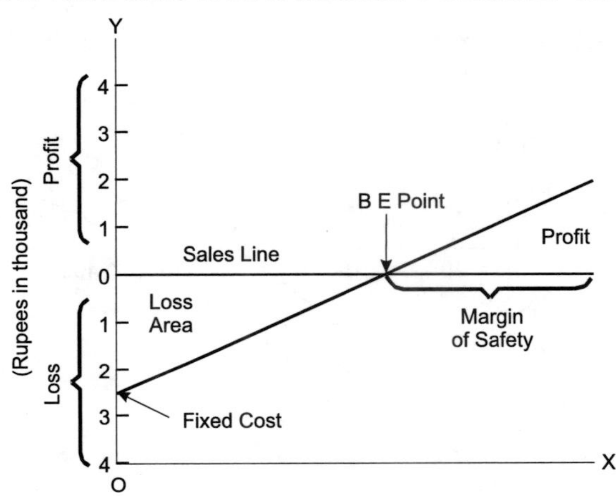

Exhibit 7.13

Effect of Changes in all Profit-Volume Factors

The P/V analysis graph can also be used to show the changes in various factors. We take an example[1] of changes in various factors i.e., sales, costs, volume and profits. If a firm sells 1,00,000 units @ ₹ 2 per unit, variable cost is @ ₹ 1 per unit, fixed costs are ₹ 80,000 and total investment ₹ 2,00,000.

Example 13

Plan I		Plan II	
Decrease in price	10%	Increase in price	10%
Increase in volume	12%	Decrease in volume	12%
Variable cost increase	4%	Variable cost decrease	4%
Fixed cost increase	5%	Fixed cost decrease	5%

The effect of these plans is shown below:

	Plan I	Present Vol.	Plan II
Units	2,24,000	2,00,000	1,76,000
Sales	4,03,200	4,00,000	3,87,200
Variable cost	2,32,960	2,00,000	1,68,960
Contribution	1,70,240	2,00,000	2,18,240
Fixed costs	1,68,000	1,60,000	1,52,000
Profit	2,240	40,000	66,240
Profit per unit	0.01	0.20	0.376
Percentage change in profit	– 94.4%	–	+65.6%
Return of investment	1.12	20%	33.1%
Break-even point	3,97,895	3,20,000	2,69,677

1. Adapted from *Cost Accounting* by Matz and Usry.

The P/V analysis graph is shown in Exhibit 7.14.

BREAK-EVEN SHOWING DIFFERENT PLANS

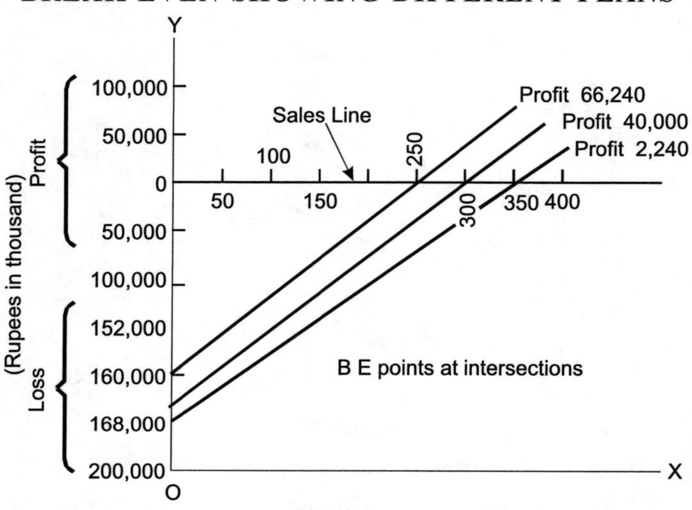

Exhibit 7.14

Sales Mix or Product Mix—Break-Even

Analysis of a firm producing two or more products: In our discussion so far, we have assumed that only one product is manufactured and sold. If more than one product is sold, the cost-volume profit analysis becomes more complex. If the products have different selling prices, the variable costs, contributions and P/V ratios shall be different. The break-even points and profits shall vary with the proportions in which the products are sold. First, take an example of a firm selling more than one product and find its break-even points.

Example 14

A firm produces two products *x* and *y*. The fixed costs are ₹ 96,800, sales prices ₹ 2 and ₹ 4 and variable costs 0.80 and 3.20 for *x* and *y* respectively. The product mix is in 3 units of *x* to 1 unit of *y*.

	Product	
	x	*y*
Product mix	3	1
	₹	₹
Sales revenue	2.00	4.00
Variable cost	0.80	3.20
Contribution	1.20	0.80
Fixed costs	—	96,800
Products P/V ratios	60%	20%

B.E. point of the firm:

Product x =	₹ 1.20 × 3	₹ 3.60
y =	₹ 0.80 × 1	₹ 0.80
	4	₹ 4.40
Average per unit (4.40 ÷ 4)	₹ 1.10	

B-E. Point is = 96,800 ÷ 1.10 = 88,000 units to be divided as follows:

	₹
Product x : ¾ × 88,000 = 66,000 units	= 1,32,000
y : ¼ × 88,000 = 22,000 units	= 88,000
	2,20,000

It should be noted that a different split would show a different profit or loss. The above is an example of product mix. If sales mix is taken, then the average P/V ratio must be taken in the analysis. Suppose the sales revenue of x is ₹ 60,000 and y is ₹ 40,000. The break-even will be as under:

Sales mix $= \frac{x}{60\%}, \frac{x}{40\%}$ i.e. in the ratio of 3 : 2

Sales revenue	=	₹ 6,00,000	₹ 4,00,000
P.V. ratio	=	60%	20%
Average ratio	=	60% × 3	= 180%
		$20\% \times \frac{2}{5}$	$= \frac{40\%}{220\%}$

= 220 ÷ 5 = 44%

Break-even point is ₹ 22,00,000 (₹ 96,800 ÷ 44%)

Product x : 66% of 2,20,000 = ₹ 1,32,000

y : 40% of 2,20,000 = ₹ 88,000

It should be remembered that the answer is not just ₹ 2,20,000 of sales revenue, but 2,20,000 split into the predetermined mix in 3:2 ratio. A different mix will give different result.

The P/V ratio of a firm can be found by following formula:

P/V ratio of each product × product or sales mix ratio of each product

The total of above ratios of products, then will be P/V ratio of the firm.

If the sales revenue of ₹ 2,20,000 is equally divided, then a loss would be expected.

Contributions:

		₹
Product:	x — ₹ 1,10,000 × 60% =	66,000
	y — ₹ 1,10,000 × 20% =	22,000
	₹ 88,000 – Fixed cost =	₹ 96,800

Loss according to B.E. analysis is ₹ 8,800.

The cause of this difference is shift in sales mix from profitable product *x* to less profitable product *y*. If the mix is equal, then average P/V will drop to 40% i.e. ₹ 88,000 ÷ ₹ 2,20,000 or

		P/V ratio	Mix	Total
Product:	*x*	60%	1	60%
	y	20%	1	20%
		40%	2	80%

Average ratio 80% ÷ 2.

The P/V analysis graph for individual product can also be prepared. Example 15 is depicted in Exhibit 7.15.

Example 15

Products	A ₹	B ₹	C ₹	D ₹	Total ₹
Sales value	60,000	70,000	45,000	25,000	2,00,000
Variable costs	50,000	30,000	15,000	5,000	1,00,000
Contribution	10,000	40,000	30,000	20,000	1,00,000
P/V ratio	17%	57%	67%	80%	50%

Fixed costs ₹ 80,000 Profit = ₹ 1,20,000
B-E. point ₹ 80,000 ÷ 50% = ₹ 1,60,000.

B/E SHOWING ANALYSIS FOR INDIVIDUAL PRODUCT ANALYSIS

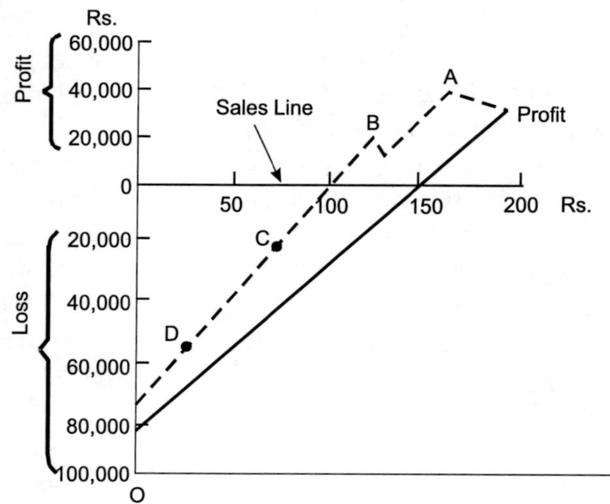

Exhibit 7.15

To find single B/E point the following formula is applied of Weighted Average C/N.

$$\text{Average C/N} = \sum_{i=1} (\text{CN} \times \text{Proportion})$$

Example 15A

Bajaj Auto manufactures three products Tyres, Tubes and Spark Plug and the % of sales of these products out of sales as 50%, 30% and 20% respectively. Following are other details:

	Products		
	Tyres	Tubs	Spark Plugs
Selling price per unit	₹ 250	₹ 216	₹ 100
Variable cost per unit	180	140	80
C/M per unit	70	70	20
C/M ratio	28%	33.3%	20%

Total Fixed Costs ₹ 4,20,000

In case only one product i.e. Tyres or Tubs or Spark Plugs are sold the B/E for Tyres $\frac{4,20,000}{70}$ for Tubes $\frac{4,20,000}{70}$ for Spark Plugs $\frac{4,20,000}{20}$ will be 6,000 units and 21,000 units respectively. Now we calculate weighted average C/M by applying the formula.

Calculation of Weighted Average C/M

	₹	Proportion	Expected Value	Total
Selling Price Tyres	250	.30	7.50	
" Tubs	210	.50	10.50	20.00
" Spark Plug	100	.20	2.00	
Variable Cost Tyres	180	.30	5.40	
" Tubs	140	.50	7.00	14.00
" Spark Plugs	80	.20	1.60	
			C/M (weighted)	₹ 6.00

$$= (7 \times .30) + (7 \times .50) + (2 \times .20)$$

$$= 2.10 + 3.50 + .40 = ₹\ 6$$

$$\text{B/E for sales mix} = \frac{\text{F.C.}}{\text{Average C / M}} = ₹\ \frac{42,000}{6} = 7,000 \text{ units}$$

$$\text{or } ₹\ \frac{42,000}{6 \div 20} = 1,40,000$$

Example 16

See the conventional break-even graph on page 176. What will be the effect of each of the following actions on total cost line and sales line and break-even point? For total expense line, state whether the action will cause line to: (1) Remain unchanged (2) Shift upward (3) Shift downward

(4) Have a steeper slope (i.e. rotate upward) (5) Have a flatter slope (i.e. rotate downward) (6) Shift upward and have a steeper slope (7) Shift upward and have a flatter slope (8) Shift downward and have a steeper slope (9) Shift downward and have a flatter slope.

In case of break-even state whether the actions will cause if (A) Remain unchanged (B) Increase (C) Decrease (D) Probably change, but the direction is uncertain.

TREAT EACH CASE INDEPENDENTLY

(a) The unit selling price is increased from ₹ 40 to ₹ 42.
(b) Unit variable costs are decreased from ₹ 25 to ₹ 23.
(c) Fixed costs are increased by ₹ 3,000 per period.
(d) Two thousand more units are sold than budgeted 25,000.
(e) Fixed costs are produced by 5,000 per period and unit variable costs are increased by ₹ 2.
(f) Both unit variable costs and selling price are increased by ₹ 5.
(g) Fixed costs are increased by ₹ 3,000 per period resulting in a 10% increase in the number of units sold.
(h) Fixed costs are increased by 10,000 per period and unit variable costs are reduced by ₹ 5.

Solution

Action No.	Effect on Total cost line	Effect on sales line	Effect on B.E.
(a)	1	4	C
(b)	5	1	C
(c)	2	1	B
(d)	1	1	A
(e)	8	1	D
(f)	4	4	A
(g)	2	1	B
(h)	7	1	D

Digits and letters as given in the question.

Assumptions of B/E Analysis

The cost-volume profit analysis is based on the following assumptions:

1. The total cost can be separated into fixed and variable elements.
2. The fixed costs are constant. The variable cost per unit does not change i.e., sales volume does not effect them, the total V.C. are directly proportional to volume.
3. The selling price per unit is constant.
4. Production and sales are same i.e., inventories are constant. No change in inventory is assumed because there are many methods used for inventory valuation.

5. Sales or product mix proportion is same.
6. Managerial policies, technological methods and efficiency of men and machines do not change.
7. The behaviour of total costs and total revenues has been reliably determined and is linear over the relevant range i.e., the normal range of output levels.
8. Revenue and costs are compared on a single activity base e.g., sales or units or produced.

Limitations

The inputs for break-even are based on historical relationships. These relationships may not be particularly stable over time. For extreme volume changes, there may be no historical precedent. We are judging future costs, volume and profits, based on past performance. The estimates are subject to risk and uncertainty. Financial short-term horizon in break-even is a limitation of long-range planning. The benefits realized from certain expenditures, such as capital expenditure and research are not likely to be realized during the period of time encompassed. "Break-even would not justify these expenditures, though they are necessary", says Van Horne.[1] But Moore, C.L.[2] and Manes, R.[3], have suggested for the use of B/E graph for investment decisions. The purpose is one of sensitivity analysis (see note) the effect on net present value of different annual outputs can be seen from Exhibit 7.15.

The limitations of cost-volume-profit analysis come because of the assumptions on which it is based. Some of the assumptions are questionable e.g., that production and sales will be same or sales mix is unchanged. Some assumptions are valid for the analysis but of no use. Actually, its use depends upon how it is constructed and applied. It is advisable to set up a series of analysis each one based on a different set of assumptions.

Utility of Break-Even Analysis

(a) *Flow of Funds*: The B/E analysis can be used for the entire company or for a particular product or division. With minor modifications, break-even analysis can be put on a cash basis instead of a profit basis. In that case from total fixed costs, deduct the non-cash expenses like depreciation first. The figure so arrived will be cash fixed costs. Cash

1. *Financial Management and Policy*, 5th Ed. Prentice Hall, p. 778.
2. 'Accounting Review', 1962, p. 721.
3. *Journal of Accounting Research*, 1966, p. 87.

Note: Sensitivity analysis is a "what-if" technique that essentially asks how a result will be changed if the original predicted data are not achieved. In the context of cost-volume-profit analysis answer questions such as "What will net income be if volume changes from that originally predicted?"

break-even analysis, though does not represent cash flows, yet provides a picture of the flow of funds from operations.

(b) *Profit Planning*: The management can know immediately answers relating to questions about income in relation to volume. For example, the difference between contribution and fixed cost will tell the pretax income expected on particular amount of sales. The change in revenue multiplied by the percentage contribution gives the idea of decrease in pretax income as a result of decrease in sales. See illustrative example.

(c) *Decision-making*: In deciding whether to add to the present capacity to meet a desired increase in sales, the expected higher income and increased cost should be compared. The fixed costs will go up. If variable costs do not go down, then B/E analysis tells us that the risk of loss is greater and so expansion will not be desirable.

(d) *Profit Performances*: Satisfaction with a higher rate of return can conceal cost increases that are creeping in with increased revenue. So, B/E analysis will help to find whether percentage of income on sales has increased, due to more sales, at the same rate or not. See illustrative example.

(e) *Price Tool*: Break-even is a pricing tool i.e., a cost plus pricing. It is desirable to compute break-even points for several different selling prices. The total demand which actually exists at different prices should be estimated. By comparing market demand and B/E point at each unit price, we can find which price will maximize profits. Following example illustrates the point, with variable cost ₹ 30 per unit and fixed costs ₹ 250.

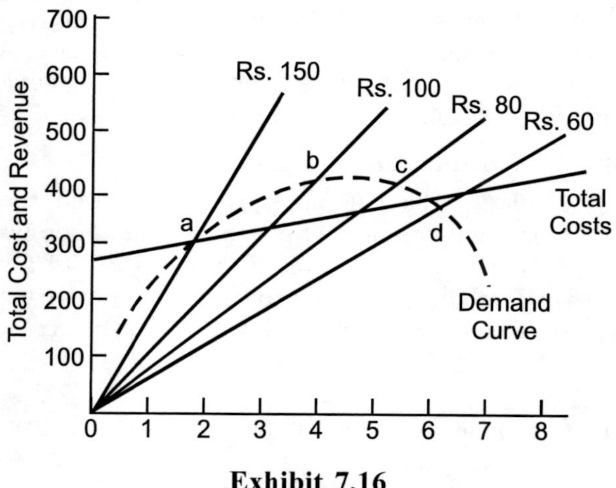

Exhibit 7.16

So, the price should be ₹ 100.

Unit Price ₹	Market Demand at the price In units	Total Revenue ₹	Total ₹	B.E. Point	Total Profit ₹
60	7	420	460	8.3	– 40
80	6	480	430	5.0	50
100	5	500	400	3.6	100
150	2	300	310	2.1	– 10

The above data is shown in Exhibit 7.16.

(f) *Goal Programming*: The technique of linear programming can be looked upon as extension of break-even analysis. Charnes Cooper and Ijiri applied goal programming, a variation of the linear programming technique to the class of problem with which break-even analysis is commonly concerned. A single break-even goal for any firm can be incorporated into a goal programming model. A break-even goal is not, of course, essential to goal programming.

Operating Leverage

Leverage is defined as relative change in profit due to change is sales. Operating leverage is defined as the extent to which fixed costs are used in operations. It tells the ratio of fixed costs and variable costs. The degree of operating leverage is the percentage change in operating income that results from a specific percentage charge in units sold. This provides a specific measure of how much operating leverage a firm is using. Break-even analysis provides a graphic view of the effects of the changes in sales on profits, the degree of operating leverage presents the algebraic terms.

A firm has a high degree of operating leverage if it uses a greater amount of fixed costs as compared to variable costs. If the firm incurs a greater amount of variable costs and smaller amount of fixed costs, the firm has a low degree of operating leverage. In case of high degree of operating leverage in a firm, profits will increase at a faster rate than the increase in sales and the firm will suffer a greater loss if the sales fall. So, highly leveraged alternative is more risky.

Operating leverage occurs any time a firm has fixed costs that must be met regardless of volume. In the very long run, of course, all costs are variable. So, this analysis also is concerned with short run. One of the best examples of operating leverage is in the airline industry, where a large portion of total costs are fixed. Beyond a certain break-even load portion of total costs are fixed. Beyond a certain break-even load factor, each additional passenger represents a straight profit.

The degree of operating leverage can be found by formula—

$$\text{Degree of O/L at } x \text{ units} = \frac{\text{Percentage change in profit}}{\text{Percentage change in output}}$$

Or

Contribution ÷ Net Income

$$\text{D.O.L. at } x \text{ units} = \frac{x\,(\text{P} - \text{V})}{x\,(\text{P} - \text{V}) - \text{F}}$$

P = Price
V = Variable cost per unit
F = Fixed costs

Suppose we want to find the degree of operating leverage of 25,000 units in Example 1, then

$$\text{D.O.L. at 25,000 units} = \frac{25{,}000\,(₹\,40 - ₹\,25)}{25{,}000\,(₹\,40 - ₹\,25) - 3{,}00{,}000} = 5$$

Or

$$\frac{3{,}75{,}000}{75{,}000} = 5$$

The further the level of output is from break-even point, the lower the degree of operating leverage.

C.V.P. and Uncertainty

Since the future sales as well as price, fixed cost and variable cost are uncertain, the accountant must assess probability distributions for these quantities. The standard deviation of expected sales and the ratio of the standard deviation to expected value must be calculated. Jaedicke and Robichek (1964) suggested a better approach to analyzing uncertainty of sales volume would be to use a continuous probability distribution. Often a normal curve-shaped distribution provides an appropriate description of the uncertainty of sales volume would be to use a continuous probability distribution. The construction of normal curve requires knowledge of mean (expected value) and standard deviation.

QUESTIONS

1. (a) If selling price is less than average cost of a unit, the firm should stop operating because it will incur losses.
   Is this statement true? Explain.
   (b) Explain the statement: "It is often said that if you lower the price, the break-even point for your business increases."

2. Fill in the blanks for each of the following independent situations:

	(a) Selling price per unit	(b) Variable cost per unit ₹	(c) Units sold ₹	(d) Contribution margin ₹	(e) Fixed costs ₹	(f) Net income ₹
1.	5	2	–	3,000	500	–
2.	5	–	2,000	4,000	–	3,000
3.	–	6	4,000	12,000	4,000	–
4.	8	5	1,000	–	–	2,500
5.	10	4	–	–	600	3,000
6.	–	6	1,000	2,000	–	1,200

3. The Singhania Company currently sells its one product for ₹ 12 and variable cost is ₹ 8. Fixed costs are ₹ 32,000. You are required to answer each question separately.
   (a) What is the break-even in rupees and units?
   (b) Calculate the new break-even point in each case if
   (i) fixed costs increase by 155, (ii) variable cost decline by 20%, (iii) selling price increase by 10%, and (iv) if all (i), (ii) and (iii) events happen together.
   (c) What sales in rupees are required to earn a ₹ 50,000 profit based on original data?
   (d) If sales are 10,000 units what is the profit?
4. (a) What is the effect on break-even point if there is increase or decrease in selling price, variable cost and fixed costs? What are the limitations of break-even analysis?
   (b) Define Margin of Safety.
5. The Registrar of FORTIS Hospital is considering methods of providing X-ray treatments to patients. The hospital now refers patients to a nearby city clinic and each treatment costs the patient ₹ 25. The hospital now refers about 120 patients monthly to the other clinic. If the clinic decides to provide the treatment, it will have to rent a machine for ₹ 1,000 per month and hire a technician for ₹ 800 per month. Variable costs are ₹ 5 per treatment. Find the profit or loss if the City Clinic charges the same fee. Also find the B.E. point.
6. The Vimpi Restaurant is now open from 8 AM to 8 PM, seven days a week. The manager is considering to open it 24 hours as it is near the railway station. He estimates that additional sales would be ₹ 20,000 per week. Additional staff, utilities and items would cost ₹ 9,000 per week. Cost of goods sold, the only variable cost, is 40% of sales.

   You are required to answer:
   (a) Should the restaurant open 24 hours?
   (b) What are break-even sales for additional hours of operation?

7. Ramanand Sagar, the Chairman of Sagar Films Ltd., a leading film producer, is trying to decide on compensation scheme for Amitabh Bachchan, the biggest star attraction. Mr. Bachchan is going to star in "Adi Ramayan". For starring in a picture he normally gets ₹ 8,00,000 plus 10% of the receipts to the producer. The producer normally receives 40% of the total paid admissions wherever the picture is shown. Bachchan is very optimistic about the film and has offered to do the picture for ₹ 3,00,000 plus 20% of the receipts to the producer. Cost of producing other than Bachchan's salary will be ₹ 25,00,000. You are required to find the break-even receipts to the producer under each compensation scheme proposed. If total paid admissions are expected to be ₹ 1,00,00,000, what will be the income to the producer under each compensation scheme?
8. "India Today" a leading magazine, takes a promotion programme to boost circulation. They want to run a contest with prizes worth ₹ 50,000 in the year. The subscription price is ₹ 2.40 per year for 12 issues and price at book stalls is 50 Paise per copy. Variable cost per copy is Paisa 10. Monthly fixed costs, without prizes, are ₹ 40,000. Find:
   (a) If there are 3,00,000 subscribers, how many copies must be sold on book stalls to break-even per month?
   (b) Assuming the subscriptions could not be affected by the contest, by how many issues per month book stalls increase sales to break-even on the contest?
   (c) Assume that 5,000 additional subscriptions and 20,000 additional copies at book stalls and increase is fixed by ₹ 2,000 per month, should the contest be sponsored?
9. Hilton Hotel has annual fixed costs applicable to room of ₹ 15,00,000 for a 300-room hotel with average daily room rates of ₹ 40 and average variable costs of ₹ 6 for each room rented. The hotel operates 365 days a year. Income-tax rate is 30%. You are to find the number of rooms the hotel must rent to earn a net income after tax of ₹ 10,00,000 and compute the break-even point in terms of the number of rooms rented.
10. A company makes two products, H and L. Both products are being sold at ₹ 20 per unit and monthly volume is 3,000 units for each. H has a variable cost of ₹ 16 per unit and L of ₹ 6 per unit. The manager believes that volume of either product could be increased by 20% if the prices were reduced by 10%. Compute that effects on monthly contribution margin if the proposed price cut were implemented for each product. Should either price be cut?
11. D.T.C. charges ₹ 10 for all rides on its buses. The city of Delhi has a quite good number of persons over the age of 65, whose income is quite lower than others. The Lt. Governor proposes that D.T.C.

should charge ₹ 5 for persons over the age of 65, whose income is quite lower than others. At present 20,00,000 ride per month on D.T.C. buses, about 10% of which are more than 65 years of age. The Lt. Governor estimates that the decrease in bus fare for older persons would increase their use by 50%. Other users would remain the same. How much will it cost per month for D.T.C. to reduce the fare? If the reduction is granted, how much would regular fare have to be increased, assuming the D.T.C. is operating at break-even?

12. A company makes two products, called B and T, with following details:

	B		T		
	Units	Amount	Units	Amount	Total
		₹		₹	₹
Sales	10,000	10,000	7,500	10,000	20,000
Costs:					
Fixed		2,000		5,600	7,600
Variable		6,000		3,000	9,000
		8,000		8,600	16,600
Income before tax		2,000		14,000	3,400

1. Find the break-even in units for B, assuming that facilities are not jointly used.
2. The break-even in Rupees for T.
3. Assuming that consumers purchase composite units of four B and three T, find the composite unit contribution and the break-even point.
4. If B and T become one to one complement and there is no change in cost function, what would be break-even volume.
5. If a composite unit is defined as one B and one T, calculate the composite contribution margin ratio.

[Hint (1) 5,000 units, (2) ₹ 8,000, (3) ₹ 4.40 and 6,909 units for B and 5,182 units for T, (4) ₹ 10,858, and (5) 4/7.]

8

Special Purpose Analysis

GROSS PROFIT ANALYSIS AND SEGMENTAL ANALYSIS

The special purpose analysis can be made by break-even analysis. Other analyses that are representative of special purpose analysis are gross profit analysis, segmental analysis and capital expenditure analysis. We shall consider the first two in this chapter.

Gross Profit Analysis

Gross profit is the difference between cost of goods sold and sales. The cost of goods sold is affected by increase or decrease in (a) cost elements i.e. material, labour and overhead costs or (b) changes in sales prices of products or (c) changes in volume sold. The volume is affected by changes in number of units sold or by change in products mix or sales mix. The gross profit analysis can be made either on the basis of previous year's figures or on the basis of Budgets and standard costs. The prices and costs of previous year (or any year selected as a base for the comparisons) are taken as the basis for the computation of variance (i.e. difference).

At the outset we shall limit the analysis of a profit change to the gross margin and assume that a single product is being manufactured and sold we take the following data:

Example 1

	2019 ₹	2020 ₹
Sales	1,00,000	10,800
Cost of goods sold	60,000	6,750
No. of Units	1,00,000	9,000
Selling price per unit	10	12
Cost per unit	6	7.50
Gross profit per unit	4	4.50

Note. If price and volume factors are to be separated, two fundamental principles must be kept in mind: (1) If the effect of a price change is being found, the volume must be kept constant, (2) If the effect of volume change is being calculated, the price must be kept constant. This is the secret to profit analysis.

Taking 2019 as a base, we convert the figure of 2020 i.e., the units of 2020 at cost and selling price of 2019. It is as follows:

Adjusted figures of 2020

	₹	
Sales	90,000	(90,000 × 10)
Cost	54,000	(90,000 × 6)
Profit	36,000	
Price changes:		
Increase in selling price:		
2020 sales at 2020 prices	1,08,000	
2020 sales at 2019 price	90,000	
Increase in gross profit	18,000	
Decrease in unit cost price:		
2020 volume at 2020 cost	67,500	
2020 volume at 2019 cost	54,000	
Decrease in gross profit	13,500	
Net increase in gross profit due to price changes	= 4,500	
OR		
Increase in selling price 2.0 × 9,000	= 18,000	
Decrease in cost 1.50 × 90,000	= 13,500	
	4,500	
Volume changes:		
Decrease in gross profit:		
2019 sales at 2019 prices	= 1,00,000	
2020 sales at 2019 prices	= 90,000	
Decrease in sales revenue	10,000	
Gross margin 40% of ₹ 10,000	4,000	
OR		
Gross margin 2020	40,000	
Gross margin adjusted	36,000	
	4,000	
OR		
1000 units @ 2019 price	10,000	
1000 units @ 2019 cost	6,000	
	4,000	

If in the above example, the number of units produced and sold is not given, the adjusted sales revenue can be found as follows:

Increase in price = 20% i.e. 120% + 1,08,000 = ₹ 90,000 or 5/6th of 1,08,000.

The total increase in gross profit of ₹ 500 can be now summarized. Decrease in sales volume ₹ 4,000 + Increase in cost = ₹ 13,500.

Increase in selling price = ₹ 18,000 i.e. 18,000 – 17,500 = ₹ 500.

Gross Profit Based on Budgeted and Standard Costs

To explain this we take an example where absorption cost concept is applied and analysis of the difference between the budgeted and reported margin is made. Further we consider an example where many products are being manufactured and sold. Consider the following:[1]

Example 2

Budgeted Income Statement (Extract)

Products	Units	Sales Price per unit ₹	Amount ₹	Cost Price per unit ₹	Amount ₹	Gross Profit (Amount) ₹
A	6,000	15	90,000	12	72,000	18,000
B	3,500	12	42,000	10	35,000	7,000
C	1,000	10	10,000	8.75	8,750	1,250
	10,500	13.52[2]	1,42,000	11.02[2]	1,15,750	26,250

Actual Income Statement (Extract)

Products	Units	Sales Price per unit ₹	Amount ₹	Cost Price per unit ₹	Amount ₹	Gross Profit (Amount) ₹
A	5,112	16	81,792	13.98	71,466	10,326
B	4,208	12	50,496	9.72	40,902	9,594
C	1,105	9	9,945	8.83	9,757	188
	10,425	13.64[2]	1,42,233	11.71[2]	1,22,125	20,108

Now we convert actual units at budgeted prices and costs. Here consider budgeted figures as base for adjustment as in Example 1.

1. Adapted from Matz and Usry, *ibid.,* p. 617.
2. Weighted average.

Adjusted Income Statement (Extract)

Products	Units	Unit Sales Price ₹	Unit Cost Amount ₹	Price ₹	Amount ₹	Gross Profit (Amount) ₹
A	5,112	15	76,680	12	61,344	15,336
B	4,208	12	50,496	10	42,080	8,416
C	1,105	10	11,050	8.75	9,669	1,381
			1,38,226		1,13,093	25,133

The difference of ₹ 6,142 between budgeted gross profit and actual gross profit is due to changes in sales prices, sales volume, sales mix and costs. The variances will be calculated as follows:

Price Changes

Sales Price Variance:

Actual Sales ₹ 1,42,233 – Adjusted Sales ₹ 1,38,226 = ₹ 4,007 (Favourable)

Cost Price Variance:

Actual Cost ₹ 1,22,125 – Adjusted Cost ₹ 1,13,093 = ₹ 9,032 (Unfavourable)

Net unfavourable price variance or decrease in gross profit = ₹ 5,025.

Volume Changes

Sales Volume Variance:

Adjusted Sales ₹ 1,38,226 – Budgeted Sales ₹ 1,42,000 = 3,774 (U)

Cost Volume Variance:

Adjusted Cost ₹ 1,13,093 – Budgeted Cost ₹ 1,15,750 = 2,657 (F)

Net unfavourable volume variance or decrease in gross profit = ₹ 1,117

Total decrease in gross profit ₹ 5,025 + 1,117 = ₹ 6,142.

Sales Mix Variance

	₹
Actual sales at budgeted prices	1,38,226
Actual sales units at budgeted cost	1,13,093
Difference	25,133
The gross profit of actual units that should be at budgeted gross profit rate per unit (10,425 × ₹ 2.50)	26.062.50
Sales Mix Variance	928.50

Final Sales Volume Variance

The final sales volume variance is the difference in the number of actual units and budgeted units sold multiplied by the budgeted average gross profit per unit.

Actual sales units – Budgeted sales units = 75 units

Budgeted average gross profit per unit = ₹ 2.50

Unfavourable final sales volume variance = ₹ 187.50

The sales mix variance and final sales mix variance above is detailed analysis of net volume variance i.e.

₹ 187.50 + ₹ 929.50 = ₹ 1,117.

Segmental Analysis

In large organisations, particularly selling more than one type of product or service, the overall operation is broken down into divisions, departments or product lines e.g. a super bazar or market. The analysis of the operations of such business sub-divisions is called segmental analysis. It is primarily useful for evaluating the profitability of the division, department or product. Sometimes separate accounts and financial reports are prepared for each segment.

Segmental analysis can be made for product planning, product pricing and advertising. Take an example of a company selling three products:

Example 3

	A ₹	B ₹	C ₹	Total ₹
Sales	4,500	4,000	2,000	10,500
Fixed expenses	2,000	1,000	1,500	4,500
Variable expenses	500	2,000	1,000	3,500
Total expenses	2,500	3,000	2,500	8,000
Net income or loss	2,000	1,000	(500)	2,500

Product Planning: It seems that product C should be discontinued because it brings loss. But on close analysis product C is contributing ₹ 1,000 i.e. difference of sales and variable expenses. If we exclude products C then the net income ₹ 1,500 because fixed expenses of ₹ 4,500 will have to be incurred. It will be like this.

Sales ₹ 8,500 minus fixed expenses ₹ 4,500 and minus variable expenses ₹ 2,500.

Product Pricing: In the above example suppose the company produced 1,000 units of product C (full capacity 1,500 units) and total expenses at full capacity are ₹ 3,000 and fixed and variable expenses being equal. Suppose there is an order for product C @ ₹ 2 per unit for 500 units. The company is to make a decision whether to accept the order because the cost of C is ₹ 2.50 per unit. At first it appears it should not accept the order. But following analysis reveals different result.

	Product C only		All Products	
	At present ₹	Including Order ₹	At present ₹	After the order ₹
Sales	2,000	3,000	10,500	11,500
Fixed expenses	1,500	1,500	4,500	4,500
Variable expenses	1,000	1,500	3,500	4,000
Total expenses	2,500	3,000	8,000	8,500
Net profit (loss)	(500)	Nil	2,500	3,000

Advertising: Segmental analysis will reveal whether advertising is useful in pushing the sales or not *i.e.* if a decision is between more sales by incurring advertising expenditure or accepting the order at low price. Suppose advertisement expenditure is ₹ 200, then the position will be as under if the sale price after advertising is ₹ 2 per unit.

Product C

	Product C		
	Present Position ₹	After order ₹	After advertising ₹
Sales	2,000	3,000	3,000
Fixed expenses	1,500	1,500	1,500
Variable expenses	1,000	1,500	1,700
Total expenses	2,500	3,000	3,200
Net income (loss)	(500)	(Nil)	(200)

QUESTIONS

1. Assuming that a firm makes and sell only one product, prepare from the following data a detailed analysis of the causes of the ₹ 7,960 change in gross margin:

	2020		2019	
	Amount ₹	Per unit ₹	Amount ₹	Per unit ₹
Sales	1,12,200	10.20	1,00,000	10
Cost of sales	64,240	5.84	60,000	6
Gross margin	47,960	4.36	40,000	4

2. The M Company, which owns and operates an office building, is considering putting certain concessions in the main lobby. The investment in equipment, which would last 10 years would be ₹ 2,000. An accounting study produces the following estimates on an average annual basis.

   Salaries ₹ 7,000, Cost merchandise sold ₹ 40,000.
   Licenses and Taxes ₹ 200 Share of Heat, light ₹ 500.

Pro rata building Depreciation ₹ 1,000. Concession advertising ₹ 100. Share of company administrative expense ₹ 400, Sales ₹ 49,000.

Assume that as an alternative a catering company has offered to rent the space for ₹ 750 per year for 10 years and to put in and operate the same concessions at no cost to the company. Heat and light are to be furnished by the office building at no cost to the catering company. Give your advice to the company.

3. The Trading Account of Mr. Baniya for 2019 showed:

	₹
Sales (90,500 units)	7,60,200
Cost of goods sold	4,52,500
Gross profit	3,07,700

For 2015, he forecasts a sales volume of 100,000 units at a sales price of ₹ 8.20 per unit. For this change of activity, variable costs are estimated to be ₹ 4.80 per unit. No fixed costs are included in the cost of goods sold.

You have to make an analysis of the variation in gross profit between two years indicating the effects of changes in sales price, sales volume and unit costs.

4. Messrs Rajiv Girish presented the following, who are engaged in grinding business:

	2019 ₹	2020 ₹	Increase (decrease) ₹
Net Sales	8,40,000	8,91,000	51,000
Cost of goods sold	9,45,000	6,88,500	2,56,500
Gross profit (loss)	(1,05,000)	2,02,500	3,07,500

On 1-1-2020 the sale price was increased from ₹ 8 to ₹ 11 per kilo. On the same day, a new machinery was placed in operation which reduced the cost of operation from ₹ 9 to ₹ 8.50 per kilo. Ending inventories, costed on Life basis, did not change. You are to analysis the effects of changes in price, volume and price-volume factors on sales and cost of goods sold.

9
Capital Budgeting

Introduction

Investment decisions in a big firm are concerned with allocation of funds, both short term and long term, to different types of assets. Capital budgeting is concerned with making decision about long term (fixed) assets. Long term effects, substantialness commitments, irreversible decisions determining the profit capacity are basic features of capital budgeting. However, capital budgeting deal with future uncertainly, time value of money and problem of measurement of future cash flows. There are two decisions (a) replacement decision or expansion decision diversification decision (b) mutually extrusive decisions in accept or reject. Three steps (i) estimation of costs and benefits of proposal (ii) estimate required rate of return (iii) using techniques cash flows may be initial cash out flow, subsequent cash inflows and out flows and last cash inflow. Cash flows are considered before tax charges Allocated overheads are ignored.

Capital budgeting is the process of deciding whether or not to invest in a project whose costs and benefits are spread over several years. The problem is how to relate the benefits to the costs in a reasonable manner with a view to maximise the shareholders' wealth. There are many methods by which the stream of cash flows or future earnings can be related to the cost of obtaining them. Four famous methods we shall discuss here.

(a) Cash Payback Method.

(b) Accounting Rate of Return Method (or Return on Investment Method).

(c) Present Value Method.

(d) Internal Rate of Return Method (or Yield Method).

The first two are traditional methods and the other two are called time adjusted methods.

Cash Payback Method

The meaning of 'cash payback' of an investment is the period for time required to recover initial investment. Thus, if an investment of ₹ 10,000 generates ₹ 5,000 in NET cash proceeds in each of the first two years of use, its cash payback period is two years. Firms accept or reject investment in any project according to the length of their payback period.

An investment with a payback period of four years may be accepted and an investment with a payback period of five years may be rejected. On the basis of payback method alone a firm should not accept or reject an investment. This method is quite old in use. Consider the following example.

Example 1

Investment Proposed	Initial outlay (period 0) ₹	Cash proceeds (period 1) ₹	Cash proceeds (period 2) ₹
A	10,000	10,000	—
B	10,000	1,000	11,000
C	10,000	5,762	5,762

According to payback period method investment A is most desirable because its payback is one year. But the weakness[1] of this position is that A returns its original investment and that is all. This method fails (i) to take into consideration the life of the investment after the payback period and (ii) to consider the timings of cash proceeds during the payback period. From timing point of view the cash inflows of C are more desirable because they come earlier than B, though the payback period of both is the same. Payback should only be used as one of the several constraints in accepting a project rather than as a sole method.

Accounting Rate of Return Method

Under this method, also called **financial statement method,** the rate of return on investment is found. Whichever investment has more rate of return that one is accepted. This is found out by forecasted average income divided by the average investment.

The rate of return for B and C are as follows:

Investment	Outlay ₹	Total Proceeds ₹	Net Income (after Tax & Depreciation ₹	Average income ₹	Average Investment ₹	Rate of Return
B	10,000	12,000	2,000	1,000	5,000	20%
C	10,000	11,524	1,524	762	5,000	15.2%

Both adjusted and unadjusted rate of return are used. The rate of return on average investment is affected by depreciation method used. In calculating average investment the scrap value of the asset must be deducted from total outlay. Sometimes some people may divide the average income by initial investment instead of average investment.

1. The payback can be used to determine a usable measure of rate of return, if net cash flows are uniform, and the economic life of assets is least twice the payback period. Payback reciprocal gives a true rate of return.
Payback Reciprocal = 1/Payback

The rate of return shows that B is more desirable than C. But this method like the earlier one fails to take into consideration the timing of the proceeds. A rupee of proceeds in period 2 is given the same weight as a rupee in period 1. This is the reason that this method should not be used as a general method of making investment decisions.

Present Value Method

What is present value? Suppose you want to buy a table which costs ₹ 700 one year from now and the rate of interest (also called discount factor) on one year deposit is 6%. How much you should invest now so that you get ₹ 700 after one year. This answer is given by following formula:

$$X = PV\ (1 + r)$$

X = amount of money you wish to have, PV = the amount you invest now,

r = rate of interest. So by putting values we get:

$$₹\ 700 = PV\ (1 + 1.06) = \frac{700}{106} = ₹\ 660.38.$$

₹ 660.38 is called present value and ₹ 700 future value i.e. ₹ 660.38 invested @ 6% P.A will be come ₹ 700. In other words, present value of ₹ 700 to be received at the end of one year @ 6% is ₹ 660.38. For finding present value of any amount, present value tables exist. One is for uneven series of amount and the other for even amounts, often called annuities. So to find present value of any amount, we multiply the amount by present value factor. The P.V. factor is found from the P.V. tables, depending on whether the amount is even or uneven. **Such tables are given at the end of the chapter.** Table A relates to uneven amounts and Table B to even amounts (annuities).

Calculation of Net Present Value: Under the present value method, cash outlays and cash inflows are both discounted back to the present period using an appropriate discount (rate of interest)[1] rate. If the net present value of the cash flow is positive the investment is accepted and if negative it is rejected normally. Take an example: A firm wants to invest ₹ 10,000 for one year in a project, discount rate 10% and the net cash inflow from the project is ₹ 11,000. Then the present value of ₹ 11,000 is ₹ 10,000 (11,000 × 0.9091). The net present value is zero. This means if firm invests there is no problem and it will not have to borrow. If the cash inflows are ₹ 20,000 instead of ₹ 10,000 then the present value of ₹ 20,000 is ₹ 18,182 and net present value (NPV) is ₹ 8,182. This thing can be expressed in either of the two ways:

(a) The present value of ₹ 20,000 @ 10% discount factor is ₹ 18,182 or (b) If the firm borrows ₹ 18,182 @ 10% interest, the total

1. The P.V. method does not calculate rate of return. It assumes a desired or required minimum earnings rate, often called cut off rate.

outlay will be ₹ 20,000 (₹ 18,182 + interest 1,818). This outlay will be equal to cash inflow of ₹ 20,000.

The N.P.V. is estimated profit of any investment. It is also the amount the firm could pay in excess of actual purchase price or cost of an investment.

In Example 1, the N.P.V. of three investments will be as follows:

Investment	P.V. @ 10%	Outlay ₹	N.P.V.
A	₹ 10,000 × 0.9091 = 9,091	10,000	-909
B	₹ 1,000 × 0.9091 + 1,100 × 0.8264 = 10,000	10,000	0
C	₹ 5,762 × 1.7355 = 10,000	10,000	0

It means investments B and C are equally desirable. With a discount rate of less than 10%. B will have a higher N.P.V. At discount rate higher than 10%, C has higher net present value, though both have negative N.P.V.

Internal Rate of Return (Yield) Method

The term 'internal rate of return' is used in three senses. It is the rate of growth of an investment. The second interpretation is that it is the highest rate of interest that an investor could pay for borrowed funds to finance the investment. The third interpretation is that the rate of discount (interest) that equates the N.P.V. of cash inflows[1] to zero. This rate is found by trial and error method by using different rates of interest. That rate, out of these different rates, which equates the cash outlay and present value of inflows to zero is the rate of return or the yield of the investment. This method is also called adjusted rate of return or discounted cash flow method.

Example 2

A machine costs ₹ 1,000. The net cash inflows for five years are ₹ 600, ₹ 50, ₹ 50 and ₹ 300. Find the I.R.R.

We try 10% and 11% discount rates.

Year	10% Discount Rate Cash inflows ₹	Discount factor	P.V.	11% Discount Rate Discount factor	P.V.
1	600	0.909	545	0.901	546
2	500	0.826	413	0.812	406
3	50	0.751	38	0.731	36
4	50	0.683	34	0.659	32
5	300	0.621	186	0.594	178
	1,500		1,216		1,198

1. The term cash inflow is a misnomer. It does not refer to increase in cash. It should be referred to as an increase or inflow of working capital.

Difference

P.V. required ₹ 1,000 >

P.V. at 10% ₹ 1,216 $\left.\begin{matrix}216\\198\end{matrix}\right]$ 1%

P.V. at 11% ₹ 1,198 >

Lower rate discount +

$$\left(\text{Difference in discount rates} \times \frac{\text{P.V. at lower discount rate}}{\text{P.V. at higher discount rate}}\right)$$

The actual rate is: 10% + $\left(1\% \times \frac{216}{198}\right)$ = 11.09% or 12%. Approx.

Exact I.R.R. can be found by COMPUTER. The rate of return of Project B and C in Example 1 is 10% and of A is zero.

CASH FLOW ESTIMATION

The computation of cash flow for capital budgeting is an important basis. The capital-budgeting analysis could be based on the working capital or the change in funds. The two methods may be equated to each other if debtors and creditors of the future are recorded today at their present value.

The cash flow procedure assumes that the moment of cash payment or receipt is the moment at which the change in financial position associated with the investment should be measured. The concept of cash flow is simple. In each time period (e.g. a year) the change in cash account caused by investing or not investing, in the asset or project under consideration, is to be estimated. The net present value of the investment whether calculated on cash flow or funds flow, will be the same. For example, assume in the first year of investment the sales are ₹ 10,000, all credit sales, to be collected at the end of second year. The cash flow and fund flow technique will record different flows, but the net present value will be the same. Both the approaches can be reconciled, the cash flow approach is used almost exclusively for investments since it is easier to apply.

A complication arises in the computation of cash flows when a new process is being considered to replace the present process (see Example 10). Should absolute revenue be used (revenues that would be earned if there was no present process) or the marginal revenues (the incremental revenues that would be earned in excess of, what could be earned using the present process)? One possibility is to calculate present value of each alternative method and choose the method with highest present value. This will solve the question whether absolute or marginal revenues are appropriate.

Cash Flows—Effect of Taxes and Depreciation

The cash flows that are estimated should be on an after-tax basis. This means that the taxable income of each period must be found. The amount of income-tax arising because of the investment should be computed and included as a decrease of cash proceeds or as an increase in liability. An interesting thing may happen when we include in the analysis both time value of money and taxes. Suppose a company has to incur ₹ 2 to collect ₹ 5 from a debtor in next two years. The discount rate is 10%. It will be better for the company not to collect the amount and let it become bad debt. It claims the bad debt as a tax deduction. The P.V. of the amount will be ₹ 2.48 [(₹ 5 – ₹ 2) (0.8264)]. If tax rate is 52%, the P.V. of tax deduction will be 0.52 (5) = ₹ 2.60.

In computing income-tax the depreciation plays an important role because tax will be charged on income after depreciation. The depreciation, a non-cash charge, will be added back to the cash inflow. There are various methods of depreciation. Complications arise in computing Income-taxes if the firm has used accelerated depreciation like sum-of-the-years' digits method. Moreover, the firm can switch over to other method of depreciation at any time. This may give rise to further difficulty. It is difficult to generalize as to which procedure will be better, because the answer depends on the amount of salvage of the asset, life of investment and the rate of discount. It is more desirable for a firm to adopt that depreciation method which results in the highest present value. Davidson and Drake found that the sum-of-the-years' digits method maximised the present value of future tax deductions, other things being equal, for longer-lived asset lives.

It is the amount of depreciation allowable and Income-tax Act is to be the relevant figure and not the amount of depreciation shown in the books of account.

From the above discussion we find that some of the difficulties in the use of P.V. method come from the problem of prediction of relevant cash flows. The rate of discount or cost of money for a firm is another difficulty to be applied to future cash flows, because it is not easily determined. One suggestion is that this rate "should be closer to a default-free interest rate than to that rate required by equity shareholders".[1] The firm should not use single discount rate for two problems (time and risk). The above discussion about Income-tax and depreciation is clear from the following example.

Example 3

A firm wants to install a machine whose cost price is ₹ 8,000 and installation expenses are ₹ 2,000. Its estimated life is five years and the rate of return is 10%. The firm pays 50% tax. The expected revenue from machine will be ₹ 4,500 in each year for five years, after which it will be of no salvage value. Calculate the net present value if (a) straight line method (b) sum-of-the-years' digits method of depreciation is used.

---

1. H. Bierman, Jr. and S. Smidt, *Capital Budgeting Decision*, 1985, Macmillan.

Solution

Net Cash Flow After-tax on Straight Line Basis

Cash flows before tax ₹	Dep. ₹	I.B.T. ₹	Tax ₹	N.I. ₹	Net cash flows after tax ₹
4,500	2,000	2,500	1,250	1,250	3,250
4,500	2,000	2,500	1,250	1,250	3,250
4,500	2,000	2,500	1,250	1,250	3,250
4,500	2,000	2,500	1,250	1,250	3,250
4,500	2,200	2,500	1,250	1,250	3,250

N.P.V. = ₹ 3,250 × 3.791 = ₹ 12,321
Cash outlay = ₹ 10,000
N.P.V. = ₹ 2,321

Net Cash Flow After-tax on sum-of-the-years' Digits Basis

Cash flows before tax ₹	Dep. ₹	I.B.T. ₹	Tax ₹	N.I. ₹	Net cash flows after tax ₹
4,500	1,500	3,000	1,500	1,500	3,000
4,500	1,200	3,300	1,650	1,650	2,850
4,500	900	3,600	1,800	1,800	2,700
4,500	600	3,900	1,950	1,950	2,550
4,500	300	4,200	2,100	2,100	2,400

N.I. = Net Income, I.B.T. = Income before tax; Dep. = Depreciation.

Depreciation formula is $\frac{5}{15} \times 4500$; $\frac{4}{15} \times 4500$ and so on

Net cash flow after tax = N.I. plus depreciation.

	₹	
N.P.V. =	3,000 × 0.909	= 2727.0
	2,850 × 0.826	= 2354.1
	2,700 × 0.751	= 2027.7
	2,550 × 0.683	= 1741.6
	2,400 × 0.621	= 1490.4
		10,340.8
	Cash outlay	10,000.0
	N.P.V.	340.8

Non-constant Cash Flows

The present value of an investments can be found estimating the cash flows for each period. A firm may wish to know the present value of cash flows with different assumptions of rates of growth (or decay) applied to the projection of initial period. Following formula gives the present value of the positive cash flows assuming a continuous rate of growth:

$$\text{P.V.} = \frac{A}{r - g}$$

where A = cash flow of the first period, g = the rate of growth, r = rate of discount.

The cash flows taken here are on an after tax basis. It is assumed that there is constant rate of growth through time, cash flows continue forever and in growth situations r exceeds g.

Example 4

Suppose A = ₹ 100, g = 0.06, r = 0.10

$$\text{P.V.} = \frac{100}{0.10 - 0.06} = \frac{100}{0.04} = ₹\ 2{,}500$$

For decreasing cash flows we assume g = – 0.15, then

$$\text{P.V.} = \frac{100}{0.01 - (0.15)} = \frac{100}{0.25} = ₹\ 400.$$

If g = 0 (i.e. constant cash flows), then the above formula gives the P.V. of a perpetuity i.e.

$$\text{P.V.} = \frac{100}{0.10} = ₹\ 1{,}000.$$

Mutually Exclusive Investments

Those investments which compete with each other are called mutually exclusive investments. One investment can be considered if there are several investments in such a case. Suppose B and C are mutually exclusive investments. Both have equal life and same initial outlays. Assume both have 10% rate of return and cost of money 6%. Following are other details.

Example 5

Period	C Cash Flows ₹	P.V. factor (6%) ₹	P.V. ₹	B Cash Flows ₹	P.V.
0	(10,000)	1.000	(10,000)	(10,000)	(10,000)
1	5,762	0.9434	5,436	1,000	943
2	5,762	0.8900	5,128	11,000	9,790
			564		733

The P.V. of B is greater than of C. The rate of return may not give correct ranking of mutually exclusive investment. As such the incremental cash flows gives the benefit to be gained by the firm from selecting one investment over another.

Incremental Cash Flows and their P.V.

Period	B ₹	C ₹	B–C ₹	P.V. factor ₹	P.V. ₹
0	(10,000)	(10,000)	0	1.000	0
1	1,000	5,762	(4,762)	0.9434	– 4493
2	11,000	5,762	5,238	0.8900	4,662
					169

If the rate of discount is 6%, then investment alternative B is better than C.

Scale Problem: Initial investments differ. Consider the following example:

Investment	Initial investment (0 year) ₹	Cash inflow (1 year) ₹	I.R.R.
X	(10,000)	12,000	20%
Y	(30,000)	35,000	16.7%

I.R.R. shows that X is better. If we assume that the difference between cash flows of X and Y are cash flows of Z i.e. outlay ₹ 20,000 and cash inflows ₹ 23,000 and I.R.R. 15%. If the rate of discount is 6% investment Z is better. The I.R.R. may be used to evaluate the incremental benefits, but here P.V. method is to be preferred. Some investments may have more than one rate of return. This occurs, if, after an outlay, there are periods of positive cash flows followed by periods of negative cash flows. This result can also occur with mutually exclusive investments. The P.V. method be used if an investment has more than one I.R.R.

Comparability of Life

In judging mutually exclusive investments with unequal lives, the P.V. method gives correct decision. It is necessary to consider what happens after the asset with shorter life is discarded. Consider the following example of two such investments.

Example 6

Investment	Initial outlay	Cash inflows			N.P.V. @ 10%
		I year	II year	III year	
	₹	₹	₹	₹	₹
C	(10,000)	12,000	—	—	909
D	(10,000)	5,000	5,000	5,000	2,434

D is better, but this analysis is not complete. If C is selected and after the end of first year again it is repeated both in second and third years, the N.P.V. will be ₹ 2,484. In that case C is desirable than D. So in mutually exclusive investment the reinvestment must be taken into account.

Investment C

Year	Cash outlay ₹	Cash inflow ₹	Net cash flow ₹
0	10,000	—	(10,000)
1	10,000	12,000	2,000
2	10,000	12,000	2,000
3	—	12,000	12,000

Amount P.V. factor @ 10% ₹
₹ 2,000 × 1.736 = 3,472
₹ 1,200 × 0.752 = 9,012
₹ 12,484 – ₹ 10,000 = ₹ 2,484.

Different Lives

If the lives of two or more mutually exclusive investments is different, there are three alternative methods of calculations and all will give same result. They are (a) Equivalent cost return per year method, (b) Return for perpetuity method, and (c) Present value of lowest common multiple (L.C.M.) of the life of investments. Take the following example of two investments.

Example 7

Investments Life	Expected years outlay	Initial inflow ₹	Net Cash ₹
E	3	10,000	5,000
F	8	30,000	6,500

Reinvestment in similar asset is assumed. Interest rate 10%. The N.P.V. is as follows:

₹ 5,000 × 2.4869 = ₹ 12,435 – ₹ 10,000 = ₹ 2,435
₹ 6,500 × 5.3349 = ₹ 34,477 – ₹ 30,000 = ₹ 4,677

The N.P.V. results can't be used because the lives of investments is not the same.

(a) *Annual cost-return equivalent*: The annual equivalent costs can be found by dividing the outlay by the annuity factor.

Net Benefit
For E it is = ₹ 4,021[1] Annual benefit ₹ 5,000 = ₹ 979
For F it is = ₹ 5,623[2] Annual benefit ₹ 6,500 = ₹ 877
So E is desirable.

(b) *Return for perpetuity method*: To find the value of perpetuity, multiply the Net benefits by the present value of perpetuity. The P.V. of

1. 10,000 ÷ 2.4869 = 4,021.
2. 30,000 ÷ 5.3349 = 5,623.

a perpetuity of ₹ 1 a period = 1/r.r = Rate of discount. So the returns for perpetuity for E and F are:

$$E = \frac{1}{(0.10)} \times 979 = ₹\ 9,790$$

$$F = \frac{1}{(0.10)} \times 877 = ₹\ 8,770$$

(c) *P.V. of L.C.M. period method*: The L.C.M. of the life of E and F is 24 years (8 years and 3 years). Compute the N.P.V. for 24 years (assuming that E is reinvested 8 times and F is invested 3 times) like we did for investments C and D in Example 6. E is more desirable by this method as well. Mostly method (B) is used because cash inflows are often difficult to associate with a given investment.

Present Value Index or Profitability Index

The P.V. Index or benefit cost ratio is a variation of present value method. It is used to rank investments, though the ranking is neither useful and nor correct. The formula for P.V. index is:

$$\text{P.I.} = \frac{\text{P.V. of cash inflows}}{\text{Initial cash outlay}}$$

The P.I. for investment E in Example 7 is $= \dfrac{12,345}{10,000} = 1.243$

If P.I. is greater than one, the investment must be accepted, otherwise not, so net P.I. in our example is 1.243 – 1.0 = 0.243. The investment is desirable. This rule is for an independent investment. The second rule for mutually exclusive investment is to rank them according to their net profitability index. This rule may lead to incorrect decisions because of scale problem or problem of classification of cash flows. This is explained by the following examples.

Example 8

There are two mutually exclusive investments.

Investment	Period	Cash inflows		P.I.	P.V.
		1	2		
	₹	₹	₹		₹
J	(1,500)	1,000	1,000	1.16	1,736
K	(3,100)	2,000	2,000	1.12	3,472

The rate of discount is 10%.

The N.P.V. shows that K is better. Profitability index shows that J is preferred. This is because of scale problem, which can be solved by comparing pairs of investments. The second problem is explained by the following example.

Example 9

Period	Cash inflows		Out-flows		P.I. Index
	L ₹	M ₹	L ₹	M ₹	
0	—	—	1,500	1,500	L = 1.16[1]
1	1,000	2,000	—	1,000	M = 1.07[1]
2	1,000	2,000	—	1,000	—

P.I. index makes a distinction between deductions from such cash inflows and investment type outlays. In this example L is better than M. But careful examination of the cashflows of the investment shows that the difference is the result of classifying the two (₹ 1,000 each) outlays of M as investments rather than as deduction from cash inflows.

Highest rank is given to the project or investment with highest P.I. But the ranking is not always reliable because index is not computed using the opportunity cost of money. P.V. methods leads to correct decisions involving choices between mutually exclusive investments.

Savage Value

The cash inflow pattern will differ if the asset is expected to have a salvage or scrap value, at the end of its estimated life. When there is a salvage value, it may affect depreciation expense as well as the last period cash inflows.

Example 10

A firm wants to replace an old machine with a new machine. The details are as under:

Old Machine		New Machine	
Present book value	₹ 70,000	Cost price	₹ 4,20,000
Estimated rest of life	10 years	Estimated life	10 years
Probable sale price	₹ 1,05,000	Depreciation	straight line
Depreciation	straight line	Salvage value	₹ 20,000
Annual cost of operation	₹ 6,00,000	Annual cost of operation	₹ 4,20,000

Tax rate 50% and rate of discount 10%.

Solution

Cash outlay = ₹ 4,20,000 – ₹ 1,05,000 = ₹ 3,15,000

$$\text{Depreciation on new machine} = \frac{4,20,000 - 20,000}{10} = ₹\ 40,000$$

1. $M = \frac{3,472}{3,236} = 1.07$ (1,500 + 1,736) = 3,236, $L = \frac{1,736}{1,500} = 1.16$

Depreciation on old machine $= \dfrac{70,000}{10} =$ ₹ 7,000

Differential depreciation = ₹ 33,000

Differential cash savings = ₹ 6,00,000 – 4,20,000 = 1,80,000

Cash inflow for nine years:	₹
Cash savings	1,80,000
Less Differential depreciation	33,000
Taxable Income	1,47,000
Less Tax 50%	73,500
I.A.T.	73,500
Add back depreciation	33,000
After Tax cash inflow	1,06,500
For tenth year cash inflow	1,06,500
Plus salvage value	20,000
	1,26,500
P.V. @ 10% for 9 years ₹ 1,06,500 × 6.145	6,54,442.50
P.V. of ₹ 1,26,500 for last year 1,26,500 × 0.386	48,829.00
Total	7,03,271.50
Cash outlay	3,15,000.00
N.P.V.	3,88,271.50

Present Value Method vs. I.R.R. Method

The present value method assumes that the net proceeds of a project are reinvested at the cost of capital rate and I.R.R. assumes that they are reinvested at the I.R.R. However, the former leads to incorrect results less often than the former. Both methods can be used for accept/reject decision in case of those projects which have two periods i.e. outlays in one period and entire inflows in the following period. The I.R.R. gives no real solution where projects are of continuous output type. In such case N.P.V. gives correct result. The I.R.R. method is also unreliable as a ranking devices for two projects which have different outlays or sometimes even when outlays are equal. The N.V.P. rule is better in such cases. Like I.R.R., the profitability index is also unreliable for ranking projects which are interdependent. Further, I.R.R. method can't be used in case of capital-rationing. When two investments are mutually exclusive, so that one may be selected, the two methods may give contradictory results.

Which method is better? The answer depends upon what is the appropriate rate of re-investment for intermediate cash flows and upon scale of investment. Theoretically N.P.V. method is superior. However, I.R.R. method is modified so that it involves incremental type of analysis, as shown in Example 5. If the I.R.R. on differential cash flows exceeds the required rate of return, the project with greater non-discounted net cash flows should be selected. This modification in I.R.R. should be done in case of mutually exclusive investment proposals, both of whose I.R.R. exceeds the required rate of return.

Miscellaneous Considerations

(a) *Working Capital*: Sometimes additional investment in working capital (stock or cash, debtors) is necessary along with investment in a project. This type of working capital requirement does not affect the total cash flows, because it will be subtracted at the beginning and added at the end. It affects the timing of cash flows and N.P.V. and I.R.R. as well. Suppose ₹ 1,000 is needed for additional stock in case of project C in Example 5. Then total outlay will be ₹ 9,000 and in second year inflow will be ₹ 6,762.

(b) *Inflation*: If an economy is facing inflation, then the cash inflows are expected to grow. This will distort the capital budgeting decision. Usually it is assumed that the price level will not change during the life of the project. So the future anticipated inflation must be taken into account when estimating cash inflows. The cash outflow and inflow will increase by more or less than rate of inflation. Some adjustment formulae are proposed by some writers.[1] If this is not done some bias will arise in the estimate of cash flows.

CAPITAL BUDGETING UNDER UNCERTAINTY

So far we have discussed capital budgeting under certainty. All investment proposals have different degrees of risk. The riskiness of an investment proposal means "Variability of its possible inflows". First of all, we should collect information (risk estimation) about the risk involved in particular investment proposal and then we must reach a decision about its desirability.

Risk is the probability of occurrence of unfavourable outcomes. Risk involves situations in which the probabilities of a particular event occurring are known. In case of uncertainty these probabilities are not known. Although frequently the terms risk and uncertainty are used interchangeably, there is a distinction between risk and uncertainty. In the context of capital budgeting risk refers to the probabilities that the returns may have alternative outcomes.

We should also draw a distinction between risk estimation and risk preference. The risk preference is concerned with the decision-maker's attitude towards risk. Decision-makers may react in three ways—risk averse, risk seeker and risk ignorers—and one may change from one type to another over time. It is assumed that mostly decision-maker's are risk-averters than risk seekers. The approach to uncertainty therefore

---

1. James Van Horne, *Financial Management and Policy* (Prentice Hall), 5th Ed., p. 134.

should include both risk estimation and risk preference with assumption that decision-makers are risk-averse.

The methods[1] of evaluating risky investments can be divided into two types:

(a) Methods not incorporating risk preference:
   (i) Risk-adjusted discount rate
   (ii) Sensitivity analysis
   (iii) Certainty equivalents
   (iv) Expected monetary value
   (v) Probability distribution of N.P.V.
   (vi) Simulation (Monte Carlo technique).

(b) Methods incorporating risk preference:
   (i) Utility analysis of risk (utility theory)
   (ii) Risk-return indifference curve and portfolio selection theory
   (iii) Capital asset pricing model (CAPM).

It may be noted that the risk measurement may be done with reference to:

(a) A single investment proposal involving:
   (i) Independence of cash flows from one future period to another, or
   (ii) Dependence of cash flows over time

(b) Multiple investment projects.

Methods not Incorporation Risk Preference

(i) *Risk-adjusted discount rate*: Under this method the discount rate is such that takes into account both for time and risk. It is a discount rate that is applicable for a particular risky stream of income; the riskless rate of interest plus a risk premium appropriate to the level of risk attached to the particular income stream. Using the N.P.V. formula for example, it would appear as follows:

$$\text{N.P.V.} = \sum_{t=1}^{n} \frac{At}{(1+i+j)\,t}$$

where i is a risk free rate and j is a risk premium; At = cash inflows; n = numbers of years of life. So risk adjusted discount rate means risk free rate plus risk premium. In Example 10 the risk free rate is 10% and say if risk premium is 2%, then the risk adjusted discount rate will be 12%. If risk is allowed for in the discount rate in this way we are assuming that it increases at a constant rate as a function of time.

(ii) *Sensitivity analysis*: The N.P.V. of a project will, in the final analysis, depend upon factors as sales volume, sales price, costs etc. If

1. For detailed discussion refer to any book on "Financial Management".

these values are favourable i.e. output, sales price are high and costs are low, then the actual N.P.V. will be high and *vice versa.* Recognizing these casual relationships the N.P.Vs. of project is calculated under alternative assumptions, then see just how sensitive N.P.V. is to changing conditions. In sensitivity analysis we regard the variables (and constants) as parameters. Sensitivity analysis is useful in establishing the range of validity of computed optimal solution.

Three useful approaches to sensitivity analysis are:

(a) the worst possible/best possible approach.

(b) to estimate by how much costs and revenues would need to differ from their estimated values before the decision would change.

(c) To estimate whether decision would change if estimated costs were higher than estimated or estimated revenues lower than estimated.

Worst possible/best possible approach: The simplest form of uncertainty analysis is to measure both most likely outcome and worst possible outcome. The following data explains it:

V.C. = ₹ 2; Fixed Costs ₹ 20,000

	₹	₹	₹
Price per unit =	4	4.30	4.40
Expected sales units:			
Best possible	16,000	14,000	12,000
Most likely	14,000	12,500	12,000
Worst possible	10,000	8,000	6,000

The highest contribution is at ₹ 4.30 i.e. ₹ 32,200. So it is best possible price. The worst possible is ₹ 4 because it guarantees that firm will not suffer loss. It gives a contribution of ₹ 20,000 i.e. equal to Fixed Costs.

Minimax/the minimax regret criteria: Mention may be made of these two criteria. Say a businessman is considering marketing one of four products. The profits for each product are classified as follows as per their outcome.

Products	Net profits if outcome turns out to be		
	I ₹	II ₹	III ₹
A	40	80	60
B	160	140	–20
C	180	20	–40
D	20	200	80

Product A should be chosen according to minimax criterion of profit that gives a profit of ₹ 40 under I. According to minimax regret criterion the idea is to minimise. The opportunity loss (as against profit in the former criterion) that could arise from selection of a particular alternative.

An example of sensitivity analysis follows:

Suppose a firm sells 2000 units @ of ₹ 2 per unit. The cost of material is ₹ 1 and of labour ₹ 0.50 per unit. Incremental fixed costs are ₹ 800, the project would be sensitive i.e. give a loss if any or the alternative situation arises.

(1) If cost of material increases by 10% or of labour by 20% or the sale price falls by 6%.

(2) If the fixed costs are more than 25% above estimate.

The remaining methods involve probability analysis.

(iii) *Certainty equivalents*: This approach bears some similarity to the risk adjusted discount rate method, except that the adjustment is made to the numerator rather than to denominator in N.P.V. formula given in (I) above.

$$\text{N.P.V.} = \sum_{t=1}^{n} \frac{xt\ At}{(1+i)^t}$$

At = the forecasts of cash flow without risk adjustment, *xt* = the risk adjustment factor (or certainty equivalent coefficient), *i* = risk free rate (e.g. government) bonds. If a project costs ₹ 5,000 and generates net cash flows of ₹ 3,000, ₹ 2,000, ₹ 1,000 and ₹ 2,000. The risk free discount rate is 10% and the *xt* factors are $x^0 = 1$, $x^1 = 0.90$, $x^2 = 0.70$, $x^3 = 0.50$, $x^4 = 0.30$.

The N.P.V. =

$$1(-5{,}000) + \frac{0.90\ (3{,}000)}{(1+0.10)} + \frac{0.70\ (2{,}000)}{(1+0.10)^2} + \frac{0.50\ (2{,}000)}{(1+0.10)^3} + \frac{0.30\ (3{,}000)}{(1+0.10)^4}$$

= ₹ 66.40

Certainty equivalent coefficient or adjustment factor is found by formula:

$$\frac{\text{Certain cash flow}}{\text{Uncertain cash flow}}$$

This method allows risk to vary from period to period. In practice the C.E. coefficient have to be determined from the market, which is problem. This method does not consider explicitly the whole range of possible outcomes.

(iv) *Expected Monetary Value*: E.M.V. is the mean of the distribution of monetary values of outcomes weighted by their probabilities i.e. weighted average return. The decision-maker, in general, prefers that outcome with the highest E.M.V. and other characteristics of the distribution will not influence him. This method, therefore, is criticised on the ground that the decision-maker is risk-neutral i.e. his utility function is linear in money.

Example 11

Suppose a firm is considering to produce a new product which once produced may be marketed nationally or regionally. The probabilities assigned are given below. The firm has to decide either to sell on the national market or to enter there regional market first and then extend to national market.

National Demand	Cost ₹	P.V. of cost flows ₹	Regional Demand	Cost ₹	P.V. of cost flows ₹	Probability
Large (N)	50,00,000	26,00,000	Large (R)	20,00,000	88,00,000	0.5 [P (n, R)]
Small (n)	35,00,000	14,00,000	Large	20,00,000	14,00,000	0.2 [p (n, R)]
Small	35,00,000	24,00,000	Small (r)	20,00,000	35,00,000	0.3 [p (n, r)]
						1.0

Solution

The expected monetary value will be calculated as follows:

	Probability	P.V. of Cash flows	Cost	Possible N.P.V.	Probable N.P.V.
		₹	₹	₹	₹
	1	2	3	4 (2–3)	5 (1×4)
National:					
Large	0.5	88,00,000	50,00,000	38,00,000	19,00,000
Small	0.2	14,00,000	35,00,000	(36,00,000)	(7,20,000)
Small	0.3	35,00,000	35,00,000	(15,00,000)	(4,50,000)
			Expected N.P.V.		7,30,000
Regional					
Large	0.5	26,00,000	20,00,000	6,00,000	3,00,000
Large	0.2	14,00,000	20,00,000	(6,00,000)	(1,20,000)
Small	0.3	24,00,000	20,00,000	4,00,000	1,20,000
			Expected N.P.V.		3,00,000

The N.P.Vs. of all alternative can be shown as a diagram (Exhibit 9.1), called decision or profitability tree diagram. It gives a visual display of possible outcomes.

DECISION TREE

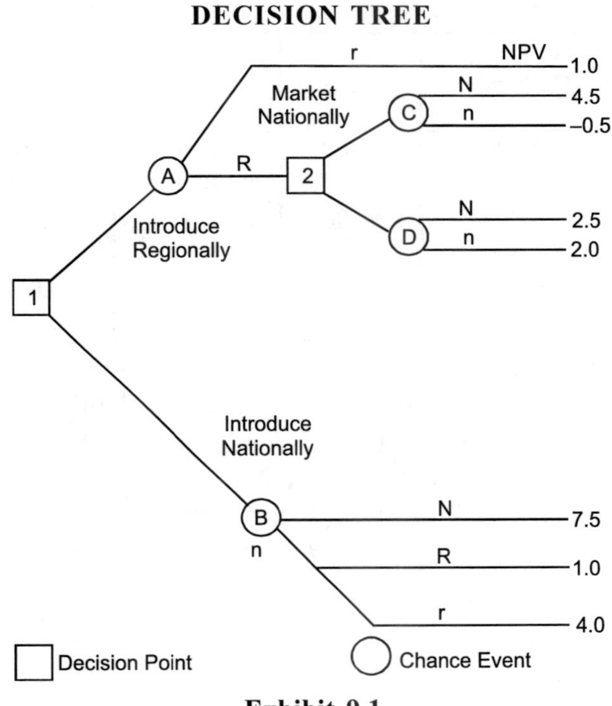

Exhibit 9.1

(v) *Probability distribution of N.P.V.*: In the normal calculation of N.P.V. the cash flows. *At* are represented by a single estimate which usually corresponds approximately to the mean or the mode of the whole distribution of cash flows in the period *t*. Actually N.P.V. must be a random variable. Two measures developed from the probability distribution have been used as measures of return and risk. These are mean and standard deviation. They are called "Bayes strategy". Any investment in a project will be preferred that has a higher expected return and lower standard deviation than others. This explains the fundamental basis for mean-variance criterion, which is based on the general idea that investors are risk averter. But sometimes two investments may have same standard deviation of returns or one investment may have higher expected return and a higher standard deviation. In that case coefficient of variation $\left(\frac{\text{Standard Deviation}}{\text{Mean}}\right)$ must be found out to select out to select any investment. This standardizes the risk.

Example 12

	Proposal C		Proposal D		
Probability	Cash flow ₹	Mean	Probability	Cash flow ₹	Mean
0.10	3,000	300	0.10	2,000	200
0.20	3,500	700	0.25	3,000	750
0.40	4,000	1,600	0.30	4,000	1,200
0.20	4,500	900	0.25	5,000	1,250
0.10	5,000	500	0.10	6,000	600
		4,000			4,000

$\bar{X}$ (Mean) = 4,000 Mean = 4,000

δ (S.D.) = 548 S.D. = 1,140

Coefficient of Variation = 0.14 C.V. = 0.29

Proposal D has greater degree of risk. Formula for δ is:

$$\delta = \sqrt{\sum_{x=1}^{n} (Axt - \bar{A}t)^2 \; Pxt}$$

Axt = Cash flow

Pxt = Probability

$\bar{A}t$ = Mean of cash flow

Variance is the square of standard deviation. The foregoing presentation represents a general method for dealing with risk. Mathematical techniques are also available for dealing with dependent and perfectly correlated cash flows over time as well as for allows that are independent for a single project or multiple investment project.[1] We shall examine later the kind of interdependence introduced by portfolio theory between the expected values of different projects.

This method provides more information for evaluating risk and considering trade offs between risk and expected value of returns.

(vi) *Simulation*: This method makes use of computer and out of purview here. It consists first of examining all the variables that influence the decision outcome and attach subjective probabilities to them. The next stage is to select a certain value of one of the variables from the distribution and using devices, such as Monte Carlo technique, combine it with certain values of all other variables, similarly chosen at random. By numerous repetitions of this procedure, recording the number of times outcomes of a given value occur, a frequency distribution of outcomes is generated which can be tabulated in the form of a probability distribution. However, this technique is not always feasible for risk analysis, except in cases of projects involving very huge amount.

1. *Financial Management & Policy,* Van Horn, Chapter 6, Ed. 5th.

Methods Incorporating Risk Preference

(i) *Utility analysis of risk or utility theory*: In economic decision-making under uncertainty the value assigned by a decision-maker to an uncertain outcome may differ from its mathematical expectation i.e. the utility of an expectation may differ from the expectation of the utility. Risk preferences can be represented in investment decision by means of utility function, utility being measures in units (called utiles) on an arbitrary scale. The utility functions are shown for a decision-maker who is (a) risk-averse, (b) risk neutral, and (c) risk seeking.

Arbitrarily, we initially assign utile values of 0 and 1 to a pair of Rupees amounts that represent extreme prospects—suppose we say Zero Rupee and ₹ 1,00,000 respectively. Further suppose a manager thinks that in any investment he has 0.5 chance of receiving no money and 0.5 chance (probability) of getting ₹ 1,00,000. He is ready to invest ₹ 33,000. It means the utile value of ₹ 33,000 is 0.5. The certainty equivalent, therefore, is ₹ 33,000 because at this amount the manager is indifferent between that sum and investment.

Suppose the probability of receiving ₹ 33,000 is 0.4 and of receiving ₹ 1,00,000 is 0.6 and suppose he invests ₹ 63,000. The utile value of ₹ 63,000 is then:

$$u\ (₹\ 63{,}000) = 0.4\ u\ (₹\ 33{,}000) + 0.6\ u\ (₹\ 1{,}00{,}000)$$
$$= 0.4\ (0.5) + 0.6\ (1.0) = 0.80.$$

GRAPH SHOWING UTILITY ANALYSIS

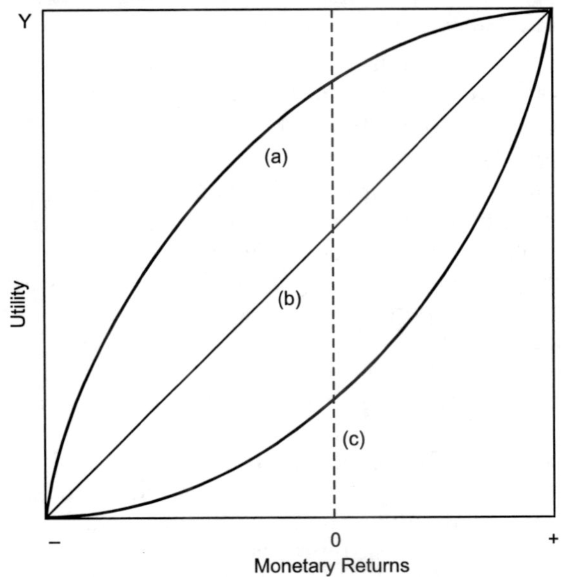

Exhibit 9.2

Consider two investments as follows:

Investment A		Investment B	
Outcome ₹	Probability of outcome	Outcome ₹	Probability of Outcome
0	0.4	33,000	0.4
33,000	0.1	63,000	0.6
1,00,000	0.5		

Expected monetary value of A = outcome × probability i.e.

0.4 (0) + 0.1 (33,000) + 0.5 (1,00,000) = ₹ 53,000 and of investment B is 0.4 (33,000) + 0.6 (63,000) = ₹ 51,000.

The expected utility of A = 0.4 *u* (₹ 0) + 0.1 *u* (₹ 33,000) + 0.5 *u* (₹ 1,00,000) = 0.55

The expected utility of B = 0.4 *u* (₹ 33,000) + 0.6 *u* (₹ 63,000) i.e. = 0.68.

B is preferred.

The procedure can be summarized as under:

1. List all the possible outcomes.
2. Determine the probability of each outcome.
3. Assign utility measures to each outcome.
4. Compute the expected utility of the investment.

The sum of money with this expected utility is called the certainty equivalent. The difference between expected monetary value and certainty equivalent is the discount for risk. Decision between alternatives can be made using expected utilities or certainty equivalent.

The utility is a function of expected monetary value and standard deviation (or variance). The greater the S.D. or variance of the probability distribution of possible returns for an investment, the less the expected utility of that investment.

(ii) *Risk-return indifference curves and portfolio theory*: The utility can be represented by means of indifference curves i.e. curves of constant utility. In this analysis risk preferences are reflected in the trade-offs a decision-maker would be willing to make between various levels of risk and return. This approach has been developed in what is called "Portfolio Selection Theory". It assumes that risk can be measured by standard deviation or variance of expected monetary returns and that investors are in general risk-averse, a conflict arises in allocating funds between investments because expected return can only be increased by incurring greater risk. This theory is based on "Expected Value Variance" rule. The variance tells how widely the actual outcomes are likely to be spread around expected value. The solution lies, first, in determining the "efficient" portfolio or the risk-return possibility curve. This is the set of investments (represented by BB^1 in Exhibit 9.3) which maximizes risk for any given level of expected return. The portfolio is efficient if no alternative combination of investments exists with either (1) the same total expected

RISK AVERSION AND PORTFOLIO BUILDING CHART

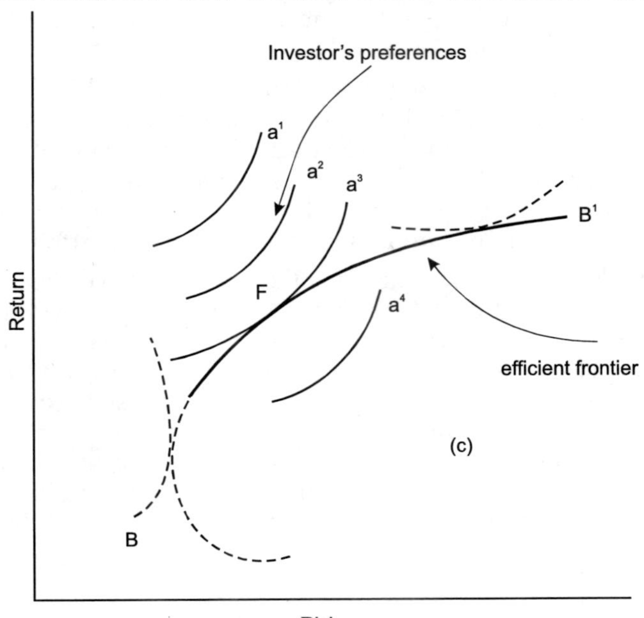

Exhibit 9.3

return and total lower variance, (2) the same total expected returns and total higher variance or (3) a higher total expected returns and a lower total variance. Hence, BB^1 is a boundary relation. The efficient combinations are represented by risk-return indifference curves (a^1, a^2, a^3 etc.). Given the investor's risk-preference, the optimal trade-off is indicated by point F, the point of TANGENCY between the risk-return possibility curve and an indifference curve.

If there are n securities the proportion of total funds for investments allocated to security j is 1. The total expected returns and total variances mathematically can be expressed as under:

$$\overline{r} = \sum_{J=1}^{n} \overline{rj}Pj$$

The total expected returns

The total variance

$\delta^2 = \sum_{j=1}^{n} \sum_{k=1}^{n} pjk\delta jk$ i.e. the variance of a portfolio is the sum of $n \times n$ matrix of covariances

pjk = coefficient of correlation between the securities j and k

δjk = standard deviation of securities

The expected returns *ui* and standard deviation of securities, *σjk* are based on statistical analysis of historical data of past. Their estimation is sometimes be a problem.

(iii) *Capital asset pricing model*: Many mathematical decision models have been developed of which this model is quite famous. It shows relationship between risk and return for efficient and inefficient portfolio. Efficient portfolio is a portfolio that has the lowest risk (Standard Deviation) for a given level of expected return. Capital market line shows the relationship between expected rate of return and risk on efficient portfolios.

This model leads to the conclusion that investors have a market basket of risky securities and can also invest in other securities with no risk of default. The risk preferences of an investor dictate a specific combination of the market basket of risk securities and risk free security. In equilibrium, the return of any security must be such that the investor expects to earn a basic return equal to return on risk free security plus an adjustment that heavily influenced by the 'Covariance' of the security's return and market's return. This adjustment is called 'risk adjustment factor'.[1] If the covariance of a security is positive, the equilibrium return of that security

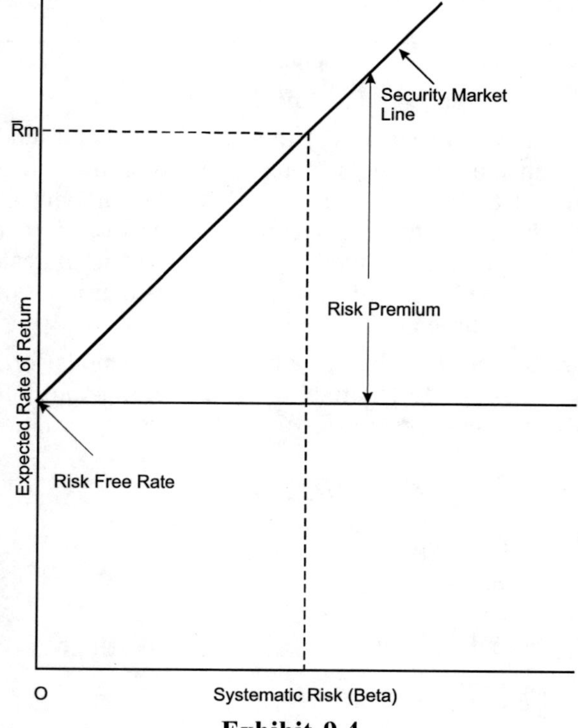

Exhibit 9.4

1. This can be obtained by multiplying the risk premium required for market return by the riskness of the individual security.

will be larger than risk-free return. If the covariance is negative, the equilibrium return will be smaller than the risk-free return. A covariance is positive if the two random variables, the returns, say from investment *j* and *m*, have a positive correlation and negative if they have a negative correlation.

The relationship between risk adjustment factor and risk of any security is expressed in security market line. This line represents the relationship between risk and return for individual and inefficient port folios. If the returns of one individual investment fluctuate by exactly the same degree as the returns on the market as a whole, the beta of the security is 1. It can be shown that *Bj*, Beta, the slope of the regression line, mathematically is:

$$Bj = \frac{\text{Cov } (j, m)}{\delta^2 m}$$

Cov (j, m) = covariance of rj, and rm and equal to E $(rj - \bar{r}j)(rm - \bar{r}m)$ $\delta^2 m$ variance of rm.

If we define $\bar{r}J^*$ to the equilibrium – required expected return for investment *J*, it can be shown that:

$$\bar{r}J^* = rj + (\bar{r}m - rj)\,Bj$$

where rj is the return on a risk-free security and $\bar{r}m$ is the expected market return. If Bj is negative, the $\bar{r}J^*$ equilibrium required expected return will be less than the return of the risk-free security.

Bj and its components are the only relevant risk factors. Only the extent to which the security's return is correlated to the market's return affects the necessary risk adjustment. The systematic risk (non-diversifiable or market risk) which is related to market, can be diversified. The non-systematic risk (diversifiable risk) cannot be diversified as it relates to a firm. Thus CAPM gives a rule for quantifying risk in terms of return and is simple. But it works under certain assumptions about market, investors and assets.

QUESTIONS

1. What are some difficulties involved in capital budgeting? Explain in three different ways, the term rate of return is used.
2. List the advantages and disadvantages of different methods of evaluating capital expenditure project.
3. Define cost of capital and sensitivity analysis. What purposes does capital budget serve?
4. What is present value index? How does cash inflow differ from net income? In what way a rate of return computed under discounted cash flow method superior to a rate of return computed on the average investment?

5. (a) Compute the rate of return on following investment:

	₹
0	3,477
1	1,000
2	1,000
10	10,000

(b) Compute the net present value of an investment that costs ₹ 800 and promises to return ₹ 1,000 three periods from now. Time value of money is 0.05 per year.

6. There are two mutually exclusive investment. Which of them you advise to choose?

Project	Cash flows Period			Yield
	0 ₹	1 ₹	2 ₹	
A	10,000	—	11,664	0.08
B	10,000	5,608	5,608	

7. Assume cash flow of the first year is ₹ 10,00,000 and the rate of discount is 0.08. What is the present value of the cash flows assuming that the:
   (a) cash flow decrease by 0.02 per year?
   (b) cash flow is constant and continue forever?
   (c) cash flow increases by 0.03 per year forever?
   (d) cash flow increases by 0.09 per year forever?

8. Assume that the life of a piece of equipment is uncertain but that management believes that the probabilities of it having different lives are as follows:

Life	Probability
0	0.00
1	0.20
2	0.30
3	0.40
4	0.10
Total	1.00

The present values of cash flows for buying and leasing for different assumed lives are as follows:

Assumed life	P.V. (Buy) ₹	P.V. (Lease) ₹
1	(10,000)	(2,000)
2	0	4,000
3	11,000	10,000
4	23,000	16,000

Is it more desirable to buy or lease?

9. A company has three investment opportunities?

	X ₹	Y ₹	Z ₹
Cost	40,000	10,000	20,000
Useful life	10	4	20
Annual cash saving	7,675	3,720	3,375

Rank the investment according to their desirability using the following:
(a) Payback period
(b) Internal rate of return
(c) Net present value discount rate 10%
Ignore depreciation and taxes.

10. Hamdard is considering a capital investment for which the initial outlay is ₹ 20,000. Net annual cash receipts, after taxes, are predicted to be ₹ 4,000 for ten years. Straight line depreciation is to be used, with an estimated salvage value of zero. Required:
    1. Payback period.
    2. Average annual return on original investment.
    3. Average annual return on average investment.
    4. Net present value of 10% and present value payback period.
    5. Discounted cash flow rate of return.

11. The Delhi Press Company is considering the purchase of a giant press costing ₹ 1,00,000. The estimated cash benefit is:

Year	Cash Benefit ₹
1	25,000
2	40,000
3	40,000
4	40,000
5	35,000
6	30,000
7	25,000
8	20,000
9	15,000
10	10,000

The press is to be depreciated on a straight-line basis over a period of ten years. The salvage value is zero. Assume a 50% tax rate and a cost of capital of 10%.

Find:
    1. Payback period.
    2. Average annual return on original investment.

3. Average annual return on average investment.
4. Net present value.
5. Discounted cash flow rate of return.

12. The Manisha Company is considering replacing an existing piece of equipment. The following data have been compiled:

		₹
(a) Old equipment:	Cost	45,000
	Accumulated depreciation	30,000
	Book value	15,000

Expected remaining life: 3 years

Current salvage value equals cost of removal. Loss on disposal of old equipment is to be recognized in the current year.

(b) New equipment: cost, ₹ 26,000 estimated life, 3 years.

(c) Capitalized cost of rearranging production line to utilize new equipment: ₹ 4,000.

(d) Estimated operating costs per year:

	Old Equipment	New Equipment	
	₹	₹	
Direct Labour	30,000	12,000	
Supplies	14,000	11,500	
Maintenance	8,000	6,000	
Supervision	6,000	6,000	
Power	4,000	7,000	
Depreciation	5,000	10,000	[(₹ 26,000 + ₹ 4,000) ÷ 3]

(e) Assume the Income-tax rate to be 50%.

Assuming a loss on the sale or disposal of equipment is treated as an ordinary tax deduction, resulting in a tax saving of 50%, should the company purchase the machine if it requires a return of 6% on investment after these considerations? Calculate (a) the net present value and (b) the discounted cash flow rate of return.

13. Write notes on (a) Decision tree and (b) CAPM.

14. A company is considering three projects:

Project	Mean	Variance
A	20	20
B	15	15
C	18	13

The company is risk averse. Comment upon this ranking of projects.

15. A company has a choice between Machine A and Machine B, either of which is satisfactory. Each machine has estimated life of three years, but Machine A will cost ₹ 4,000 and B ₹ 10,000. The operating costs are A ₹ 1 and B 0.50 Paise, excluding depreciation. The product is sold for ₹ 3.

    The number of units required for next three years may be 2,000, 3,000 or 5,000 units.

    The following table shows probabilities.

Annual requirements (units)	Probability
2,000	0.2
3,000	0.6
5,000	0.2

    Calculate N.P.V. for each three activity levels for Machine A and Machine B using a discount rate of 6%. Calculate expected N.P.V. for each machine. Which machine would you recommend?

TABLE-A
Present Value of ₹ 1

Future Years	1%	2%	4%	6%	8%	10%	12%	14%	15%	16%	18%	20%	22%	24%	25%	26%	28%	30%	35%	40%	45%	50%
1	0.990	0.980	0.962	0.943	0.926	0.909	0.893	0.877	0.870	0.862	0.847	0.833	0.820	0.806	0.800	0.794	0.781	0.769	0.741	0.714	0.690	0.667
2	0.980	0.961	0.925	0.890	0.857	0.826	0.797	0.769	0.756	0.743	0.718	0.694	0.672	0.650	0.640	0.630	0.610	0.592	0.549	0.510	0.476	0.444
3	0.971	0.942	0.889	0.840	0.794	0.751	0.712	0.675	0.658	0.641	0.609	0.579	0.551	0.524	0.512	0.500	0.477	0.455	0.406	0.364	0.328	0.296
4	0.961	0.924	0.855	0.792	0.735	0.683	0.636	0.592	0.572	0.552	0.516	0.482	0.451	0.423	0.410	0.397	0.373	0.350	0.301	0.260	0.226	0.198
5	0.951	0.906	0.822	0.747	0.681	0.621	0.567	0.519	0.497	0.476	0.437	0.402	0.370	0.341	0.328	0.315	0.291	0.269	0.223	0.186	0.156	0.132
6	0.942	0.888	0.790	0.705	0.630	0.564	0.507	0.456	0.432	0.410	0.370	0.335	0.303	0.275	0.262	0.250	0.227	0.207	0.165	0.133	0.108	0.088
7	0.933	0.871	0.760	0.665	0.583	0.513	0.452	0.400	0.376	0.354	0.314	0.279	0.249	0.222	0.210	0.198	0.178	0.159	0.122	0.095	0.074	0.059
8	0.923	0.853	0.731	0.627	0.540	0.467	0.404	0.351	0.327	0.305	0.266	0.233	0.204	0.179	0.168	0.157	0.139	0.123	0.091	0.068	0.051	0.039
9	0.914	0.837	0.703	0.592	0.500	0.424	0.361	0.308	0.284	0.263	0.225	0.194	0.167	0.144	0.134	0.125	0.108	0.094	0.067	0.048	0.35	0.026
10	0.905	0.820	0.676	0.558	0.463	0.386	0.322	0.270	0.247	0.227	0.191	0.162	0.137	0.116	0.107	0.099	0.085	0.073	0.050	0.035	0.024	0.017
11	0.896	0.804	0.650	0.527	0.429	0.350	0.287	0.237	0.215	0.195	0.162	0.135	0.112	0.094	0.086	0.079	0.066	0.056	0.037	0.025	0.017	0.012
12	0.887	0.788	0.625	0.497	0.397	0.319	0.257	0.208	0.187	0.168	0.137	0.112	0.092	0.076	0.069	0.062	0.052	0.043	0.027	0.018	0.012	0.008
13	0.879	0773	0.601	0.469	0368	0.290	0229	0.182	0.163	0.145	0.116	0.093	0.075	0.061	0.055	0.050	0.040	0.033	0.020	0.013	0.008	0.005
14	0.870	0.758	0.577	0.442	0.340	0.263	0.205	0.160	0.141	0.125	0.099	0.078	0.062	0.049	0.44	0.039	0.032	0.025	0.015	0.009	0.006	0.003
15	0.861	0.743	0.555	0.417	0.315	0.239	0.183	0.140	0.123	0.108	0.084	0.065	0.051	0.040	0.035	0.031	0.025	0.020	0.011	0.006	0.004	0.002
16	0.853	0.728	0.534	0.394	0.292	0.218	0.163	0.123	0.107	0.093	0.071	0.054	0.042	0.032	0.028	0.025	0.019	0.015	0.008	0.005	0.003	0.002
17	0.844	0.714	0.513	0.371	0.270	0.198	0.146	0.108	0.093	0.080	0.060	0.045	0.034	0.026	0.023	0.020	0.015	0.012	0.006	0.003	0.002	0.001
18	0.836	0.700	0.494	0.350	0.250	0.180	0.130	0.095	0.081	0.069	0.051	0.038	0.028	0.021	0.018	0.016	0.012	0.009	0.005	0.002	0.001	0.001
19	0.828	0.686	0.475	0.331	0.232	0.164	0.116	0.083	0.070	0.060	0.043	0.031	0.023	0.017	0.014	0.012	0.009	0.007	0.003	0.002	0.001	
20	0.820	0.673	0.456	0.312	0.215	0.149	0.104	0.073	0.061	0.051	0.037	0.026	0.019	0.014	0.012	0.010	0.007	0.005	0.002	0.001	0.001	
21	0.811	0.660	0.439	0.294	0.199	0.135	0.093	0.064	0.053	0.044	0.031	.0.022	0.015	0.011	0.009	0.008	0.006	0.004	0.002	0.001		
22	0.803	0.647	0.422	0.278	0.184	0.123	0.083	0.056	0.046	0.038	0.026	0.018	0.013	0.009	0.007	0.006	0.004	0.003	0.001	0.001		
23	0.795	0.634	0.406	0.262	0.170	0.112	0.074	0.049	0.040	0.033	0.022	0.015	0.010	0.007	0.006	0.005	0.003	0.002	0.001			
24	0.788	0.622	0.390	0.247	0.158	0.102	0.066	0.043	0.035	0.028	0.019	0.013	0.008	0.006	0.005	0.004	0.003	0.002	0.001			
25	0.780	0.610	0.375	0.233	0.146	0.092	0.059	0.038	0.030	0.024	0.016	0.010	0.007	0.005	0.004	0.003	0.002	0.001	0.001			
26	0.772	0.598	0.361	0.220	0.135	0.084	0.053	0.033	0.026	0.021	0.014	0.009	0.006	0.004	0.003	0.002	0.002	0.001				
27	0.764	0.586	0.347	0.207	0.125	0.076	0.047	0.029	0.023	0.018	0.011	0.007	0.005	0.003	0.002	0.002	0.001	0.001				
28	0.757	0.574	0.333	0.196	0.116	0.069	0.042	0.026	0.020	0.016	0.010	0.006	0.004	0.002	0.002	0.002	0.001	0.001				
29	0.749	0.563	0.321	0.185	0.107	0.063	0.037	0.022	0.017	0.014	0.008	0.005	0.003	0.002	0.001	0.002	0.001					
30	0.742	0.552	0.308	0.174	0.099	0.057	0.033	0.020	0.015	0.012	0.007	0.004	0.003	0.002	0.001	0.001	0.001					
40	0.672	0.453	0.208	0.097	0.046	0.022	0.011	0.005	0.004	0.003	0.001	0.001										
50	0.608	0.372	0.141	0.054	0.021	0.009	0.003	0.001	0.001	0.001												

TABLE-B

It is Zero Present Value of ₹ 1 Received or Paid Annually for each of the next N years

Years	1%	2%	4%	6%	8%	10%	12%	14%	15%	16%	18%	20%	22%	24%	25%	26%	28%	30%	35%	40%	45%	50%
1	0.990	0.980	0.962	0.943	0.926	0.909	0.893	0.877	0.870	0.862	0.847	0.833	0.820	0.806	0.800	0.794	0.781	0.769	0.741	0.714	0.690	0.667
2	1.970	1.942	1.886	1.833	1.783	1.736	1.690	1.647	1.626	1.605	1.566	1.528	1.492	1.457	1.440	1.424	1.392	1.361	1.289	1.224	1.165	1.111
3	2.941	2.884	2.775	2.673	2.577	2.487	2.402	2.322	2.283	2.246	2.174	2.106	2.042	1.980	1.952	1.923	1.868	1.816	1.696	1.589	1.493	1.407
4	3.902	3.808	3.630	3.465	3.312	3.170	3.037	2.914	2.855	2.798	2.690	2.589	2.494	2.404	2.362	2.320	2.241	2.166	1.997	1.849	1.720	1.605
5	4.853	4.713	4.452	4.212	3.993	3.791	3.605	3.433	3.352	3.274	3.127	2.991	2.864	2.745	2.689	2.635	2.532	2.436	2.220	2.035	1.876	1.737
6	5.795	5.601	5.242	4.917	4.623	4.355	4.111	3.889	3.784	3.685	3.498	3.326	3.167	3.020	2.951	2.885	2.759	2.643	2.385	2.168	1.983	1.824
7	6.728	6.472	6.002	5.582	5.206	4.868	4.564	4.288	4.160	4.039	3.812	3.605	3.416	3.242	3.161	3.083	2.937	2.802	2.508	2.263	2.057	1.883
8	7.652	7.325	6.733	6.210	5.747	5.335	4.968	4.639	4.487	4.344	4.078	3.837	3.619	3.421	3.329	3.241	3.076	2.925	2.598	2.331	2.108	1.922
9	8.566	8.163	7.435	6.802	6.247	5.759	5.328	4.946	4.772	4.607	4.303	4.031	3.786	3.566	3.463	3.366	3.184	3.019	2.665	2.379	2.144	1.948
10	9.471	8.983	8.111	7.360	6.710	6.145	5.650	5.216	5.019	4.833	4.494	4.192	3.923	3.682	3.571	3.465	3.269	3.092	2.715	2.414	2.168	1.965
11	10.368	9.787	8.760	7.887	7.139	6.495	5.988	5.453	5.234	5.029	4.656	4.327	4.035	3.776	3.656	3.544	3.335	3.147	2.752	2.438	2.185	1.977
12	11.255	10.575	9.385	8.384	7.536	6.814	6.194	5.660	5.421	5.197	4.793	4.439	4.127	3.851	3.725	3.606	3.387	3.190	2.779	2.456	2.196	1.985
13	12.134	11.348	9.986	8.853	7.904	7.103	6.424	5.842	5.583	5.342	4.910	4.533	4.203	3.912	3.780	3.656	3.427	3.223	2.799	2.468	2.204	1.990
14	13.004	12.106	10.563	9.295	8.244	7.367	6.628	6.002	5.724	5.468	5.008	4.611	4.265	3.962	3.824	3.695	3.459	3.249	2.814	2.477	2.210	1.993
15	13.865	12.849	11.118	9.712	8.559	7.606	6.811	6.142	5.847	5.575	5.092	4.675	4.315	4.001	3.859	3.726	3.483	3.268	2.825	2.484	2.214	1.995
16	14.718	13.578	11.652	10.106	8.851	7.824	6.974	6.265	5.954	5.669	5.162	4.730	4.357	4.033	3.887	3.751	3.503	3.283	2.834	2.489	2.216	1.997
17	15.562	14.292	12.166	10.477	9.122	8.022	7.120	6.373	6.047	5.749	5.222	5.775	4.391	4.059	3.910	3.771	3.518	2.295	2.840	2.492	2.218	1.998
18	16.398	14.992	12.659	10.828	9.372	8.201	7.250	6.467	6.128	5.818	5.273	4.812	4.419	4.080	3.928	3.786	3.529	3.304	2.844	2.494	2.219	1,999
19	17.226	15.678	13.134	11.158	9.604	8.365	7.366	6.550	6.198	5.877	5.316	8.844	4.442	4.097	3.942	3.799	3.539	3.311	2.848	2.496	2.220	1.999
20	18.046	16.351	16.590	11.470	9.818	8.514	9.469	6.623	6,259	5.929	5.353	8.870	4.460	4.110	3.954	3.808	3.546	3.316	2.850	2.497	2.221	1.999
21	18.857	17.011	14.029	11.764	10.017	8.649	7.562	6.687	6.312	5.973	5.384	4.891	4.476	4.121	3.963	3.816	3.551	3.320	2.852	2.498	2.221	2.000
22	19.660	14.658	14.451	12.042	10.201	8.772	7.645	6.743	6.359	6.011	5.410	4.909	4.488	4.130	3.970	3.822	3.556	3.323	2.853	2.498	2.222	2.000
23	20.456	18.292	14.857	12.303	10.371	8.883	7.718	6.792	6.399	4.044	5.432	4.925	4.499	4.137	3.976	3.827	3.559	3.325	2.854	2.499	2.222	2.000
24	21.243	18.914	15.247	12.550	10.529	8.985	7.784	6.835	6.434	6.073	5.451	4.937	4.507	4.143	3.981	3.831	3.562	3.327	8.855	2.499	2.222	2.000
25	22.023	19.523	15.622	12.783	10.675	9.077	7.843	6.873	6.464	6.097	5.467	4.948	4.514	4.147	3.985	3.834	3.564	3.329	2.856	2.499	2.22	2.000
26	22.795	20.121	15.983	13.003	10.810	9.161	7.896	6.906	6.491	6.118	5.480	4.956	4.520	4.151	3.988	3.837	3.566	3.330	2.856	2.500	2.222	2.000
27	23.560	20.707	16.330	13.211	10.935	9.237	7.943	6.935	6.514	6.136	5.492	4.964	4.524	4.154	3.990	3.839	3.567	3.331	2.856	2.500	2.222	2.000
28	24.316	21.281	16.663	13.406	11.051	9.307	7.984	6.961	6.534	6.151	5.502	4.970	4.528	4.157	3.992	3.840	3.568	3.331	2.857	2.500	2.222	2.000
29	25.066	21.844	16.984	13.591	11.158	9.370	8.022	6.983	6.551	6.166	5.510	4.975	4.531	4.159	3.994	3.841	3.569	3.332	2.857	2.500	2.222	2.000
30	25.808	22.396	17.292	13.765	11.258	9.427	8.055	7.003	6.566	6.177	5.517	4.979	4.534	4.160	3.995	3.842	3.569	3.332	2.857	2.500	2.222	2.000
40	32.835	27.355	19.793	15.046	11.925	9.779	8.244	7.105	6.642	6.234	5.548	4.997	4.544	4.166	3.999	3.846	3.571	3.333	2.857	2.500	2.222	2.000
50	39.196	31.424	21.482	15.762	12.234	9.915	8.304	7.133	6.661	6.246	5.554	4.999	5.545	4.167	4.000	3.846	3.571	3.333	2.857	2.500	2.222	2.000

10
Budgeting

PLANNING OF PROFITS, SALES AND COSTS

A plan precedes the formation of a business. In chronological order plans precede decisions and decisions precede controls. It is sometimes said that plans are *ex ante* decisions. Plans can be classified in three distinct categories:[1]

(a) *Operating plans*: These plans relate to production, marketing, investment and financing.

(b) *Administrative plans*: They are concerned with developing and maintaining an organizational structure.

(c) *Strategic plans*: Such plans relate to firm's objectives, nature of its activities and external environment. We may call them strategies.

In accounting, business plans are usually thought of as being represented in budgets, which serve both as plans and controls. All managements make plans. If these plans are explicit and are set out in quantitative terms they are called budgets.

In accounting, plans are mostly static under certainty, are not optimal plans and are not perfectly realized. A plan is a broad statement of policy governing the future conduct of the business. Every plan implies a series of decision to implement it.

The terms "profit planning" and "budgeting" are used as synonyms. The profit planning may be a long-range plan or short-range plan. The long-range plan, in accounting terms, may be drawn in the form of a prospective income statement and balance sheet and cash flow statement. The rate of return on capital (assets) employed is an important statistic in long-range profit planning. The short-term plan (or budgets) is a plan for one year. Long-range plans must be incorporated in short-term plan. For their implementation there must be a follow-through. There are advantages of planning, but its limitations depend upon methods of production, quantities to be produced and prices to be charged and the combination of the products to be produced.

---

1. *Budgeting* by Ansoff, H.I., p. 6.

The accountant helps to bring together the budget estimates and coordinates them into a comprehensive plan for the future. Production requirements are planned, costs are determined and all phases of the business operating are interlocked to form a master guide. The management will be able to predict the results of business operation and the financial position at some later date.

BUDGETING

A budget is a coordinated financial programme or plan of operations segregated into responsibility areas, indicating amounts expected to be required for specific purposes or received from specific sources. A budget is a quantitative expression of a plan of action and an aid to coordination and implementation. Budgets may be prepared for the organisation as a whole or for any sub-unit e.g., department. The budgets of sub-units, covering their sales, production, distribution and finance can be summarized in a MASTER BUDGET. This budget summarizes the future expected income, cash flows, financial position and supporting plans in terms of figures. Budgets serve many functions: planning, evaluating performance, coordinating activities, implementing plans, communicating and motivating and authorizing actions. The last function of budgets is very important in non-profit organizations and government.

A budget is a planned event usually expressed in financial and quantitative terms. First, a budget, therefore, is a collection of forecasts. Second, it represents an attempt to organise and aggregate various individual forecasts into consistent overall expectation about a future period. Third, it serves to mediate and to transmit sub-goals to various managers in harmony with overall goals. The nature of budgetary system is governed by the size of the business. It uses the language of accounting and gives added purpose to accounting by increasing its effectiveness. The act of preparing budget is collied budgeting.

Principles of Budgeting

The budget process is usually directed by a budget committee, which is composed of managers incharge of different activities. The committee decides on policies, reviews budget estimates, suggests revisions, analyses budget reports and recommends actions.

The following are the fundamental principles of budgeting:

(A) *Human Behaviour*: The success of budgetary system depends upon its acceptance by the firm's members who are affected by budgets. One should be aware of the irrational and often obstinate behaviour of certain supervisors with respect to the contemplated budget programme. Budget place managers in spotlight, in some firms, budgeting may be most unpopular. Budgeting plays an important role in influencing individual and group behaviour at all states of management process. Therefore, one should not ignore the behavioural function of the people. Good budgeting will depend greatly upon the existing relationship within the management group. Budget should not be an instrument of torture and it can be successful only when people are willing to accept it. Head of each department must participate in making the budget estimates.

(B) *Clear Objectives*: It takes time to install a budget system because it may not be understood by manager. For this, the existing managerial responsibilities may be clarified. The objectives of budgeting must be clear and explicit. There should, for example, be a correct choice of budget period, the use of a realistic preparation time-table and clear instructions to executives to assist them in preparing the budgets.

(C) *Top Management Support*: The reluctance of manager to submit their thinking to the discipline required for budgeting may only be overcome by top management support. The discipline of recording executive commitments on paper usually makes the intentions more definite and comprehensive in their coverage. To establish a budgetary control system the top management should prepare an organisational chart for the business and sort out overlapping operations and overlapping responsibilities.

(D) *Assignment of Authority and Responsibility*: The structure of budgets follows the organisational lines of authority of the company since it reflects the quantification of delegated responsibility. Budgets exist to help managers. Managers supervise subordinates. To improve performance, top managers design an organisational structure i.e. an arrangement of lines of authority and responsibility. The organisational structure is typically hierarchical. It is desirable to have organisational structure and designations of authority and responsibility in writing. The budget manual is a written set of instructions and pertinent information that serves as a rule book and a reference for the implementation of a budget programme. It tells what to do, how to do it, when to do it and which form to do it on. Budgets spell out quantitatively what is expected of each member of management at every level in terms of expected goal.

(E) *Specific Goals and Flexibility*: The budget must be directed towards the desired goals and as far as possible should be flexible. A.C. Stedry observes that level of the budget has an impact on aspiration level i.e. the goals hoped for rather than the goal aimed for. For achieving organisation's goals, motivation is necessary. The consent and cooperation of subordinates must be attained. There are many ways of obtaining goal congruence. Incentive plans and managerial audit technique (auditing the performances of supervisors and others) are some of them.

(F) *Communication and Feedback*: The budget and its related decisions should be communicated to all concerned to give rise a feeling of participation. It is important for individuals to learn about their success or failure. More feedback is required particularly if performance is slightly below expectations. Feedback is needed so that employees will continue to work for budgeted goals. A related point concerns the matching of input and output data with the period budget. Budgets may, sometimes, produce side effect if the people concerned are not communicated decisions about budget. Small informal groups be formed, who may have their own goals. A supervisor may distort the measurement process, there may be overemphasis of departmental performance, undue publicity be given to individual performance and stifling of initiative.

Functions, Advantages and Limitations of Budgets

A modern budget is a managerial tool incorporating organisational and financial planning, analysis of the behaviour characteristics of costs, setting of objectives and evaluation of performance.

Functions: Budgets are major features of most control systems. Budgets (a) compel planning, (b) provide performance criteria, and (c) promote communication and coordination. Budgets formulate expected performance; they express managerial targets. Without such targets, operations lack directions, problems are not foreseen, results lack meaning, and the implications for future policies are dwarfed by the pressure of the present. The planning role of all levels of management should be accentuated and enlarged by a budgetary system. Managers will be compelled to look ahead and will be ready for changing conditions. This forced planning is by far the greatest contribution of budgeting to management. As a basis for judging actual results, budgeted performance is generally viewed as being a better criterion than past performance. In practice, it needs plenty of intelligent administration to use budgets for improving coordination and communication. So, the top management must understand and enthusiastically support the budget and all aspects of the control system. Thus the budgets perform five functions i.e., planning, coordinating communication, motivation, and control.

Advantages: Budgeting, sometimes called profit planning, has the following advantages:

(a) Provides a disciplined approach to solution of problems.
(b) Coordinated managerial activity is facilitated.
(c) Identifies the part each executive must play and assists in using the resources of the business in the most possible economical way.
(d) Encourages an attitude of cost consciousness.
(e) Affords the opportunity of appraising systematically every facet of the organization, examining periodically the policies and guiding principles.
(f) Coordinates and correlates all efforts and directing efforts into profitable channels.
(g) Provides yardsticks for measuring performance and provides a basis for review and modifications.

(h) Provides information as a routine and the decisions reached are likely to be more accurate.

(i) It forms the vary basis of profitability studies, make or buy decisions and micro-economic knowledge of the company.

Limitations: Any budgetary system will be effective if certain basic principles are followed. Sometimes there are some pitfalls and limitations. They are:

(a) Forecasting is not an exact science. So the budgets must be revised because they are merely estimates.

(b) Staff regard the technique as a pressure instrument. So cooperation and participation of all members of management is essential.

(c) Installation takes time. Management often becomes impatient and loses interest. So the motivation may be misplaced.

(d) The checking of estimates may be difficult.

(e) The supporting accounting system may not be sufficiently effective. There may be deficiencies in the organisational structure of the business.

(f) Not enough time may be allowed for the system to be developed and managers gain the necessary experience to use the technique to maximum advantage.

Types of Budgets

Budgets may cover a period of one year or less or sometimes upto ten or more years. It may be short-term or long-term budget. The usual budget period is one year and is broken down by months. The budgeted data for a year are often revised as the year ends. Continuous budgets are increasingly used.

The budgets are called by various names like targeting, profit planning and proforma statements. There are many forms of budget. A master budget may contain the following:

(A) *Operational Budgets*:	Sales budget, Production budget, Direct material budget, Direct labour budget, Factory overhead budget, Cost of goods sold budget, Selling expense budget, Administrative expense budget.
(B) *Financial Budgets*:	Budgeted statement of Income capital budget, Cash budget, Budgeted Balance Sheet budget, Budgeted statement of changes in financial position.

A master budget may be and (a) static or fixed budget and (b) flexible budget or variable budget. A static budget is not adjusted or altered, regardless of changes in volume or other conditions during the financial period. It is a set of specific monetary allowances. A flexible budget is adjusted for changes in volume. It is a budget that creates ex-post budget from ex-ante budget. It is a budget that is tailored to any volume level. It is based on a knowledge how revenue and costs should behave over a range of activity. The difference between the static and flexible budgets amounts is called sales volume variance. Unit prices are held constant. Government budgets are almost always static budgets. In industry, fixed budgets are appropriate for those departments whose workload does not have a direct current relationship to sales or production e.g. administrative department. Continuous budgets, also called rolling budget, are budgets that have a short period say two months and is a type of fixed budget. Budgets may also be clarified according to type of activity or flexibility or budget cycle.

Example 1

Following is static budget of a machine department. It shows indirect factory cost expected at a single level of activity at 100% capacity of 10,000 labour hours.

Machining Department

Overhead or Indirect Factory Costs Budget

(at 10,000 direct labour hours)

Fixed Costs:	₹
Supervisor	20,000
Light	3,000
Depreciation (Equipment)	1,000
Taxes Property	7,000
Maintenance	1,600
Employees State Insurance	1,000
Total Fixed Costs	33,600
Variable Costs:	
Indirect labour	2,000
Electricity (Power)	5,000
Depreciation machine	10,000
Supplies	4,800
Repairs	3,000
Total variable cost	24,800
Total factory overheads costs	58,400

Static budget can be easily converted into flexible budget. The expenses are to be separated first into fixed and variable like above based on some method (see Chapter 11). The fixed costs do not change over a normal range of operations or a level of activity. Variable expenses increase or decrease in direct proportion to volume. The above static budget is converted into a flexible budget as three levels of activity. It shows overhead costs expected at those levels.

Machining Department

Overhead Factory Flexible Budget

Based on direct labour hours Percentage of capacity	8,000 80% ₹	10,000 100% ₹	12,000 120% ₹
Fixed Costs:			
Supervisor	20,000	20,000	20,000
Light	3,000	3,000	3,000
Depreciation equipment	1,000	1,000	1,000
Taxes (Property)	7,000	7,000	7,000
Maintenance	1,600	1,600	1,600
Employees State Insurance	1,000	1,000	1,000
Total fixed costs	33,600	33,600	33,600

Based on direct labour hours Percentage of capacity	8,000 80% ₹	10,000 100% ₹	12,000 120% ₹
Variable Costs:			
Indirect labour	1,600	2,000	2,400
Electricity (Power)	4,000	5,000	6,000
Depreciation Machine	8,000	10,000	12,000
Supplies	3,840	4,800	5,760
Repairs	2,400	3,000	3,600
Total variable costs	19,840	24,800	29,760
Total factory overhead	53,440	58,400	63,360
Fixed Factory overhead rate per DLH	4.20	3.36	2.80
Variable Factory overhead rate per DLH	2.48	2.48	2.48
Total Factory overhead rate per DLH	6.68	5.84	5.28

The formula for calculating fixed or variable or factory overhead rate is:

$$= \frac{\text{Budgeted fixed or variable or total overheads}}{\text{Some pre-selected activity level for the year}}$$

The pre-selected activity level, also called volume, is the denominator. The rate calculated is called 'predetermined overhead rate'. It is to be noted that the variable overhead rate is different at different levels of activity. The selection of overhead rate depends upon following factors:

(a) *Base to be used*: In our example we have used direct labour hours as denominator. But units of production, direct material cost, direct labour cost or machine hours can also be used as a base.

(b) *Inclusion or exclusion of fixed overhead*: In factory overheads, fixed overheads are included if absorption costing is adopted. They are not included if factory overheads are calculated on the basis of direct costing method.

(c) *Use of single or many rates*: The rate may be calculated at plant wide (blanket rate) or department or at centre or at operational level. For services activities separate set of rates may be used.

(d) *Activity level to be used*: In our example we have used different activity levels i.e. 80%, 100%, and 120%. The activity level or capacity is used in four senses:

(i) Maximum or ideal or theoretical capacity

(ii) Practical capacity or volume.

(iii) Normal capacity or volume (some call it standard production or average volume or capacity or activity)

(iv) Expected actual capacity or expected annual activity (or volume) or Master budgeted activity (volume).

Ideal or theoretical capacity is calculated on the assumption that the factory is working without any interruption, e.g., electricity or material shortage or strike or even holidays or for repairs. This is not practically possible.

Practical capacity is calculated by making allowances and deductions on account of these factors. Normal capacity is based on a long period e.g. average of five years. Actual or master budgeted is annual capacity. There is a difference of opinion as to which capacity be used. Maximum capacity is not attainable and expected capacity demands too little. So choice should be between normal or practical capacity.

Example 2

A factory works 10 hours per day for six days a week on a single shift. The factory is closed or idle for 20 working days in a year due to holidays or other interruptions. The normal five years average sales are 4,000 units and expected sales in the current year is 3,000 units. Two units of the product are made in one hour.

		Total capacity
(a)	Ideal or Maximum capacity 365 days × 10 hours per day	= 3650 Hours
(b)	Practical capacity 365 days less 52 Sundays and 20 days for other = 293 × 10	= 2930 Hours
(c)	Normal capacity 4000 units ÷ 2 units per hours	= 2000 Hours
(d)	Master budgeted or annual/ Expected capacity 3000 ÷ 2	= 1500 Hours

Idle capacity will be different. It is found by deducting the expected actual capacity. So in first three cases it will be:

3650 – 1500 = 2150 Hours

2930 – 1500 = 1430 Hours

2000 – 1500 = 500 Hours.

Budgeting Techniques

In commercial organisations, there are three approaches to the budgeting process:

1. The sales approach
2. The manufacturing facilities approach
3. The action programme approach

The sales approach is given below:

	Budgeted sales	....
Less	Budgeted variable costs	....
	Budgeted contribution	....
Less	Budgeted fixed costs	....
	Budgeted profit	....

The budgeted sales are based on an analysis of the market. This approach is based on marginal cost concept. The manufacturing facilities approach works in opposite direction i.e. we start from budgeted profit and end with budgeted sales. The two methods are two sides of the same coin.

The third approach, as described by B.J.M. Edmunds, is given below:

(A)	Profit on the basis of the operations of current year	....
(B)	*Add/deduct* the effect of action programmes originated in the current years on operations for the budget year (called carry over effect)	....
(C)	*Add/deduct* the effect of environment factors affecting the business in the budget year not experienced in the current year	....
(D)	*Add/deduct* the effect of action programmes originated in the budget year	....
(E)	Budgeted Profit	....

The approach to be adopted depends upon the key factor like customer demand, shortage of materials or labour or cash and manufacturing facilities.

In case of government and non-profit organisations the approach may be of two types:

(a) Input-oriented approach
(b) Output-oriented approach

(a) *Input-oriented approach*: It is also called 'incremental approach'[1] or 'item line' approach. It is a traditional approach. Under it the existing base is accepted and only the difference between existing budget appropriation

1. Negotiated static budget may be incremental or zero base. This budget is a technique for controlling discretionary costs (also called managed or programmed costs). These costs have no relationship between inputs and outputs and arise from periodic appropriation decisions.

and proposed expenditure is taken into account i.e. only increment involved is considered. It is simple and easy and required little paper work. But there is a difficulty in adding any new function in case of any change. It is also difficult to find new resources for new functions as old ones are not dropped.

(b) *Output-oriented approach*: This is also known as "programme budget". It is of various types:

(i) Zero-base budgeting (ZBB)
(ii) Performance budgeting
(iii) Planning, programme budgeting system

(i) *Zero-base budgeting*: This technique, first introduced by Peter Pyhrr in 1970 in U.S.A., is based on assumption that zero will be spent on each programme or activity. Zero is the beginning point and not the previous budget. The basic steps in this technique are:

1. Describe the programme in "decision packages".
2. Evaluate and rank the packages.
3. Allocate the resources.

A decision package is a document that describes the programme in a manner that the management may decide whether to approve it or not. It may be a mutually exclusive package or incremental package. The decision package is formulated at level which is responsible operationally for the approved budget. Ranking means listing of all identified packagers in order of decreasing benefit. The ranking may be done at top or ground level by managers. Thus in ZBB all activities are evaluated every time budget is prepared.

The zero[1] base budgeting has the following advantages:

1. It provides the manager, at each level, a mechanism for identifying, evaluating and communicating his activities to higher levels.
2. It directs the attention to the whole activity and its feasibility only to the change or difference between the existing and planned expenditure.
3. It provides a tool to view the activities objectively.
4. Managers are eager to execute the budget as they are involved in ranking process.
5. It provides necessary data for measuring effectiveness of any programme or activity.

This technique, however, is expensive. Paper work is more and ranking is difficult for want of information or expertise or time. Some government departments in India has adopted it since 1987.

1. Change justification budgeting and review period budgeting ideas originated from ZBB. Former is based on previous year figures and latter reviews budget of several years.

(ii) *Performance budgeting*: Under this system, the emphasis is on "measurable performance of activities and work-in-progress". This technique uses cost accounting or work measurement as its tools. It can be described by following steps:

(a) It classifies the budgetary accounts by function and activity as well as by organisation unit.
(b) It investigates and measures the existing activity in order to obtain maximum efficiency and to establish cost standards.
(c) It bases the budget of next year upon unit cost standard multiplied by expected number of units of activity estimated in that period. Total budget is the sum total of standard unit multiplied by expected unit of activity.

This technique has the advantage of having narrative description of every proposed activity, measures cost and output and provides detailed data. It provides the way to control the subordinates and to evaluate their performance.

But sometimes data on cost basis may not be available and there may be a shortage of staff that has knowledge of cost benefit analysis or standard cost.

(iii) *Planning-programme budget system (PPBS)*: Under this system, that lays emphasis on long run considerations, following steps are taken:

(a) First identify the objectives and goals of the government or the non-profit organisation. Relate all the activities to these objectives.
(b) Identify the future year implications explicitly.
(c) Consider all pertinent cost.
(d) Analyse systematically alternative programmes on relational basis considering revenues available and other factors.
(e) Evaluate on continuing bases the budgetary and management performance.

This system makes the long-range planning a routine. Plans and programmes are reviewed continuously under it. It strengthens inter-governmental coordination and inter-departmental planning is improved.

But it is difficult to formulate a meaningful explicit statement of governmental goals. Goals change from time to time and there is political interference. Government officials have limited time and there are measurement problems. There is little follow up and it may take years to implement it.

Budgeting Procedure—Preparation of an Operating Budget

First, the management must be told the advantages of budgeting and secondly the accounting systems must be tailored. The operating budget shall be shown as a part of Master Budget in the following section. For designing an operating budget first of all forecast of sales be made. Forecasts of sales and of operating conditions will probably be uptodated from time to time during the year. Sales forecasts be obtained either by product line managers or by field sales force according to geographical territories or through statistical calculations. Using the best possible sales forecast is useful, but they must be uptodated periodically. The operating budget may be variable or fixed budget.

To achieve a variable budget it is necessary to segregate fixed and variable expenses. This may be done from chart of accounts, designating each expense account as either fixed or variable. The other method is segregating by performance analysis in the budgeting process i.e. review the changes in expenses due to change in facilities or methods. Anything new will affect operating costs.

Variable budgets are more intricate than fixed ones. Usually, they pertain to departments whose work is much more insulated from financial presentations than is the case within fixed budget areas. Variable budgets can be profitably employed in mercantile, services, and even financial institutions. The budget person begins by outlining the general programme, the expected economic conditions and the general budgetary principles involved. He will then present the budget estimate sheets. The estimate sheet shall show the expenses like indirect labour, repairs and maintenance etc., volume factor (rupees of direct labour), estimated cost at current volume, high volume and low volume. The budget person discusses each expense account. A specimen is given below:

Exhibit 10.1

BUDGET ESTIMATE SHEET

Department			Year		
Particulars	Average Monthly Cost ₹	Notes	Estimated cost at		
			Current Volume ₹	High Volume ₹	Low Volume ₹
Volume factor (₹ of direct labour)	50,000		90,000	1,12,000	60,000
No. of shifts	1½		1½	2	1
Expenses:					
1. Indirect Labour	15,000	New machine	16,000	18,000	13,000
2. Repairs	2,000	Old Machine needed repairs at high volume	2,000	3,200	2,000
3. —	—				
4. —	—				
Total cost	1,67,000		1,65,000	1,80,000	1,05,000

The total cost is merely an assumption. The indication of the reasonableness of each expense estimate is its relation to past experience.

The fixed budget estimate sheet should also be prepared. A specimen is given:

Exhibit 10.2

BUDGET ESTIMATE SHEET (FIXED BUDGET)

Department ....

Designation	Current Year Estimated		Estimated Cost for current year	Budget for current year	First half	Second half	Total
	Expenses for months of 2015	Expenses for other months					
1. No. of workers at the end							
2. Expenses							
a.							
b.							
c.							
Totals							

The assembly and testing of the budgets of all phases of operations are done with annual figures only. The reasonableness of budgets should be tested by a check list. When the budget estimates have been completed for each department, a proforma profit and loss account and a proforma balance sheet can be prepared.

The Master Budget

It summarises the objectives of all sub-units of an organisation—sales, production, distribution and finance. Mechanically, preparation of a master budget involves a set of technical procedures that generate the supporting schedules and aggregate them into a comprehensive statement of expected income and a new balance sheet for the end of the period. To make easy a period of one year, divided into quarterly data, has been taken.

Usually, the starting point in preparing the master budget is the sales forecast for the period. It is assumed that expected sales is a variable factor to the firm. The sales forecast serves as the basis for developing production budget for the period. After production budget the cash and non-cash expenditures can be estimated. These estimates can be summarized into raw material purchases, direct labour cost and manufacturing overhead budgets. Total selling and production activities indicate the amounts of selling and administrative expenses that should be incurred. These individual budgets may be consolidated into cash budget, projected income statement and projected balance sheet.

Sales budget: It is based on simple forecast of past sales. It depends upon many factors such as competition, seasonal variation, production capacity, price, advertisement and so on. The sales data may be based on estimates provided by salesmen. Sales personnel deliberately bias their estimates downward. The format selected depends upon the structure of the firm. The sales budget shown in Exhibit 10.3 is based on classification by responsibility units i.e. areas and articles. If possible budget data should flow from individual sales personnel upward to the chief sales officer. Statistical approach like correlation analysis between sales and economic indicators, trend and cycle projection should be made. Lastly, all top officers should use their experience and judgement to project sales.

Exhibit 10.3

SALES BUDGET

	Area 1		Area 2		Area 3		Totals	
	Units	Amount ₹	Units	Amount ₹	Units	Amount ₹	Units	Amount ₹
Articles A (₹ 3 per unit)								
1st Qtr.	7,000	21,000	10,000	30,000	9,000	27,000	26,000	78,000
2nd Qtr.	8,000	24,000	11,000	33,000	9,000	27,000	28,000	84,000
3rd Qtr.	11,000	33,000	14,000	42,000	9,000	27,000	34,000	1,02,000
4th Qtr.	9,000	27,000	9,000	27,000	8,000	24,000	26,000	78,000
Totals	35,000	1,05,000	44,000	1,32,000	35,000	1,05,000	1,14,000	3,42,000
Article B (₹ 4 per unit)								
1st Qtr.	40,000	1,60,000	75,000	3,00,000	50,000	2,00,000	1,65,000	6,60,000
2nd Qtr.	50,000	2,00,000	80,000	3,20,000	70,000	2,80,000	2,00,000	8,00,000
3rd Qtr.	55,000	2,20,000	75,000	3,00,000	80,000	3,20,000	2,10,000	8,40,000
4th Qtr.	50,000	2,00,000	60,000	2,40,000	75,000	3,00,000	1,85,000	7,40,000
	1,95,000	7,80,000	2,90,000	11,60,000	2,75,000	11,00,000	7,60,000	30,40,000

Production budget: The sales budget is the basis for preparing production budget. The number of units to be produced is the number of units to be sold plus ending inventory desired minus the number of units available in beginning inventory. The forecast of the level of ending inventory desired is based on the estimated sales in future periods. The production budget is shown in Exhibit 10.4. Not that the production budget is stated in finished physical units.

Materials budget: The production budget indicates the number of units to be produced in each quarter and it is the basis for developing amounts of material labour and overhead necessary during a particular period. The materials budget (Exhibit 10.5) summarises the amounts of material needed to produce the desired production budgeted in each quarter. These items are priced and a purchase budget is shown also in Exhibit 10.6. The purchases are equal to materials needed for production plus ending inventory desired minus materials in hand. All purchases are on credit.

Exhibit 10.4
PRODUCTION BUDGET

Article A	Qtr. 1	Qtr. 2	Qtr. 3	Qtr. 4
Units to be sold (see Exhibit 10.3)	26,000	28,000	34,000	26,000
Add: Planned ending inventory	1,000	1,300	1,000	1,200
Units needed during the period	27,000	29,300	35,000	27,200
Less: Beginning inventory	700	1,000	1,300	1,000
Units to be produced	26,300	28,300	33,700	26,200
Article B				
Units to be sold (Exhibit 10.3)	1,65,000	2,00,000	2,10,000	1,85,000
Add: Planned ending inventory	10,000	12,000	15,000	20,000
Units needed during the period	1,75,000	2,12,000	2,25,000	2,25,000
Less: Beginning inventory	5,000	10,000	12,000	15,000
Units to be produced	1,70,000	2,02,000	2,13,000	1,90,000

Exhibit 10.5
MATERIALS BUDGET

Plastic	Qtr. 1	Qtr. 2	Qtr. 3	Qtr. 4
Units to be used	1,00,000	3,00,000	2,00,000	50,000
Add: Planned ending inventory	10,000	5,000	4,000	10,000
Units needed during the period	1,10,000	3,05,000	2,04,000	60,000
Less: Planned beginning inventory	15,000	10,000	5,000	4,000
Units to be purchased	95,000	2,95,000	1,99,000	56,000
Total: 6,45,000 units				
Steel				
Units to be used	1,00,000	1,00,000	1,75,000	1,50,000
Add: Planned ending inventory	10,000	7,500	10,000	10,000
Units needed during the period	1,10,000	1,07,500	1,85,000	1,60,000
Less: Planned beginning inventory	10,000	10,000	7,500	10,000
Units to be purchased	1,00,000	97,500	1,77,500	1,50,000
Total: 5,25,000 units				
Wood				
Units to be used	1,00,000	1,00,000	50,000	50,000
Add: Planned ending inventory	10,000	10,000	8,000	20,000
Units needed during the period	1,10,000	1,10,000	58,000	70,000
Less: Planned beginning inventory	15,000	10,000	10,000	8,000
Units to be purchased	95,000	1,00,000	48,000	62,000
Total: 3,05,000 units				

The example is adapted from
Cost Accounting—Accounting Data for Management's Decisions by N. Dopuch, J.G. Bimberg and J. Demski Harcourt Brace. Jevanorich Inc. 3rd Ed. Chapt. 10.

Exhibit 10.6
PURCHASES BUDGET

	Qtr. 1 ₹	Qtr. 2 ₹	Qtr. 3 ₹	Qtr. 4 ₹
Cost of materials to be used	2,00,000	3,00,000	3,00,000	2,00,000
Add: Planned ending inventory	20,000	15,000	16,000	25,000
Cost of materials need	2,20,000	3,15,000	3,16,000	2,25,000
Less: Planned beginning inventory	25,000	20,000	15,000	16,000
Cost of materials to be purchased	1,95,000	2,95,000	3,01,000	2,09,000
Total purchase : ₹ 10,00,000				

Exhibit 10.7
DIRECT LABOUR

	Qtr. 1 ₹	Qtr. 2 ₹	Qtr. 3 ₹	Qtr. 4 ₹	Standard
Article A (Hours)[1]	26,300	28,300	33,700	26,200	1 hour/unit
Article B (Hours)[1]	85,000	1,01,000	1,06,500	95,000	½ hour/unit
Total hours	1,11,300	1,29,300	1,40,200	1,21,200	₹ 1.50 per hour

Total labour budget = ₹ 7,53,000 1. From Exhibit 10.4

Exhibit 10.8
MANUFACTURING OVERHEAD BUDGET

	Qtr. 1 ₹	Qtr. 2 ₹	Qtr. 3 ₹	Qtr. 4 ₹	Total ₹
Heat	5,000	3,000	1,000	4,000	13,000
Light	3,200	3,000	2,800	3,000	12,000
Power	5,895	6,235	6,399	6,094	24,623
Supplies	2,945	3,455	3,701	3,243	13,344
Maintenance	12,000	13,000	15,000	12,300	52,300
Rent	15,000	15,000	15,000	15,000	60,000
Depreciation	23,500	23,500	23,500	23,500	94,000
Indirect labour	3,926	4,606	4,934	4,324	17,790
Insurance	1,000	1,000	1,000	1,000	4,000
Totals	72,466	72,796	73,334	72,461	2,91,057
Less: Depreciation	23,500	23,500	23,500	23,500	94,000
Cash payments	48,966	49,296	49,834	48,961	1,97,057

Average overhead per unit of production is $\frac{2,91,057}{8,89,500}$ = ₹ 0.327 Approx.

1. ₹ 0.02 per unit sold.

Exhibit 10.9

SELLING EXPENSE BUDGET

	Qtr. 1 ₹	Qtr. 2 ₹	Qtr. 3 ₹	Qtr. 4 ₹	Total ₹
Salaries	25,000	25,000	25,000	25,000	1,00,000
Commissions[1]	20,800	24,900	26,500	23,000	95,200
Travelling	16,000	17,000	17,000	16,000	66,000
Advertising	50,000	50,000	50,000	50,000	2,00,000
Telephone	1,000	1,000	1,000	1,000	4,000
Shipping expenses[2]	3,820	4,560	4,880	4,220	17,480
Rent	6,250	6,250	6,250	6,250	25,000
Carriage out	4,000	5,000	6,000	5,000	20,000
Total	1,26,870	1,33,710	1,36,630	1,30,470	5,27,680

Exhibit 10.10

GENERAL AND ADMINISTRATIVE BUDGET

Officers salaries	45,000	45,000	45,000	45,000	1,80,000
Office salaries	27,500	27,500	27,500	27,500	1,10,000
Audit fee	8,000	—	—	—	8,000
Taxes	14,000	14,000	14,000	14,000	56,000
Supplies	2,000	2,000	2,000	2,000	8,000
Light & Heat	3,000	500	500	2,000	6,000
Rent	9,500	9,500	9,500	9,500	38,000
Telephone	1,000	1,000	1,000	1,000	4,000
Donations	500	500	500	500	2,000
Depreciation	1,500	1,500	1,500	1,500	6,000
Totals	1,12,000	1,01,500	1,01,500	1,03,000	4,18,000
Less: Depreciation	1,500	1,500	1,500	1,500	6,000
Cash payments	1,10,500	1,00,000	1,00,000	1,01,500	4,12,000

Direct labour budget: The production of articles A and B each requires one hour and half hour of direct labour hours respectively. The direct labour budget can be prepared showing the standard labour rate. The labour hours required for each article in any quarter is based on the expected production as shown by production budget. The budget is shown in Exhibit 10.7.

1. App. 2.8% of sales.
2. ₹ 0.02 per unit sold.

Manufacturing overhead budget: This budget is a summary budget of all overhead activities, and therefore, not disaggregated enough for detailed control purposes. The sample budget is shown in Exhibit 10.8. Some items are fixed and some are variable. The heat and light are affected by environmental conditions and the rate of production. Power, a semi-variable item, changes with volume. Rent, depreciation and insurance are fixed expenses. The pattern for maintenance cost is usually less clear. This is probably budgeted on the basis of the amount of production. The depreciation is not included for calculation of cash outflow as it is a non-cash expense.

Selling and administrative budgets: The example of these budgets is shown in Exhibits 10.9 and 10.10. The administrative expense budget mostly showing cost that are fixed. In selling expense budget shows both fixed and variable costs. Commissions and shipping expenses are variable, others are fixed except delivery expense. The delivery expense is a step cost with no cost equation specified.

Cash budget: There are three methods of its preparation: (a) The Receipt and Payment Method, (b) The Adjusted (Budgeted) P&L method and (c) The Balance Sheet Method (Budgeted). While preparing the cash budget by Receipt and Payment method, the total cash receipts and cash payments along with opening and closing balance are shown. Particular attention must be given to the amount of net sales i.e., after bad debts and returns and allowances (discount). Moreover, the debtors (accounts receivables) may not be paying regularly. From past experience it should be found out what is the pattern of payments by debtors. A firm may not have actual experience but we may illustrate by an Example 3.

Example 3

Past collection experience indicates that the firm can expect to collect 88% of a quarter's net sales within the quarter in which sales are made, another 10% in following quarter, and remaining 2% in the quarter after that. The discount on sales is 4% and bad debts assumed are 2% of gross sales. The net sales shall be calculated as follows:

	Qtr. 1	Qtr. 2	Qtr. 3	Qtr. 4	Total
Gross sales (Exhibit 10.3)	7,38,000	8,84,000	9,42,000	8,18,000	33,82,000
Discounts	29,520	35,360	37,680	32,720	1,35,280
Bad debts	14,760	17,680	18,840	16,360	67,640
Total deductions	44,280	53,040	56,520	49,080	2,02,920
Net sales	6,93,720	8,30,960	8,85,480	7,68,920	31,79,080

The estimated cash collection from the debtors on the basis of above assumption can be calculated as shown in Exhibit 10.11.

Exhibit 10.11

	Qtr. 1 ₹	Qtr. 2 ₹	Qtr. 3 ₹	Qtr. 4 ₹
Net Debtors at the beginning of quarter				
Previous quarter (12%)	72,000[e1]	83,246	99,715	1,06,258
Second previous quarter (2%)	12,000[e1]	12,000	13,874	16,619
Plus net current sales	6,93,720	8,30,960	8,85,480	7,68,920
Total due	7,77,720	9,26,206	9,99,069	8,91,797
Less: Collections:				
88% of current quarter	6,10,474	7,31,245	7,79,222	6,76,650
10% of previous quarter	60,000[e2]	69,372	83,096	88,548
2% of second previous quarter	22,000[e2]	12,000	13,874	16,619
Total collections	6,82,474	8,12,617	8,76,192	7,81,817
Ending balance debtors	95,246	1,13,589	1,22,877	1,09,980

The cash budget can now be presented in the form shown in Exhibit 10.12.

Exhibit 10.12

CASH BUDGET

	Qtr.1 ₹	Qtr. 2 ₹	Qtr. 3 ₹	Qtr. 4 ₹	Total ₹
Beginning Balance	90,000	75,063	28,224	99,052	90,000
Budgeted receipts:					
Collection of debtors	6,82,474	8,12,617	8,76,192	7,81,817	31,53,100
Other incomes[e*]	5,000	6,000	3,000	3,000	17,000
Sales of assets[e*]	20,000	—	—	10,000	30,000
Totals	7,07,474	8,18,617	8,79,192	7,94,817	32,00,100
Budgeted disbursements:					
Material (10.6)	1,95,000	2,95,000	3,01,000	2,09,000	10,00,000
Labour (10.7)	1,66,950	1,93,950	2,10,300	1,81,800	7,53,000
Manufacturing O.H. (10.8)	48,966	49,296	49,834	48,961	1,97,057
Selling expenses (10.9)	1,26,870	1,33,710	1,36,630	1,30,470	5,27,680
Administrative exp. (10.10)	1,10,500	1,00,000	1,00,000	1,01,500	4,12,000
Capital expansion	28,000	12,000	7,000	12,000	59,000
Interest payments	2,125	—	3,600	—	5,725
Income tax	44,000	44,000	—	—	88,000
Dividends	—	37,500	—	37,500	75,000
Govt. Bonds	—	—	—	75,000	75,000
Totals	(7,22,411)	(8,65,456)	(8,08,364)	(7,96,231)	(31,92,462)
Net change	14,937	46,839	70,828	1,414	7,638
Ending balance	75,063	28,224	99,052	97,638	97,638

e* Amount and/or period assumed. (see Exhibit 10.12)

---

e1. Assumed to be from balance sheet.

e2. 10% is ₹ 60,000 from previous quarter sales and entire amount of second previous quarter will be collected in this quarter. (see Exhibit 10.11 for e[1] and e[2])

The cash budget tells us the importance as well as difficulty of budget preparation. Various budgets are important because they permit management to anticipate its problems. The preparation of budgets is difficult because a substantial amount of effort is required to assess the desirability of various courses of action available to management. Recently, two approaches have been suggested to assist the management and simplify the problem.

They are:

(a) Mathematical programming models.

(b) Simulation models (computer based). They are out of purview of this chapter.

The second method of preparing cash budget by "adjusting P&L method" is also called cash flow statement method and explained in Chapter 6 on page 140.

Budgeted Income Statement

In operating budget, the last step is to prepare a budgeted income statement after the aforesaid budgets. Proforma budgeted income statement is prepared in the same manner as if actual figures were used. Items of other income and expense and income taxes are tentatively estimates. The statement should be in detail. As a part of preparation of this statement the fixed and variable expenses should be made to total separately. A specimen is given in Exhibit 10.13.

Budgeted Balance Sheet

A proforma (projected) balance sheet as at the end of the budgeted year is prepared to show the effect of the budgeted transactions on the financial condition and to indicate cash requirements. It is the last method of preparing cash budget. A projection of the balance sheet as at the beginning of the budgeted period (end of the current year) must be made. A work sheet for the forecast balance sheet is prepared. The balance sheet accounts are still in a raw state and need adjustment. The cash account is the residue account, all other transactions affecting it, so it is scrutinized. The budgeted balance sheet affects the next year's budget and financial flow. A specimen is given in Exhibit 10.14.

Installing and Administering the Budget

It is necessary that while installing and administering the budget, budget reports must be issued usually monthly to every unit for which a budget was established. The following points may be noted in this connection.

(a) *Accounting system*: The accounting system and the budgetary system should be in accordance with organisation structure. Usually, budgets are used for comprehensive control, if not for planning always, along with accounting system. So the accounting and budgeting systems must be linked together. This will help in control of activities.

(b) *Budget committee*: For better and efficient administration of budget, there must be a director/manager (budgeting). He is a staff expert. He should consult a budget committee constituted of top level line executives. There may be special budget committee as well. This committee has an advisory role to play. It assembles, reviews, transmits and makes recommendations about budget data.

(c) *Budget manual*: It is highly desirable to have a budget manual that contains instructions, information, procedures, rules, etc. for implementation of budget. It tells what to do, how to do it, when to do it and in which way to do it. The budget manual should be made available at the desk of all concerned.

(d) *Revision and follow up*: It is the duty of the line manager to investigate the deviation in budget.

Exhibit 10.13

BUDGETED INCOME STATEMENT

	Qtr. 1 ₹	Qtr. 2 ₹	Qtr. 3 ₹	Qtr. 4 ₹	Total ₹
Budgeted sales—units	1,91,000	2,28,000	2,44,000	2,11,000	8,79,000
Budgeted production—units	1,96,000	2,30,000	2,46,700	2,16,200	8,88,500
Sales (net) (10.3) A	6,93,720	8,30,960	8,85,480	7,68,920	31,79,080
Cost of sales (10.5):					
Materials	2,00,000	3,00,000	3,00,000	2,00,000	10,00,000
Direct labour	1,66,950	1,93,950	2,10,300	1,81,800	7,53,000
Totals	3,66,950	4,93,950	5,10,300	3,81,800	17,53,000
Indirect Mfg. Costs (10.8):					
Fixed	39,500	39,500	39,500	39,500	1,58,000
Variable	32,966	33,296	33,834	32,961	1,33,057
Total	72,466	72,796	73,334	72,461	2,91,057
Total costs of sales (B)	4,39,416	5,66,746	5,83,634	4,54,261	20,44,057
A – B = x	2,54,304	2,64,214	3,10,846	3,14,659	11,35,023
Selling expenses (10.9)					
Fixed	57,250	57,250	57,250	57,250	2,29,000
Variable	69,620	76,360	79,380	73,220	2,98,680
Total (C)	1,26,870	1,33,710	1,36,630	1,30,470	5,27,680
Gen. & Adm. Expenses (10.10)					
Fixed	1,09,000	1,01,000	1,01,000	1,01,000	4,12,000
Variable	3,000	500	500	2,000	6,000
Total (D)	1,12,000	1,01,500	1,01,500	1,03,000	4,18,000
Total operating expense (C + D) = y	2,38,870	2,35,210	2,38,130	2,33,470	9,45,680
Net operating income (x – y)	15,434	29,004	63,716	81,189	1,89,343
Other income (10.11)	5,000	6,000	3,000	3,000	17,000
	20,434	35,004	66,716	81,189	2,06,343
Interest expense	1,125	1,125	2,475	3,375	8,100
Pretax income	19,309	33,879	64,241	80,814	1,98,243
Tax (50%)	9,654	16,939	32,120	40,407	99,121
Net Income	9,645	16,940	32,121	40,407	99,122

Exhibit 10.14

BUDGETED BALANCE SHEET

	Jan. 1 ₹	March. 31 ₹	June 30 ₹	Sept. 30 ₹	Dec. 31 ₹
Assets:					
Current Cash (10.11)	90,000	75,063	28,224	99,052	97,638
Govt. Bonds (10.11)	4,000	4,000	4,000	4,000	79,000
Debtors (10.12) (net)	84,000	95,246	1,13,589	1,92,877	1,09,980
Stock:					
Material (10.6)	25,000	20,000	15,000	16,000	25,000
Finished goods	28,500	28,500	28,500	28,500	28,500
Inventory changes[1] (Adj.)	—	274	25,133	40,078	27,938
Net current assets	2,31,500	2,22,525	2,14,446	3,10,507	3,68,101
Fixed Assets (net)	15,00,000	14,83,000	15,60,000	16,02,000	15,79,000
Total	17,31,500	17,05,525	17,74,446	19,12,507	19,47,101
Liabilities:					
Accounts payable	35,000	35,000	35,000	35,000	35,000
Interest due	1,000	—	1,125	—	3,375
Taxation due (10.13)	88,000	53,654	26,593	58,713	86,521
Total current liabilities (10.11)	1,24,000	88,654	62,718	93,713	1,24,896
Loan	75,000	75,000	1,65,000	2,25,000	1,37,904
Total liabilities	1,99,000	1,63,654	2,27,718	3,18,713	2,62,800
Authorised and paid up capital	14,00,000	14,00,000	14,00,000	14,00,000	14,00,000
Reserves	1,32,500	1,32,500	1,42,964	1,46,728	1,93,794
Quarterly earnings (10.13)	—	9,645	13,940	32,121	40,407
Dividend (10.11)	—	—	37,500	—	37,500
Tax credit	—	—	—	—	12,600
Total	17,31,500	17,05,525	17,74,446	19,12,507	19,47,101

The budgets are not merely for planning, they are an effective control tool also. They should not be just in files or wrongly interpreted. About revision of the budget most authorities agree that except in unusual circumstances, a budget should not be revised during the year. If the budget line constantly changes, it becomes more difficult to interpret the overall performance and to make accurate projections.

(e) *Budget period*: The length of the budget period varies with the company and also with nature of the budget. It can be for a short period of one year or for a long period say upto twenty years. Both have their respective advantages and disadvantages. It depends upon the circumstances which period should be choosen. However, the budget should be available in time for the commencement of the budget period.

1. The difference has been debited to inventory account, which is due to production exceeding sales.

Principal Budget Factor

This is also called key or limiting budget factor. The first step in budgeting is to identify the factor which imposes a limitation or ceiling on the level of activity. The level of activity refers to the amount of work done, or the number of events that have occurred. The key factor is usually sales demand, but it may also be limitations on any resource—materials, labour, machine time, working capital, etc. Once this factor is defined, the rest of the budget can be prepared. Production resources usually exceed sales demand. If sales demand is more than the key budget factor is any other resource.

If we assume that fixed costs will remain unchanged by the decision to produce more or less of a product, the production budget which maximises profit will also maximise contribution. The contribution (then profit) will maximise by making most profitable use of the scarce resource.

Suppose a firm produces two products *X* and *Y*. Both have unlimited demand and use same type of labour, that is in restricted supply, other details are:

	X ₹	*Y* ₹
Sale Price		
V.C.	30	30
Contribution	18	20
	12	10
Hours per unit	3 hrs.	2 hrs.
Contribution per labour hour	₹ 4	₹ 5

Product *Y* is more profitable. But this decision will be affected if sales price of either product is raised or production of *Y* only will have adverse effect on sales demand or stopping *X* will have no effect on fixed costs or it will affect long and short term plans.

In the above example, we assume that all relationship is linear, variable costs are constant and sales demand and resources required to make are known with certainty.

Probabilistic Income Budget

It is a method which combines the concept of flexible budgets with an estimate of the probability that each level of activity will be achieved. Its purpose is to provide an analysis of the uncertainty or risk within the budget by providing estimates of likely variations from the master plan. The approach is called ‘single figure expected values’. More common technique is to calculate expected values (or weighted average values) for sale price, sales volume, fixed and variable costs, and then to construct a budget using these single value figure.

Example 4

Akamba Company is preparing a budget for next year. Three estimates have been prepared with following additional information:

	Probability	Sales units	Price sales unit ₹	V.C. ₹	F.C. ₹
Worst	0.3	1,600	3.80	2.6	1,400
Likely	0.6	2,000	4.00	2.2	1,200
Best	0.1	2,200	4.40	2.0	1,100

The sale price is ₹ 3.98 and 950 units have been sold.

First, we should calculate expected value of each by multiplying the concerned figure with probability value.

Expected value of:

	Sales Price ₹	V.C. ₹	F.C. ₹	Sales units
Worst	1.14	0.78	420	480
Likely	2.40	1.32	720	1,200
Best	0.44	0.20	110	220
	3.98	2.30	1,250	1,900

Profit = Sales – V.C. = Contribution
₹ 3,781.0 – 2,185.0 = 1,596
or Contribution – F.C. = Profit
= 1,596 – 1,250 = ₹ 346.

The probabilistic income budget figure for expected profit is ₹ 346. Alternatively, we may calculate expected value only of profit figures by multiplying the three profit figures with their respective probabilities.

Responsibility Accounting and the Budget

Budgets take many forms, but basically they consist of sets of standards indicating the level of activity expected from each responsible person or decision unit and the amounts of resources that should be consumed to achieve that level of activity. Such a system of budgets constitutes a responsibility accounting system or profitability accounting or activity accounting systems.

Responsibility accounting is often focused primarily on the lowest level managers who have the most day-to-day influence on the operations. The basic focus should be on knowledge or information and not control.

Responsibility accounting systems differ from firm to firm because no two organisations can be expected to delegate responsibilities for decision implementation in exactly the same way. However, the principles of responsibility accounting are the same. First, an attempt is made to determine the decision points within an organisation. Once these have been isolated, the extent of responsibility for each decision point is defined. We should inquire who should be asked in a particular situation—not who should be blamed. Responsibility may be limited or extensive. Basically the responsibility accounting systems are usually designed around cost centres, profit centres and investment centres.

Responsibility accounting is difficult to implement in practice. Ideally, responsibility for implementing all of an organisation's decisions is broken down in such a way that the responsibility for each input cost incurred and each output achieved can be traced to a single responsibility head. Unfortunately, the activities of most organisations are so interrelated that it is too costly and often not humanly possible to achieve this type of break down. For responsibility accounting the costs be divided into controllable and non-controllable costs. They may further be divided into fixed and variable costs.

QUESTIONS

1. Discuss the need for planning and budgeting in business organisations.
2. A company seeks assistance in developing cash and other budget information for May, June and July of 2021. On April 30, 2021, the company had cash of ₹ 5,500, debtors ₹ 4,37,000, Stock ₹ 3,09,400. The budget is to be based on the following assumptions:

   Sales:

   (a) Each month's sales are billed on the last day of the month.

   (b) Customers are allowed a 3% discount if payment is made within 10 days after the billing date. Debtors are recorded at gross selling price.

   (c) 60% of the billings are collected within the discount period, 25% are collected by the end of the month, 9% are collected by the end of the second month, and remaining prove bad debts.

   Purchases:

   (a) 54% of all purchases of material and a like percentage of marketing and administrative expenses are paid in the month purchased with remainder paid in the following month.

   (b) Each month's units of ending inventory are equal to 130% of the next month's units of sales.

   (c) The cost of each unit of inventory is ₹ 20.

   (d) Marketing, general and administrative expenses (of which ₹ 2,000 is depreciation) are equal to 15% of the current month's sales.

Actual and projected sales are as follows:

2020	Amount ₹	Units
March	3,54,000	11,800
April	3,63,000	12,100
May	3,57,000	11,900
June	3,42,000	11,400
July	3,60,000	12,000
August	3,66,000	12,200

Prepare a statement showing: (i) Budgeted cash disbursements during June 2020, (ii) Budgeted cash collections during May 2020, and (iii) Budgeted units of inventory to be purchased during July 2020.

3. The Budget department of A Company Ltd. prepared these estimates for the coming year:

	Beginning	Ending
Inventories (Annual):		
Raw Material (in units)	5,000	6,000
Finished goods (in units)	10,000	7,000
Sales (Gross)		1,00,000 units
Average sales price per unit		₹ 4
Raw materials, units usage rate and cost		2 units of material for each finished unit @ 0.25 each

Direct labour, per unit of finished product is 150% of direct labour cost.

Marketing and administrative expenses are budgeted at 16% of gross sales.

Prepare: (i) A production budget (annual basis) indicating units to be manufactured.

(ii) A forecast income statement.

4. Prepare a purchase budget for first three months of 2020 from the following data:

Sales Forecast 2020	₹
January	40,000
February	55,000
March	70,000
April	60,000

Other data:

1. Cost of sales 40% of sales.
2. Inventory is 1½ times budgeted sales for the coming month (at cost).
3. The beginning inventory is ₹ 30,000.

5. The following information has been made available from the records of Incheape Precision Tools Limited for the last six months of 2020 (and of only the sales of January, 2021) in respect of product x:
   (i) The units sold in different months are:

July	1,100	November	2,500
August	1,100	December 2015	2,300
September	1,700	January 2016	2,000
October	1,900		

   (ii) There will be no work-in-progress at the end of any month.
   (iii) Finished units equal to half the sales for the next month will be in stock at the end of every month (including June 2020).
   (iv) Budgeted production and production cost for the year ending 31-12-2020 are thus:

Production (units)	22,000
Direct materials per unit	₹ 10
Direct wages per unit	₹ 4

   Total factory overhead apportioned to produce ₹ 88,000. You are required to prepare a production of last six months of 2020 and a production cost budget for that period.

6. The following is an income statement of a company for the year 2020A:

	₹	₹	₹
Sales			6,00,000
Cost of sales:			
Materials		1,50,000	
Direct labour		1,30,000	
Overheads (Factory)			
Fixed	45,000		
Variable	65,000	1,10,000	3,90,000
			2,10,000
Selling and administrative expenses:			
	₹		₹
Fixed	75,000		
Variable	55,000		1,30,000
Net Income			80,000

For the year ending December 31, 2020B, it is expected that the sales will increase 20% in volume while variable production costs and selling and administrative expenses will advance in price as follows:

Materials	20%
Labour	20%
Factory overheads	10%
Selling and administrative expenses	20%

No change in the fixed production cost and selling and administrative costs. A 10% reduction in material content is expected. It is desired that the net income for 2020B shall exceed that of the year 2020A by 25%. The selling price of the company's product will be increased as much as necessary to bring the desired profit.

You are required to draw an estimated net income statement for the year ending December 31, 2020B. By what percentage must selling price of product be increased?

11

Cost Estimation Techniques

One of the assumptions required for the use of break-even analysis is that all costs are either fixed or variable within a relevant range. Depreciation or insurance expenses are fixed, whereas cost of goods sold is variable. A cost is classified either as fixed or variable, according to whether the total amount of cost changes as volume changes. The simplest and fastest technique for obtaining first estimates of these costs is by direct analysis of each component of cost. This account classification method has these limitations:

1. It classifies costs as fixed or variable.
2. It relies on only a single observation at a single activity level to determine the cost.
3. It does not give insight as to whether some costs are partially fixed and partially variable.
4. The first two objections can be overcome if we have estimates of costs at more than one activity level.

MIXED COSTS

Some costs contain both fixed and variable element and are called mixed costs or semi-variable costs, e.g. salaries, maintenance. The determination of the fixed and variable element of a semi-variable cost is necessary in order to plan, analyze, control or evaluate operating efficiency, profit structure, capital expenditures, utilization of facilities and break-even point, etc. The following statistical methods are used in determining the fixed and variable elements of a semi-variable cost:

1. High and low point method.
2. Statistical scatter graph method (or the Visual Inspection Method).
3. Correlation-regression analysis.

High and Low Point Method or Range Method

This method relies on two extreme activity levels—the highest and the lowest—to reflect change in cost that results from change in activity.

Formula: $TC = F + Vx$

V = variable cost

x = no. of units
F = fixed cost

This technique can best be explained by using an example.

Example 1

Following are the extracts from the cost accounting records of a company:[1]

Month	Overhead Cost ₹	Direct Labour Hours
1	25,200	840
2	24,800	830
3	20,800	740
4	27,500	1,130
5	23,300	770
6	26,900	910
7	24,800	950
8	26,100	1,170
9	29,100	1,160
10	27,300	1,030
11	27,600	1,200
12	21,100	780
13	21,700	750
14	30,200	1,290
15	27,300	1,060
	Total 3,83,700	14,610
	Mean 25,580	974

We have to take two extreme activity levels—the highest and the lowest—to reflect the change in cost that results changes is activity.

Activity Level

	Overhead cost		DLH
High	30,200	100%	1,290
Low	20,800	68.87%	740
	9,400	31.13%	550

Variable cost 9,400 + 550 = ₹ 17.1 per DLH approx.

1. Adapted from R.S. Kaplan, *Advanced Management Accounting*, Prentice Hall, p. 58.

	High	Low
Total expenses	30,200	20,800
Variable cost @ ₹ 17.1 per DLH	(1290) 22,050	(740) 12,650
Fixed element	8,150	8,150

The 31.13% difference between the activity levels selected in the example is 550 hours, with a cost variation of 9,400. It can be calculated also as under:

$$F + 1{,}290v = ₹\ 30{,}200$$
$$\underline{-F - 740v = -20{,}800}$$
$$550v = 9{,}400$$
$$v = \frac{9{,}400}{550} = ₹\ 17.1 \text{ DLH approx.}$$

Note. Sometimes, highest and next lowest items may be taken, e.g. 30200-29100 and DLH 1290-1660. This method will give different result and so is not used.

Example 2

Following is the data of a firm:

Year	Output (units)	Total Cost ₹	Average Price Level Index
2016	65,000	1,45,000	100
2017	80,000	1,79,000	112
2018	90,000	2,09,100	123
2019	60,000	2,01,600	144
2020	75,000	2,48,000	160

What cost should be expected in 2021 if output is 85,000 units and average price level index is 180. Use High and Low method.

Solution

	Output	Total cost	Cost at price level ₹
(a) High	90,000	$2{,}09{,}100 \times \frac{100}{123}$	1,70,000
Low	60,000	$2{,}01{,}600 \times \frac{100}{144}$	1,40,000
Variable of cost	30,000 units		₹ 30,000 i.e. ₹ 1 per unit

(b) Substituting	₹
Total cost of 90,000 units at P.L.I. 100 =	1,70,000
Less variable cost of 90,000 units @ ₹ 1	90,000
Fixed cost at P.L.I. 100 =	80,000
(c) Cost in 2020 for 85,000 units	
Variable cost @ ₹ 1. At P.L.I. 100	85,000
Fixed cost at P.L.I. 100	80,000
Total cost	1,65,000

But the P.L.I. in 2020 is 180. So this cost will be $1,65,000 \times \frac{180}{100}$ = ₹ 2,97,000.

Example 3

The following are condensed income statements prepared on an 'actual cost' basis for Manisha Co. Ltd. for the year 2019 and 2020:

	2019 ₹	2020 ₹
Sales revenue @ 10 per unit	1,00,000	80,000
Cost of sales	70,000	59,000
Gross profit	30,000	21,000
Selling and Administrative expenses	21,000	23,000
Net profit (loss)	9,000	(2,000)

The following information is also available:

(a) There were no changes in selling price in 2020.

(b) There was no changes in cost structure (manufacturing and operating expenses) during 2020.

(c) Except for a commission of 5% paid to salesman, all the selling and administrative expenses are fixed.

(d) Manufacturing cost incurred in 2020 were according to budget.

(e) There were no significant changes in inventories in 2020.

You are required to find:

(a) Variable manufacturing cost per unit.

(b) Fixed manufacturing cost per year.

(c) Variable selling and administrative expenses per unit.

(d) Fixed selling and administrative expenses for 2020.

Solution

(a) Variable manufacturing costs using high and low method.

	Units sold	Costs of goods sold ₹
2019	10,000	70,000
2020	8,000	59,000
	2,000	11,000

i.e. V.C. per unit ₹ 11,000 + 2,000 + ₹ 5.50

(b) Fixed cost per year:

	₹
Total cost of sales 2019	70,000
Less V.C. 10,000 units @ ₹ 5.50	55,000
Fixed costs	15,000

(c) Variable selling and administrative cost per unit.
Commission 5% × ₹ 10 = 50 Paisa.

(d) Fixed selling and admn. expenses for 2020:

	₹
Total selling and admn. expenses 2019	21,000
Less V.C. i.e. 5% of ₹ 1,00,000	5,000
	16,000

THE SCATTER GRAPH METHOD

Under this method all costs are plotted on a graph on vertical axis of ox and units axis of oy. Then a line in drawn by free hand in such a way that it passes through the scattered points that come reasonably close to most of them. This line in called 'Regression line' or trend line. Where the line intercepts the axis of ox is the level of fixed costs.

To find the V.C. any level is selected and the cost at that level are deducted from the level of fixed costs at the line. The difference is divided by the volume. The data in example is shown on the scatter graph below:

SCATTER GRAPH

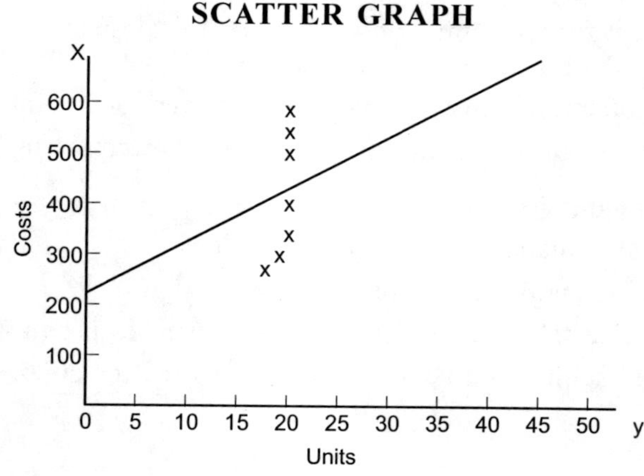

Exhibit 11.1

The line cuts at 230. It is fixed costs. To find V.C. take total cost say at 15 units. It is ₹ 310. So from ₹ 310 deduct ₹ 230 = 80, divide by 15 = ₹ 5.30 App. V.C.

The trend line introduces a subjective element into analysis that can be removed only by fitting the line mathematically.

The disadvantage of this method is that every body will not draw the same line by free hand and different estimates will be derived from the total cost function. It may be a "tight or a loose fit". However, the method is easy.

Method of Least Squares—Linear Regression Analysis

The most widely used regression model is ordinary least squares. The predicting equation used is $Y' = a + bx$. Here Y' is calculated value as distinguished from the observed value Y. The numerical values of the constants a and b that minimise $\Sigma (Y - Y')^2$, the difference between actual Y to changes in x is to be found out. This is found by using two equations, called normal equations.

$$\Sigma y = xa + b\,(\Sigma x)$$

$$\Sigma xy = a\,(\Sigma x) + b\,(\Sigma x^2).$$

Example 4

Following are the data of a firm; find the fixed costs and variable cost per unit by least square method.[1]

Volume units x	cost y
	₹
15	310
15	320
20	370
25	350
40	440
25	370
50	540
30	370
35	430
45	500
300	4,000

1. Adapted from *Cost Accounting*, G.R. Growning Shield and K.A. Gorman, p. 724.

Applying the equation, we get:

x^2	xy		
225	4,650	4,000 = 10*a* + 300 *b*	(*i*)
225	4,800	1,28,100 = 300*a* + 10,350 *b*	(*ii*)
400	7,400	multiplying (*i*) by 30 we get	
625	8,750	1,20,000 = 300*a* + 9,000 *b*	(*iii*)
1,600	17,600	Deducting (*iii*) from (*ii*)	
625	9,250	8,100 = 1,350 b	
2,500	27,000	b = ₹ 6 variable cost estimated	
900	11,000	a = ₹ 220 estimated fixed cost	
1,225	15,050		
2,025	22,500		
10,350	1,28,100		

It can be found by following method as well: $y = a + bx$
where b is given by following formula

$$b = \frac{\Sigma xy}{\Sigma x^2}$$

and a is given by following formula

$$a = \bar{y} - b\bar{x}$$

Deviations from $\bar{x}$, *Deviation from* $\bar{y}$

X	Y	X^2	XY	Y^2
–15	–90	225	1,350	8,100
–15	–80	225	1,200	6,400
–10	–30	100	300	900
–5	–50	25	250	2,500
+10	+40	100	400	1,600
–5	–30	25	150	900
+20	+140	400	2,800	19,600
0	–30	0	0	900
+5	+30	25	150	900
+15	+100	225	1,500	10,000
0	0	1,350	8,100	51,800

$b = \frac{8{,}100}{1{,}350} = ₹\ 6$ $\quad a = 400–6\ (30) = ₹\ 220$ (see question no. 7)

Standard Error of Estimate: The application of the above method reveals fixed cost ₹ 220 and variable cost ₹ 6 per unit. These are average expenses based on a calculated regression line. There is likelihood that actual unit cost will be different from what might be estimated using the calculated fixed cost and variable cost rate [e.g. for 15 units it is ₹ 220 + 15 (6) = ₹ 310]. Some difference can be expected and an acceptable range of tolerance is given by standard error of estimate. It is the standard deviation about the regression line.

Actual cost y	Expected Average cost ye	Difference	Squared $(y-ye)^2$
₹	₹	₹	₹
310	310	0	0
320	310	+10	100
370	340	+30	900
350	370	–20	400
440	460	–20	400
370	370	0	0
540	520	+20	400
370	400	–30	900
430	430	0	0
500	490	+10	100
4,000		0	3,200

Standard error of estimate, $et^1 = \sqrt{\dfrac{(y-ye)^2}{n-2}} = \sqrt{\dfrac{3,200}{10-2}} =$ ₹ 20.

In accordance with normal curve distribution probabilities 68% of data points lie within plus and minus one standard error. For example, if in future 50 units are produced, the cost estimated to be ₹ 500 [₹ 220 + 50 × 6] can be expected to lie between ₹ 500 (520 – 20) and ₹ 540 (520 + 20) about 68% (two-third) of the time. Same way, two standard error about 95% of the data points and three standard error 99% of data points lie within plus and minus two or three standard error. For 95% probability the cost will lie between ₹ 180 [₹ 220 – (2 × 20)] and ₹ 260 [220 + (2 × 20)]. We assume equal dispersion and equal standard error of estimate at all points along the regression line.

The adjusted standard error of estimate can be computed by the formula

$$\sqrt{1+\frac{1}{N}+\frac{(x-\overline{x})^2}{\Sigma(\overline{x}-x)^2}}$$

where x is the specified independent variable data points (say 35 units in future), x is the mean of independent variable (30 in our example) and $\Sigma(x - x)^2$ is the difference of each x variable in the sample from the average squared and totalled. Thus:

$$\sqrt{1+\frac{1}{10}+\frac{(35-30)^2}{1,350 \text{ (see on previous page)}}}$$

1. Another formula is $et = \sqrt{\dfrac{\Sigma y^2 - a\Sigma y - b\Sigma xy}{x-2}}$

[y^2 = 16,51,800, y = 400 Σxy = 1,28,100.]
Here y = cost, x = units

$$= \sqrt{1 + 0.1 + 0.185} = \sqrt{1.285} = 1.1335$$

This value is called computed correction factor.

So if 35 units are produced then the adjusted standard error of estimate is (₹ 20 × 1.1335) = ₹ 22.67.

The Standard errors of *a* and *b* can be found.

The formulae are:

$$et\ a = et\sqrt{\frac{1}{n} + \frac{(x)^2}{\Sigma x^2}} \qquad et\ b^2 = et\sqrt{\frac{1}{\Sigma x^2}}$$

In our example the standard error is:

$$et\ a = (20)\sqrt{\frac{1}{10} + \frac{(30)^2}{1{,}350}}$$

$$= ₹\ 17.51$$

$$et\ b = (20)\sqrt{\frac{1}{1{,}350}}$$

$$= ₹\ 0.54.$$

The standard errors, *et a* and *et b*, are multiplied by a confidence[1] factor *t* at a particular level of confidence say at 90%. The value of this factor be found from statistical table given in any book. The value of this factor at 90% level of confidence for 8 degrees of freedom (as in our example) is 1.86.

The fixed cost estimated by us is in error by no more than 1.86 × 17.51 = ₹ 32.57 (₹ 220 × 32.57) and of variable cost is an error by not more than 1.86 × 0.54 = ₹ 1 (₹ 6 + ₹ 1). Thus, standard error of regression coefficient and value of *t* helps to assess the probability that marginal cost is within specified limits.

Correlation Analysis

This analysis establishes the relationship between the values of two attributes—the independent variable (the units) and the dependent variable (*y* or the cost)—before finding the fixed and variable elements. The coefficient correlation '*r*' is a measure of the extent to which these two variables are related linearly. If *r* = 0, it means there is no correlation. If *r* = + 1, it means the correlation is positive and – 1 means correlation

1. Without confidence internal *t* value = coefficient + standard error of the coefficient, so *t* value of $a = \frac{220}{17.51}$ = 12.56 and *b* = 6 + 0.54 = 1.11.

is negative. The coefficient of determination, often called r square (r^2), tells us the proportion of variance in y that can be explained by the least squares line. The formula for coefficient of correlation is:

$$r = b\sqrt{\Sigma x^2 \Sigma y^2} \quad \text{...(i)}$$

Or

$$r = \frac{\Sigma xy}{\Sigma x^2}\sqrt{\frac{\Sigma x^2}{\Sigma y^2}} \quad \text{...(ii)}$$

Or

$$r = \frac{\Sigma xy}{\sqrt{\Sigma x^2 \Sigma y^2}} \quad \text{...(iii)}$$

Or

$$r = \frac{\Sigma(x-\overline{x})\,(y-\overline{y})}{\sqrt{\Sigma\,(x-\overline{x})^2\ \Sigma(y-\overline{y})^2}}$$

You can apply any formula.

Applying each formula one by one,

(i) $b\sqrt{\frac{1,350}{51,800}}$ $= 0.969$

(ii) $\frac{8,100}{1,350} \times \sqrt{\frac{1,350}{51,800}}$ $= 0.969$

(iii) $\frac{8,100}{\sqrt{(1,350)\ (51,800)}}$ $= 0.\ 969$

coefficient of determination r^2 is $= (0.069)^2$

$= 0.939$ i.e. 93.9%.

It means that 93.9% of the variation in y can be explained by the least squares and about 6% of the variation is unexplained. The larger is r^2, the closer it comes to coefficient of correlation until both coefficients equal 1. The word explained means that the variations in the dependent variable are related to, but not necessarily, caused by, the variation in the independent variable. The coefficient of determination can also be expressed as:

$$r^2 = 1 - \frac{\text{Unexplained variance}}{\text{Explained variance}}$$

or

$$r^2 = 1 - \frac{\Sigma(y-ye)^2}{\Sigma(y-\overline{y})^2} = 1 - \frac{3,200}{51,800} = 0.939.$$

MULTIPLE REGRESSION analysis is an extension of method of least squares when there are more than more independent variable. The equation is $y = a + bx + cz$ and c is the degree of variability for an additional independent variable z. The multiple regression is calculated with the help of a computer.

Regression is the most systematic approach to cost estimation. It involves considerable amount of calculations, the restriction due to the nature of regression line itself and the time frame of the data.

QUESTIONS

1. (a) For what purpose might an organisation want to know how costs react to change in the level of activity?
   (b) Explain the meaning of 'multiple regression analysis'.
   (c) What is the purpose of a statistical correlation analysis in cost behaviour analysis?
2. Why is it important to classify factory overhead as variable and fixed. Should semi-variable expense be separated into its fixed total and its variable percentage? What methods are available to separate semi-variable expenses?
3. Given the data below, calculate fixed and variable costs using high-low approach.

Manufacturing Overhead ₹	Units produced
10,00,000	14,500
9,25,000	13,050
8,00,000	12,000
7,50,000	11,500
9,00,000	12,900
7,00,000	10,000
8,40,000	11,800
9,70,000	14,200

   How would you assess the reliability of the estimates?
4. Because sealing department of Mohammed & Peter Co. Ltd. works on several of the firm's products in one period, there is some questions of the relevant base for cost estimation. Each of four different department supervisors suggested a different basis for cost-volume analysis. The departmental overhead costs and four possible indices of activity are shown below.

   You are to resolve the conflict by finding what appears to be the best index of volume (*Hint*: use graph analysis).

Overhead cost Per quarter ₹	Units produced	Direct labour hours	Machine hours	Weight of units
12,500	1000	4,090	750	15,000
18,000	1075	3,700	1,725	23,000
16,000	1130	3,750	875	21,800
19,200	1060	5,350	2,050	20,050
11,800	1050	1,600	1,660	12,000
14,900	1080	3,100	1,720	17,000
17,600	1010	3,320	1,950	16,000
13,800	1080	2,490	1,550	19,300
15,400	1020	2,980	1,100	13,900
14,200	1050	2,500	1,240	21,400
13,000	1010	4,100	960	13,250
16,500	1060	4,150	1,470	14,100

Fit also a straight line to the cost function to the data using DLH as index of volume. Calculate it by (a) Visual fit to the graphed data; (b) The High low method; (c) Least Square Let x = DLH, y = cost, Σx^2 = 15,18,58,500, Σxy 64,13,96,000. Compare the three results.

5. Three independent variables are used in a correlation-regression analysis. The ranges of observations on each are as follows:

   x_1 : 15 – 83; x_2 : 25 – 52; x_3 : 6 – 11

   Assuming that each independent variable has the same regression coefficient, which one is most important in explaining changes in the dependent activity variable? Would it be appropriate to use the regression equation to predict the activity level for values of $x_1 = 70$, $x_2 = 50$ and $x_3 = 10$?

6. From following data of Messrs. Govinderan and Basu, you are required to find the fixed costs and variable cost per labour hour using least square method.

Month	Labour Hours	Production Costs ₹
September	2,500	20,000
October	3,500	25,000

November	4,500	30,000
December	3,500	25,000
Total	14,000	1,00,000

7. In order to determine the strength of the linear relationship between monthly sales and advertising expenses, the following data have been collected over six-month period.

Month	Advertising expenses ₹	Sales ₹
1	200	12,000
2	100	22,000
3	500	20,000
4	1,000	65,000
5	1,000	70,000
6	800	15,000

Compute the coefficient of determination without computing the least square and interpret the result.

8. Mr. Careless spilled tea over a solution and following solution is left with missing figures, which you have to find.

Month	Units sold (x)	Total cost (y)	xy	x^2
1	3	₹ 1,600	₹ 4,800	9
2	5	M	M	M
3	M	3,200	25,600	M
4	9	3,700	33,300	81
5	7	M	M	M
6	M	M	18,000	36
7	M	M	9,600	M
Total	M	M	1,26,000	M

M stands for missing

Hint:

Equation: (1) ₹ 1,26,000 = Ma + Mb

(2) M = Ma + Mb

Multiply equation 2 by 6 and substract from equation 1.

V.C. = M

F.C. = ₹ 1,000.